THE COLLABORATORS

THE COLLABORATOR

ALSO BY IAN BURUMA

The Churchill Complex: The Curse of Being Special,
from Winston and FDR to Trump and Brexit

A Tokyo Romance: A Memoir

Their Promised Land:
My Grandparents in Love and War

Theater of Cruelty:
Art, Film, and the Shadows of War

Year Zero: A History of 1945

Taming the Gods:
Religion and Democracy on Three Continents

The China Lover: A Novel

Murder in Amsterdam:
Liberal Europe, Islam, and the Limits of Tolerance

Conversations with John Schlesinger

Occidentalism:
The West in the Eyes of Its Enemies (with Avishai Margalit)

Inventing Japan: 1853–1964

Bad Elements: Chinese Rebels from Los Angeles to Beijing

Anglomania: A European Love Affair

The Missionary and the Libertine: Love and War in East and West

The Wages of Guilt: Memories of War in Germany and Japan

Playing the Game: A Novel

God's Dust: A Modern Asian Journey

Behind the Mask: On Sexual Demons, Sacred Mothers,
Transvestites, Gangsters, Drifters and Other
Japanese Cultural Heroes

The Japanese Tattoo (text by Donald Richie;
photographs by Ian Buruma)

THE
COLLABORATORS

Three Stories of Deception and
Survival in World War II

Ian Buruma

PENGUIN PRESS
NEW YORK
2023

PENGUIN PRESS
An imprint of Penguin Random House LLC
penguinrandomhouse.com

Photo credits appear on page 281.

LIBRARY OF CONGRESS CATALOGING-IN-PUBLICATION DATA
Names: Buruma, Ian, author.
Title: The collaborators / Ian Buruma.
Description: New York : Penguin Press, 2022. |
Includes bibliographical references and index.
Identifiers: LCCN 2022005097 (print) | LCCN 2022005098 (ebook) |
ISBN 9780593296646 (hardcover) | ISBN 9780593296653 (ebook)
Subjects: LCSH: World War, 1939–1945—
Collaborationists—Biography. | Kersten, Felix, 1898-1960. |
Weinreb, Friedrich, 1910-1988. | Kawashima, Yoshiko, 1906?-1948.
Classification: LCC D810.C696 B87 2022 (print) |
LCC D810.C696 (ebook) | DDC 940.53092/2 [B]—dc23/eng/20220328
LC record available at https://lccn.loc.gov/2022005097
LC ebook record available at https://lccn.loc.gov/2022005098

Printed in the United States of America
1st Printing

Designed by Amanda Dewey

For Hilary

Contents

PROLOGUE *1*

One. PARADISE LOST *11*

Two. IN ANOTHER COUNTRY *25*

Three. MIRACLES *39*

Four. A LOW, DISHONEST DECADE *61*

Five. CROSSING THE LINE *89*

Six. BEAUTIFUL STORIES *117*

Seven. THE SHOOTING PARTY *143*

Eight. THE ENDGAME *171*

Nine. FINALE *207*

Ten. AFTERMATH *241*

EPILOGUE *275*

Acknowledgments *279*
Credits *281*
Notes *283*
Index *291*

The Collaborators

PROLOGUE

⊚⊚⊚

O n the face of it, the three main characters in this book have very
little in common: Felix Kersten was a plump bon vivant who became famous, or notorious, as the personal masseur of Heinrich Himmler,
mass murderer and head of the SS. Himmler's fond nickname for him
was the Magic Buddha. Aisin Gyoro Xianyu, or Jin Bihui, or Dongzhen
("Eastern Jewel"), but best known by her Japanese name Kawashima Yoshiko, was a cross-dressing Manchu princess who spied for the Japanese
secret police in China. Friedrich, or Frederyck, or Freek Weinreb, was a
Hassidic Jewish immigrant in Holland who took money from other Jews
by pretending to save them from deportation to the death camps, but in
fact ended up betraying some of them to the German police.

In May 1947, Weinreb was about to be sentenced for his wartime behavior. A stocky, slightly stooped figure with thick glasses, he had the air
of a Talmudic scholar whose mind floated high above worldly affairs. His
judges belonged to the Special Court for cases of treachery and collaboration during the Nazi occupation of the Netherlands. The public prosecutor accused Weinreb of the most fantastic swindle ever perpetrated in
his country. Defenders of Weinreb saw him as a modern-day Dreyfus, a
Jewish scapegoat for crimes committed by Gentiles. Some Jews who had

survived the war and known Weinreb during the occupation regarded him as a ruthless fraudster who collaborated with the Gestapo. Weinreb himself liked to compare the story of his life to a Hassidic miracle tale.

The trial of Kawashima Yoshiko, in October 1947, was a much more raucous affair. The court in Beijing was overwhelmed by huge crowds who wanted to get a glimpse of the "Mata Hari of the Orient." Pandemonium inside the courtroom prompted the judges to shift the action to the gardens outside, where thousands more people were pressing to get in, some to find a precarious perch in the plane trees surrounding the court. Tofu and watermelon vendors were doing brisk business.

Kawashima, her hair cut short like a man's, wearing purple slacks and a white polo sweater, was accused of betraying her native country of China, organizing a private army in support of the Japanese invasion of Manchuria, and spying for the Japanese in Shanghai. Her exploits as the lover of senior Japanese officers and swaggering around occupied China like a wild samurai were reported in lurid detail in all the papers. Most of her alleged misdeeds took place in the 1930s, when Japanese armies marauded across China with great savagery.

The oddest thing about Kawashima's trial was that many of the accusations against her were lifted straight from movies, novels, and other fictions, concocted during the war by Japanese propagandists and sensation-mongers, often with her full collaboration. Kawashima was at least partly a fictional figure. The peculiar mixture of fabrication and facts resulted in her execution on a bleak early morning in Beijing.

Himmler's masseur, Felix Kersten, was never put on trial. Born in Estonia but naturalized as a Finnish citizen, Kersten didn't betray his country, since Finland cooperated with Nazi Germany, only changing sides quite late in the war. But Kersten was certainly a collaborator. Still, taking care of a genocidal murderer's mental and physical well-being, as his masseur and confidant, was reprehensible, perhaps, but not a war crime. Kersten's myths were largely made up after the war, when he reconstructed his past as a story of brave resistance, claiming to have used his unique position in Himmler's court to save millions of innocent lives.

All three were what Germans call a *Hochstapler*. The word originally referred to a beggar who, when cornered in an awkward situation, puts on the airs of a high-class person. The usual translations in English are "fraud," "bluffer," or "con artist." They were in some ways like the famous fictionalized eighteenth-century *Hochstapler* Baron von Münchhausen, who claimed, among other feats, to have traveled to the moon, ridden a cannonball, and wrestled a giant crocodile. They were such successful storytellers that some of their most outlandish claims were still widely believed long after the war was over, in Kersten's case even by some highly respected historians.

As some of Weinreb's defenders quite rightly pointed out, fraud, fake identities, made-up stories, and other forms of deceit were an inextricable part of wartime culture. Members of the resistance in occupied countries adopted false names. Subterfuge was the essential nature of their business. But the same was true of the regimes they fought. Dictatorship rules by terror and propaganda. A lie repeated often enough becomes the truth. Was it Joseph Goebbels who said that, or was it Vladimir Lenin? Conspiracy theories and other fantasies thrive when accurate information is lacking, either because the truth is suppressed or too dangerous to speak about openly. Wars offer the ideal conditions for mythomaniacs, self-invented figures, chancers who live their real lives as fictional characters, but they are not the only such conditions.

Much about the three subjects in this book seems alarmingly contemporary, at a time when a typical *Hochstapler* from reality TV shows can become president of the United States, when critical information is dismissed as "fake news," and large numbers of people believe in plots and conspiracies that bubble up from the collective imagination of the internet. Weinreb, Kersten, and Kawashima thrived in World War II, but one can easily imagine them as avatars in the social media world. The conditions of war, in other words, are not so remote.

I grew up in an atmosphere thick with tall tales, boys' stories, movies, sonorous memorial speeches, and unreliable personal memories that gave a patently bogus account of the dark war years preceding my birth. In some countries this was a matter of government policy. General de Gaulle, presiding over a deeply wounded society, where rancor over wartime behavior, in collaboration or resistance, could easily have boiled over in civil war, used his authority as a resister of the first hour to paint a picture of an "eternal France," whose citizens had been staunch in their opposition to the German foe. This eternal France had been liberated by its own people, he claimed, its own army, with "support and help of all of France"—and, yes, of course, it had to be admitted, almost as an afterthought, also with the "help of our dear and formidable allies." This was a myth, a falsehood, a fraud if you like.

In France, it was perhaps a necessary fraud. I was born in a country, the Netherlands, where Weinreb arrived as an immigrant from Lwów in 1916, and Kersten had lived happily and profitably before 1940, and after 1945. The Netherlands was not about to erupt in civil war. But the myth of nationwide resistance was as potent during my childhood as it was in France. Maybe this, too, was necessary in a way. Occupation by a foreign enemy is a humiliating experience. In a term that would now strike people as old-fashioned, it was as though the nation, after surrendering to superior German force in May 1940, had been emasculated. The stories of resistance, told over and over in my youth, were a way to cope with that humiliation, to regain national pride, to rebuild a patriotic spirit, to feel good about who we were, a people of heroic resisters. No doubt a similar process, just as deceptive, played out in all countries that had been under occupation.

In no country has the truth about the wartime past been more contested and elusive than in Japan. Kawashima Yoshiko is remembered as a tragic rather than a culpable figure in Japanese movies, musicals, manga, novels, and history books. Guilt can result in just as many myths as subjugation.

The sinister figure of the *collabo*, as such people were called in France, was an essential element in the national morality tales of the late 1950s. God cannot exist without Satan. We were aware that a minority had committed the cardinal sin of collaborating actively with the enemy. They were the fallen ones, the symbols of depravity, whose crimes served to highlight the glowing virtuousness of the plucky majority. The word in Dutch for those who opposed the Germans was *goed*, that is "good" or "decent," and those who didn't were *fout*, "wrong," not just politically but morally. These were absolute categories. You were either good, or you were not. There was no in-between.

It took at least a decade for countermyths to appear, cracking the facade of postwar self-delusions. New histories, novels, movies, and television programs revealed, cautiously at first, but then with more and more vehemence as the protest movements of the 1960s accelerated, that the story of societies under German occupation had been far less heroic than we had been led to believe. It also dawned on us that the complexities of resistance and collaboration made simple morality tales of good versus evil seem inadequate, even trite.

People joined the resistance for all kinds of reasons. Some did it because they felt morally compelled by their religious or political beliefs, and some out of a sense of common (or not so common) decency. Others, not necessarily any less decent, joined because they craved adventure. Some enjoyed the thrill of danger and violence. The consequences of violent action could be severe for other people who were less drawn to adventure but were caught in brutal reprisals. For this reason, resisters often became romantic heroes after the war, long after their righteous deeds sometimes did more harm than good. In any case, active resisters were a minority everywhere.

Reasons for collaboration were just as diverse. Some of the harshest vengeance after the war was meted out to the least serious offenders, especially women who had slept with the enemy, out of desire, loneliness, ambition, pleasure in the good life, or indeed, who knows, out of love—but rarely because of any profound ideological commitment. Again, the sense of national humiliation, especially among men, inflamed the jeering crowds who humiliated these women in turn: parading them through the streets, heads shaven, covered in filth, spat on, and sometimes raped. The cruel faces of such gleeful mobs are familiar from any number of paintings of Christ's road to Calvary. The fact that Kawashima Yoshiko was the only one of the three collaborators in this book to have been executed for what she did owed something to the violence of such emotions.

Many collaborators did far worse things than sleep with the enemy. Occupation armies and criminal regimes invariably provide a chance for all kinds of people to rise from dark corners of society and lord it over others with vengeful glee: failed artists become arbiters of official taste; petty criminals acquire fancy ranks and run prison camps; disbarred lawyers, corrupt bureaucrats, doctors with troubled histories, and marginal politicians are able to form a new elite and enjoy the trappings of high office under a foreign tyranny. This is what made the fascist years ideal for *Hochstapler*, fantasists who entered a world of violent make-believe. And, of course, there is often a great deal of dishonest profit to be made out of other people's misfortunes.

But not all collaborators were gangsters, grifters, or corrupt opportunists. Mayors clung to their positions while telling themselves that resigning would open the door to successors who would surely be worse. Factory owners cooperated because they didn't want their companies to be confiscated; and, after all, they might claim, they treated slaves from local concentration camps better than Nazi bosses would have done. Lawyers and judges acquiesced to Nazi laws and regulations citing their belief in the rule of law. To salvage their conscience, they consoled themselves with the thought that the exact nature of those laws was not up to them to determine. As for the buyers and sellers of looted properties, or providers of all manner of services to the new rulers, well, someone had to keep the economy going.

But there were also people, some of them highly educated, who believed that a new Europe, led by Germany, would stand firm against the twin evils of "Judeo-Bolshevism" and "Judeo-American-capitalism." Such alleged dangers, usually minus the obsession with Jews, inspired similar bonds of brotherhood in Asia, where the Japanese empire embarked on its brutal campaign to liberate fellow Asians from communism, as well as from Western imperialism. The Japanese occupation of China and other parts of Asia gave rise to the same kinds of criminal types, deluded idealists, social and professional failures, vengeful brutes, chancers, businessmen, and other opportunists who operated in Europe under Hitler's flag. But just as some people suffering the depredations and humiliations of Soviet rule cooperated with the Germans, because Stalinism seemed worse, some prominent Asians collaborated with the Japanese out of a genuine desire to rid their countries from Western colonial rule.

None of these three figures neatly fit into any of these types. Very few people, collaborators or resisters, can be reduced to single types. Human beings, even malicious or craven ones, are too complicated for that. But the highly eccentric lives of Kersten, Kawashima, and Weinreb contain elements that mark the stories of many collaborators: greed, idealism, thrill seeking, power hunger, opportunism, and even a conviction, not always misplaced, that they were doing some good.

To say that collaboration and resistance cannot be pressed into morality tales of good versus evil doesn't mean that these characteristics are always evenly distributed. Bad things can be done with good intentions, and bad people can sometimes do good. Moral judgment has to deal with degrees. Felix Kersten certainly did some good, even as he played his role as a member of a mass killer's court. But none of the three was utterly depraved. They were all too human, especially in their frailties. Similar frailties can be seen in many figures strutting around the public sphere today. That is why I chose to write about them, and by doing so to reflect on the question of collaboration: human weakness is more interesting to me than saintliness or heroism, perhaps because it is easier to imagine oneself as a sinner than as a saint.

Another reason for my interest in these three people is the complexity of their backgrounds. Kersten, the Baltic German, was first a Finn and then, after the war, a Swede, who lived at various times in The Hague, Berlin, and Stockholm. Kawashima was born in China, as the daughter of a Manchu prince, but raised in Japan as the adopted child of a Japanese ultranationalist. Weinreb moved with his parents from Lwów to Vienna, and then to a seaside resort in Holland, where he grew up. He died in Switzerland, a fugitive from Dutch justice and a revered dispenser of religious wisdom derived from obscure readings of the Bible.

Since the question of resistance and collaboration played such a large part in the patriotic education of my generation, it is tempting to conclude that a cosmopolitan milieu or muddled provenance would necessarily result in divided loyalties. But this is a temptation to be resisted. Multifarious loyalties don't have to be in conflict. And an exaggerated patriotism is often the mark of a person with more than one nation in his or her background, if only because of a conviction that loyalty to one or the other needs to be proven. Whether this stems entirely from one's own heart or is the result of social pressure is a question that cannot be answered in general terms. People may not even know themselves.

But the tangled international lives of Kersten, Weinreb, and Kawashima are not irrelevant. Emerging from mixed cultural and national backgrounds, they were swept up by world events in complicated ways. Great art can emerge from uncertain and multifarious identities, but so can more sinister forms of self-invention. I am writing this at a time of deep social and political divisions, in a society where collective identities are insisted upon, while individual identities are increasingly fluid and mixed, where a constant barrage of conspiratorial fantasies is replacing political debate, and where people inhabit not just different places but different conceptual worlds. I have chosen my leading figures, then, not as typical examples of treachery, but as figures who reinvented themselves in a time of war, persecution, and mass murder, when moral choices often had fatal consequences but were rarely as straightforward as we were told to believe after the dangers had lifted.

*H*ochstaplers are by definition unreliable narrators of their own stories. There is much about the lives of Kersten, Kawashima, and Weinreb that will remain unknowable. All three wrote personal accounts, but always with a particular purpose in mind: to embellish their biographies with exotic tales of adventure, or with demonstrations of great courage and gallant acts of resistance.

Of course, all memories are endlessly reedited, in the minds of individuals as much as in the histories of nations. Political fashions and new discoveries, changing tastes and shifting rules of moral conduct, all these factors affect our views of the ever-receding past. This doesn't mean that everything is fiction, as some theorists, no less influenced by fashion than anyone else, would have us believe. There are factual truths. People *were* gassed. Cities *were* sacked. Atom bombs *were* dropped. We need to be reminded of these facts; they tell us much about why we are who we are. Much of what most people know about the past, however, is based on fiction: movies, novels, comic books, computer games. Collective memories are shaped by scholarship, but even more by the imagination. That is why made-up stories are worth paying attention to. They tell us much about who we are too.

The life stories of my three subjects are by no means entirely imagined. All three contain factual truths. Even critics of Weinreb admit that while he told many fibs about himself, his descriptions of daily life under German occupation often ring true. I set myself the task of telling their stories, because the facts they reveal about how people lived through some of the most horrific times of the last century are illuminating. But so are the lies.

One

PARADISE LOST

1: Helsinki

After the war, when Felix Kersten was anxious to settle with his wife and three sons in Sweden as a Swedish citizen, his previous occupation as the private masseur of Heinrich Himmler was a problem. The Swedes, already a trifle defensive about their neutral position during the war, when business relations with Germany had been profitable and useful services had been rendered to the Third Reich, were not especially keen to bestow nationality upon a man who had been in the thick of the Nazi elite.

The swift publication in various languages of Kersten's memories and wartime notes, all heavily edited, must be read in this light. What makes his accounts especially confusing is that they are so different from one another. *The Kersten Memoirs*, first published in the United States in 1947, reads like a series of short essays about Himmler's character, and his disobliging views on such subjects as Jews and homosexuals. Much of the rest of the book is about Kersten's heroic interventions on behalf of political prisoners, the Dutch population, Scandinavians, and Jews. The Swedish translation is similar but gives conflicting accounts on various matters.

The German edition omits Kersten's most dramatic feat (dramatic, but not necessarily true): how he persuaded Himmler (and by extension Hitler himself) not to carry out a plan to deport the entire Dutch population to Poland in 1941. Himmler (so Kersten tells us) was ready to abandon this grandiose and no doubt murderous project if only Kersten could relieve his intolerable stomach pain through the magic of his healing hands. The story is of course included in the Dutch edition of 1948, entitled *Clerk and Butcher* (*Klerk en beul*), edited and amended by a young man who had worked for the underground resistance press during the war—"good" in other words. This man, Joop den Uyl, would one day be the socialist prime minister of the Netherlands.

The picture of Kersten's childhood, as conveyed in the Dutch edition (the others don't go into his youth), is idyllic, almost like a fairy tale of a "good" man who loved people of all races and creeds. He was born in 1898, in Dorpat, a town in Livonia, part of Estonia, once ruled by the Swedish king, but then a province of the tsar's Russian empire. In the sixteenth century, Kersten's paternal ancestors had moved from Holland to Germany, where they lived as farmers until Kersten's grandfather Ferdinand was killed by an angry bull. His widow then moved to a huge baronial estate in Livonia, where her son, Friedrich Kersten, met a Russian woman named Olga Stubbing, whose family owned quite a lot of land. They flourished, and Olga gave birth to Felix, who was named after the French president Félix Faure by his godfather, the French ambassador in Petersburg. The family had done well.

Kersten describes the sleepy environment of his childhood as a kind of cosmopolitan paradise, a cultural crossroads combining the best of everything: Scandinavian individualism, Russian grandeur, and European humanism and enlightenment. German was the dominant language of his class, but Kersten's idea of Germany, he assures his readers, had nothing to do with Prussian militarism. Rather, it was the land of Goethe that was cherished, with its culture of "freedom, education, universality and love." His school friends were Baltic Germans, like himself, as well as Russians and Finns. They all got along fine. And the "Jewish problem" didn't exist at all. Kersten remembers the Jewish milliners and tinsmiths in his town with great fondness. He could still taste the delicious matzos handed out by Jewish friends during Passover. He often mused, later in life, why the whole of Europe could not be as peaceful as the lovely Livonian countryside of his childhood.

This rather pink-spectacled vision of his Baltic Garden of Eden leaves out certain things that are revealed in an admiring account of Kersten's life, entitled *The Man with the Miraculous Hands* (*Les mains du miracle*), by Joseph Kessel, himself a fascinating figure. He was a Jewish member of the French resistance during the war, and author of, among other books, *Belle de Jour*, which Luis Buñuel made into one of his greatest films. Kessel, although skeptical at first, decided to believe Kersten's stories, many of which Kessel heard firsthand. It is not immediately clear why. Kessel cannot have been naive. Kersten must have appealed to his romantic imagination. He liked heroic tales. Apart from *Belle de Jour*, Kessel is also the author of one of the best books written about the French resistance during the war, *Army of Shadows* (*L'armée des ombres*). Unlike his later book on Kersten, this was meant to be an imaginary account based on true facts. It was published in London before the end of the war. Fiction came easily to this superb journalistic storyteller. *Army of Shadows*, too, was the source of a cinematic masterpiece, made in 1969 by Jean-Pierre Melville, the great director of French gangster pictures.

Kessel paints the Estonia of Kersten's youth as a Gogolesque outpost of the Russian empire, where the peasants would drop to their knees whenever families of Kersten's rank passed them on the road. Kersten, he says, used to a life of ease, would have been oblivious to the misery of the people around him. He also mentions that Kersten's mother, Olga, sang beautifully at charity parties, earning her the name of Livonian Nightingale. Her other talent was for massage. She is said to have had the power to cure people of all kinds of ailments with her expert hands, a gift inherited by her son.

The Livonian idyll came to a sudden end in the revolutionary era of the early twentieth century. Kersten writes that armies from different countries brought death and destruction to his native land, and that hatred was sown between the different peoples by their rulers. Estonia was an important base for the Russians during World War I, and Estonians first fought on the Russian side. Then, after the tsar's regime was toppled in 1917, Estonian nationalists attempted to establish an independent Republic of Estonia. They were opposed by Estonian Bolsheviks, who wanted to be with their Russian comrades, as well as by Baltic Germans, who hoped to be the rulers of a German-dominated United Baltic Duchy. In 1918, German troops occupied the country, but not for long. They were soon replaced by Russian Bolsheviks, and Estonia became part of a Russian empire once again. Kersten's parents lost their properties and were deported to a remote village on the Caspian Sea.

Kersten himself was in Germany when the war began. He had done poorly at school. A spoiled, lazy youth clinging to his indulgent mother, Kersten mainly took pleasure in eating too much. His reputation as a gourmand started early. As a teenager, he already looked and acted the part. His father thought he needed a firmer hand and sent him first to a boarding school in Riga, where the boy failed to shine, and then decided that he should study agriculture in Germany. This, too, was not much to his liking, but cut off from his family by the war, he somehow finished his studies and found a job on a large estate in Anhalt, in the eastern part of the country.

What happened to Kersten then is very hazy. One version—Kessel's—has it that Kersten was drafted into the kaiser's army, since the German government considered the Baltic Germans to be compatriots, as they would in World War II. Another book mentions a claim that Kersten won the Iron Cross at the Battle of Verdun. The author speculates that Kersten might have invented this feat himself to gain a smooth entry into the Finnish army. In yet another account, by the German writer Achim Besgen, Kersten became a soldier only when a German army, led by General Rüdiger von der Goltz, entered Finland to fight with the Finns against Russia. It is possible that he was part of a regiment of Finns in the German army, or he might have joined the Finnish army.

This was Kersten's first experience of confused loyalties and collaboration. As a Baltic German, he was on the German side; as a subject of the tsar, he was on the Russian side; and as an Estonian, he would, at different times, have been opposed to both powers. In any event, he did take some part in the struggle for independence in Finland and the Baltic states. Collaborating with Germany would have been the best way to confront the common Russian enemy. But it wasn't quite so simple. Finland, like Estonia, had been part of the Russian empire and declared independence only in 1917, the year of the Russian Revolution. "Red" Finns, supported by the Russians, then fought a civil war with the "whites," supported by Germany. When Kersten entered Finland and the Baltic states as an officer in a Finnish army, not only was he was fighting for independence from Russia, but he was doing so as an anti-Communist ally of Germany. Allegiance to this cause did not end with the defeat of imperial Germany in 1918.

Kersten's military career was short. After spending much of the winter of 1918 in the freezing Nordic marshes, his legs were paralyzed by rheumatism, and he spent several months in a hospital in Helsinki. "I entered my new fatherland on crutches," is how he put it. Again, his manner of leaving the army is controversial: he claimed that he did so of his own free will, but there are Finnish reports that say he was dismissed for forging documents to get a promotion. He was in any case now a Finnish citizen, and terribly bored. Lying in bed, Kersten watched the doctors tending to the wounded men, and, as he later recalled, childhood memories of the helplessness of injured people came back to him. He wanted to help. This would be his stated mission in life, helping the suffering and the wounded.

Massage was a popular form of therapy in Finland at the time, and one of the top practitioners was a Dr. Ekman, a major in the Finnish army, and head of the hospital in Helsinki. In Kersten's own story, Major Ekman took one look at Kersten's big, powerful hands and said they were worth a fortune. Joseph Kessel's book, unusually, is slightly less dramatic. In his version, Kersten told Ekman that he wanted to be a surgeon. Ekman said that that would take years of study. Kersten was not the studying type. No, he said, grasping Kersten's meaty palm, these hands are perfect for massaging, not surgery.

2: Lwów

Friedrich ("Freek") Weinreb freely admits that his memoirs are subjective and that to look for factual accuracy would be missing the point. He tells his readers: "If you wish to hear the story of my life, or rather of a certain period of my life, you will have to get used to accepting strange events as the truth. However you wish to interpret them, they are true to me."

It all began in the city of Lemberg (in German), or Lwów (in Polish), and now Lviv (in Ukrainian), where Weinreb was born in 1910. Lwów was a lively cultural center in the Galician part of the Austro-Hungarian empire. This "Little Paris," with its Belle Epoque opera house, its grand cafés, its Viennese-Renaissance buildings, its Polish universities, its Yiddish newspapers, its Ukrainian churches, and its fine Jewish musicians, was a model of cosmopolitanism. First German and then Polish were the main common languages. Yiddish and Ukrainian were spoken as well, though not in the most highly educated circles.

"Only in Lwów!" ("Tylko we Lwowie!") was the biggest hit song of the 1930s, known to all Poles: "Where else do people feel as good as here? / Only in Lwów . . ." The hit was sung by two radio comedians known as Szczepko and Tońko. Tońko's real name was Henryk Vogelfänger, a Jewish lawyer, who escaped to London, where he became Henry Barker. My friend, the British journalist Anthony Barker, remembers visits as a child to the Polish Hearth Club in London, where, to the young boy's astonishment, middle-aged ladies would swoon at the sight of his father, reliving in their minds a little bit of the lost world of prewar Lwów.

About 30 percent of the population of Lwów was Jewish, until the Germans came in 1941. In the years that followed, almost all the Jews were slaughtered, either in Bełżec, the nearest extermination camp, or in Janowska, a camp outside Lwów, where members of the National Opera were ordered to provide musical accompaniment to torture and mass shootings, before being shot themselves. There are photographs of Heinrich Himmler visiting the latter camp in 1941 or 1942. Smiling in his raincoat, full of bonhomie, Himmler shakes hands with Fritz Katzmann, the camp commander, who wrote an official report in June 1943 on "the Solution to the Jewish Question in the District of Galicia." By the time Katzmann was finished there, 434,329 Jews had been killed. When Lwów was *Judenrein*, "cleansed of Jews," Himmler ordered his SS men on the spot to make sure all traces of mass murder were eliminated.

Friedrich Weinreb remembers his childhood as "a lost paradise." One thing that was lost, once his parents decided to flee Lwów in 1914, when Russian troops chased out the Austro-Hungarian army and people were afraid that the Cossacks were about to start a pogrom, was something that Weinreb later dismissed as a dangerous illusion: the idea that secular liberal Jews could assimilate into a humane world of reason and enlightenment. The setting for his childhood paradise was a large, comfortable, well-furnished family house in a nice neighborhood, where Yiddish was seldom heard, and the sight of bearded Jewish beggars was rare. In fact, in his recollection, Weinreb as a child had no concept of Jews, or any other distinctions based on background or ethnicity. His parents believed that this was what modern, European, civilized life was all about. German was the only language spoken in the Weinreb home. Weinreb's father, David, who had studied business in Czernowitz, that other great multiethnic, multicultural, multilingual, multireligious Habsburg town that would lose most of its original inhabitants, had worked hard to replace his native Yiddish with the language of High Culture, which could only be German. Hermine Sternhell, Weinreb's mother, grew up in Wiznitz, not far from Czernowitz, where Jews once made up almost 90 percent of the population. But she never doubted that their culture was German, rooted in the Germany that Felix Kersten recalled as the land of freedom, education, universality, and love. As keen members of the German *Kultur*, these cultivated, idealistic Jews could feel superior to the Ukrainian peasants, not to speak of the unenlightened, poor, religious Jews.

Weinreb had vivid memories of the day when his childhood world collapsed. He was on holiday with his mother in Jaremca (now Yaremche), a lovely spa in the Carpathian Mountains with gold-domed Orthodox churches and charming wooden houses. The smell of pine forest and the sweet sounds of birds and waterfalls were as unforgettable to him as the taste of those matzos on Passover in Kersten's memories of Livonia. After a leisurely picnic in the woods, he and his mother returned by carriage to a graceful little hotel belonging to his aunt. That is when he heard the words "war" and "mobilization" for the first time. The Russians were coming. Men were being called up. Pogroms might follow. There was panic everywhere. Families were escaping in horse-drawn carts filled with everything they could carry. Weinreb's father turned up from Lwów with terrifying tales of soldiers shooting in the streets. They found a place on a crowded freight car bound for the Hungarian border. The life of exile, of moving from one seedy hotel to another, of being an unwanted guest, of having to learn the codes of new cultures, and of viewing the past in the dense mist of nostalgia, had begun. His mother blamed the Russians and the cowardly French. She still believed in the Austrian kaiser and the civilizing influence of German culture. Weinreb claims that it was then that he had his first intimation of how cold, cruel, and stupid the world really was.

3: Beijing

Kawashima Yoshiko—or Dongzhen, as she was still called as a child—was the fourteenth daughter of Aisin Gyoro Shanqi, or Prince Su, a member of the Manchu imperial family that ruled China as the Qing Dynasty for more than two and a half centuries. She, too, had hazy memories of a charmed world that collapsed around her when she was a mere toddler. What she didn't recall (and given her age, she couldn't have recalled very much) was instilled in her, like a family myth, as she grew up.

Kawashima's sparse memories of her early childhood are related in her memoir, *In the Shadow of Chaos* (*Doran no kage*), published in Japan in 1937, the year that Japanese Imperial Army troops occupied China's major cities and committed some of their worst crimes. She starts her account with detailed descriptions of her father, Prince Su, and the Japanese man who would later adopt her, Kawashima Naniwa. A little oddly, she apologizes to her readers for spending so many words on her two fathers, but this, she says, is because she must first explain how her cossetted world was shattered by "rebellions, riots, revolutions and counterrevolutions." Which is really a roundabout way of explaining her own story of collaboration with Japan, and the men who put her on that path.

Prince Su, a small, plumpish, round-faced man, had once been a very grand figure in the imperial court. His household in Beijing matched his high status. With a wife, thirty-eight children, and four concubines, he lived in a mansion with two hundred rooms, many in the gilded French style, with cascading chandeliers, Louis XV furniture, and a pipe organ. The compound also had several fine gardens with beautiful fountains, a well-stocked stable, and a private theater. The family had its own running water system and supply of electricity. Like all Manchu grandees, whose ancestors were tribal chieftains from the drab northeastern plains, dusty and hot in summer, and swept by freezing Siberian winds in winter, Prince Su combined elements of his Manchu heritage with high Chinese culture. He continued to wear his queue, a Manchu custom that had also been imposed on the Han Chinese, much to their loathing, and he had a romantic attachment to horse riding and falconry, but he was also a proud connoisseur of the Peking Opera, regular performances of which took place in his private theater.

The prince held a succession of important positions, in charge at various times of taxes, the police, and the Ministry of the Interior. He was a traditionalist but not in his prime a reactionary. As interior minister, he tried to improve hygienic conditions in the capital. He was responsible for such innovations as public toilets. When a plague reached Beijing from Manchuria in 1910, he made sure that bodies were cremated, and he stopped the trade in white mice, which were suspected of carrying the disease.

Although China had been ruled by dynasties that originated in the barbarian wilds beyond the Great Wall before, the Manchus had been resented as vulgar foreign upstarts from the time they took power in 1644. Loyalists of the Chinese Ming Dynasty resisted the Qing in the seventeenth century and dreamed of restoring native Chinese rule. The Taiping Rebellion in the mid-nineteenth century, led by a messianic figure who believed he was the brother of Christ and promised to lead the Chinese people to the Kingdom of Heaven, was infused with Han Chinese animus against the supposedly decadent Manchus. The uprising ended in failure, but once it was suppressed, up to thirty million people had died, often horribly. Han chauvinism also fired up activists in the early twentieth century. They were excited by Western notions of nationhood, revolution, and the Darwinian struggle for national survival. These modern ideas mostly came to them via Japan, where many of the Chinese Nationalists went to study.

In 1905, Sun Yat-sen, commonly known as the Father of the Nation, and a Christian convert, organized a revolutionary movement with Chinese students in Tokyo. His Revolutionary Alliance was supported by Japanese who dreamed of purging the Asian continent of Western colonial powers and giving it back to the Asians. Some were Sinophiles and romantic pan-Asian dreamers, some were right-wing gangsters with fascist ideals. Sun himself devised a vague set of principles, combining nationalism, democracy, and socialism, that made up his vision of China's future.

The main reason Japan appealed to Chinese revolutionaries was its success in turning a quasi-feudal samurai junta into a modern nation-state. When, in the Russo-Japanese War of 1904–1905, Japan became the first Asian nation in centuries to defeat a Western power, Asians rejoiced. Russian government propaganda described the war as a clash between Christians and Buddhists. Leo Tolstoy, a pacifist, saw it differently. The Japanese, he lamented, had learned the lessons too well from rapacious modern Western nations who had lost their spiritual bearings.

Many modern Chinese felt inspired by Meiji Japan and its Western culture in translation. Their ideals were in many ways "progressive." Women insisted on getting a proper education and refused any longer to hobble around on bound feet (hitherto, only Manchu women exempted themselves from this custom, something that made conservative Chinese men recoil from their "big feet"). One of the women who joined Sun Yat-sen's Revolutionary Alliance arrived in Japan to escape from an unhappy arranged marriage. Her name was Qiu Jin. She liked to dress up in men's clothes, was drawn to military action, and experimented with bombs. Back in China, she became a radical schoolteacher and entered the dense world of secret societies plotting to overthrow the imperial government. She got caught, was tried, and was executed for sedition.

Whether Kawashima Yoshiko ever regarded Qiu as a model can't be known—she never mentioned her in her writings, and they espoused opposite causes—but their lives followed a similar course, including a taste for men's clothes and military action. Born in 1907, Kawashima was just four years old when the Qing Dynasty came to a violent end. But the *ancien régime* lived on as a legend in her mind, fed by the people around her, not least her two fathers, Manchu and Japanese, who dreamed of bringing it back one day. This would continue to haunt her. Ever since she could clearly remember, she heard talk about restoring the Qing Dynasty and her family's fortunes with Japanese help.

Prince Su was a member of the same regime that people like Qiu Jin wished to topple. And yet he admired modern Japan as much as they did, not so much because of any progressive ideals, even though he might have subscribed to some of them, but because of Japan's growing power. Like the Japanese backers of Sun Yat-sen's Revolutionary Alliance, he, too, despite his questionable taste for French rococo opulence, wanted to purge Asia from Western domination, but by strengthening the Qing empire, not destroying it.

Alas for him, the empire began to unravel very swiftly in the late autumn of 1911. It began with a bomb going off by accident in Wuhan, where revolutionary agitators had been trying out explosive devices in the Russian concession area. This set the uprising in motion: Manchu officers were assassinated, revolutionaries took over cities, more and more government troops went over to the rebels.

Prince Su, like many ousted Manchu aristocrats, fled Beijing in February 1912. Disguised as a poor Chinese merchant, accompanied by a Japanese army captain dressed in similar garb, he escaped to the port of Shanhaiguan, where he boarded a Japanese naval ship bound for Port Arthur, the former Russian naval base in Manchuria, now firmly under Japanese control. A little more than a week later, the Qing imperial court ceded all political authority to the Republic of China.

Other Manchu officials fled to different parts of China, but none, except Prince Su, chose to live in an area controlled by the Japanese. The prince offered a complicated explanation. He had intended to make his way to Mukden (today's Shenyang, the seat of the original Manchu imperial court), to reach out to the powerful local warlord. Together they would raise enough troops to topple the new republic. But his way to Mukden had been blocked, possibly on Japanese orders, so he had no choice but to go to Port Arthur. This does not sound quite right. He was probably drawn to the Japanese, because he hoped to get their support for his antirepublican resistance. He had been led up this particular garden path by Japanese friends, who fed his revanchist fantasies. To make the story even more convoluted, these friends included some of the same activists who had supported Sun Yat-sen's revolutionary project in Tokyo. One of them was Kawashima Naniwa, a pan-Asianist adventurer who would end up adopting Prince Su's daughter as his own, which is how Dongzhen became Kawashima Yoshiko.*

Prince Su never gave up his dream of restoration and vowed never to set foot on republican soil, except under the banners of the Qing Dynasty. His children, including Dongzhen/Yoshiko, followed their father to Port Arthur on another Japanese ship, amid sobbing retainers. This is the atmosphere, thick with intrigues and betrayals, in which they grew up, pining for a world that was lost forever.

---

*Not out of disrespect or false familiarity, but to avoid confusion with her adoptive father, I shall follow the example of other biographers and refer to her as Yoshiko from here on.

Two

IN ANOTHER COUNTRY

∞

1: *Vienna*

Hitler had left Vienna two years before the Weinreb family arrived there from Hungary in 1915. A failed artist who had been staying in a flophouse and made a kind of living by drawing mawkish postcards of Viennese tourist spots, Hitler called the city a "racial Babylon." He didn't mean this kindly. The notorious mayor of Vienna, Karl Lueger, much admired by the young Hitler, had been an antisemitic demagogue who ranted for years about the "Jewish grip" on the press, higher education, the arts, and so on.

Vienna was still the capital of a great empire in 1915, but it was a decaying empire, with the hapless Emperor Franz Joseph fast losing control of Czech, Hungarian, Polish, German, Serbian, and other ethnic groups agitating for national independence. Only the Jews had no nation to agitate for, unless one includes the distant dream of Zion, and so they were the last and most loyal of Franz Joseph's subjects. Hence the emperor's reputation in antisemitic circles for being under the influence of nefarious Jewish interests; he was, in a popular expression of the time, "Jewified."

Joseph Roth, the great Jewish writer born in a small town near Lwów, who became a Viennese Francophile and died of alcoholism in Paris, wrote beautifully about the question of belonging. Jews, he wrote, "don't have a home anywhere, but they have graves in every cemetery." Czechs, Slovenes, Germans, Hungarians, have their own soil. Jews don't. And so, in Roth's analysis, they would have done much better if Franz Joseph's relatively benign cosmopolitan empire had stuck together. Roth's best novel, *Radetzky March*, is a tribute to this imperial polity, the k. and k., *Kaiserlich und Königlich*, Imperial and Royal, also known as Kakania. The end of empire was a disaster for the Jews.

They came streaming into Vienna's North Station, often with fake papers, or invented names to make things easier for the immigration officers, or stories that didn't quite hold up under scrutiny. But, as Friedrich Weinreb said in the memoir of his youth: "Identity documents are untouchable, they are sacred, they are taboo." The unlucky ones were sent back, only to return for another try with a different set of documents. The lucky ones lived in poor Viennese districts, large families stuck in one room, in cramped, filthy apartments, sewing clothes, changing currencies, peddling stuff in the streets, or selling their bodies. It was these poor Jews who shocked Hitler when he first came to the "racial Babylon." They were the Jewish proletariat, the flotsam of empire, the unwanted gate-crashers, despised by the non-Jewish Viennese bourgeoisie, as well as the less prosperous Christians, and, perhaps even more, by members of the wealthy Jewish bourgeoisie, who viewed these *Ostjuden*, these impoverished newcomers from east and central Europe, in their threadbare kaftans, shabby suits, beards, and black hats, as an embarrassing and disruptive nuisance.

Elevated way above the Jewish proletariat, living in another country, as it were, high Jewish Vienna—wealthy, secular, proudly assimilated—still flourished, despite Karl Lueger's demagoguery. Sigmund Freud gave lectures on psychoanalysis; Arthur Schnitzler wrote plays about the erotic entanglements of the upper classes; Karl Kraus was the most celebrated journalist in town; and Arnold Schoenberg, experimenting with atonal music, vowed to give the decadent French a lesson in the true German spirit—ironic in the light of what was soon to come when Germans called his atonal music an example of "Jewish degeneracy." Schnitzler and Schoenberg were born in Leopoldstadt, a part of Vienna where many Jews lived. Freud and Kraus came from small towns in Moravia and Bohemia.

In 1922, after the war and the end of empire, Hugo Bettauer wrote an extremely popular novel entitled *The City Without Jews (Die stadt ohne Juden)*. Two years later it was made into an expressionist film. The city is called Utopia, but it is in fact Vienna. The antisemitic government decides that Jews have too much influence and need to be expelled. But life and culture after the Jews are gone proves to be so dull and mediocre that they are asked to come back again. The novel was really a piece of wishful thinking. Shortly after the movie came out, Bettauer was murdered by a Nazi dental technician named Rothstock, who wanted to save German culture from Jewish influence. Proud of having killed the "slimy Jewish swine," the assassin was confined to a mental institution but was pronounced "cured" after little more than a year, upon which he decided to move to Germany.

When the Weinreb family arrived at the North Station, not knowing where to park their suitcases or how to survive, about 10 percent of Vienna's more than two million citizens were Jews. Quite where the Weinrebs thought they belonged in the pecking order was unclear, probably even to themselves. They had lived in Lwów, but they weren't Poles, let alone Ukrainians. They weren't Zionists or religious Jews. The harsh but warm comforts of *shtetl* culture were closed to them. They were loyal subjects of k. and k., when Kakania was dying. Mrs. Weinreb never stopped believing in the beneficence of Emperor Franz Joseph. And something Joseph Roth wrote about eastern European Jewish illusions about the West, the promised land of freedom, opportunity, and justice, applied to David and Hermine Weinreb as well. To the *Ostjuden*, Roth said, "Germany is still the country of Goethe, Schiller, and the German poets, whose works every studious Jewish youngster knows better than our Nazified high school graduates."

Friedrich Weinreb, whose full Jewish name was Ephraim Fishl Jehoshua Weinreb, then only five years old, had no idea where he was, or so he wrote in retrospect. He was "hanging in the air." His parents "represented a disappointed Western idealism and longed for something vague." Quite what they were longing for is not spelled out. In the literal sense of losing their status and material comfort, as well as a home, the Weinrebs were *déclassé*, neither proletarian nor part of a settled Viennese middle class, and far removed from the upper class. Karl Kraus, the literary scourge of antisemites who himself dabbled in antisemitic tropes, might have made fun of Hermine Weinreb's pretentious Germanophilia, that eminently vulnerable trait of trying too hard to assimilate, but neither she nor her husband was anywhere near to being powerful or influential enough to attract Kraus's scorn.

Then, still holed up in a dark house on the Odeongasse in Leopoldstadt, where hungry children cried all the time, and women screamed when they heard about a husband or brother killed in the war, the child Weinreb had a kind of epiphany. That, at any rate, is how he would describe it. His father, David, a nervous and now sickly man, had been called up to serve in the Austrian army but was soon invalided out and sent to a sanatorium.

It was just when the precocious child was wondering where he belonged that his maternal grandfather, Nosen Jamenfeld, came for a visit. He wasn't always called Jamenfeld. This was another one of those names that emerged from the lazy pen of some petty immigration officer. Benjamin Feld had been contracted to Jamenfeld. Jamenfeld or Feld came from a "dreamworld" of which Weinreb had been entirely unaware: the old world, so often sentimentalized (Chagall paintings, *Fiddler on the Roof*, and the like), of revered scholars of the Torah, cherished traditions, and Hassidic dances. Listening to his grandfather's stories of illustrious ancestors and miraculous wonder rabbis, Weinreb claims that for the first time he felt a sense of security in the midst of confusion and pandemonium. Perhaps, he writes, "the downfall of the world my parents had longed for had restored the links to the world of their parents."

From his grandfather, Weinreb heard stories full of wonder and mystery passed on by wise men in every generation. His grandmother, Channa, spoke of 127 famous sages, leaders, and scholars in her family. One great-grandfather, Avreimel, was so learned that scholars came to visit him in remote Bukovina from as far away as Jerusalem. The family also vaunted a relation to Shaul Wahl Katzenellebogen, the Jew who occupied the Polish throne for one day in 1587 because the electors couldn't agree on any of the candidates. Even King David himself was said to be an ancient ancestor. In a bizarre but not untypical flight of fancy, Weinreb wonders in his memoir whether the power of these distinguished ancestors might now have been concentrated in him alone.

One thing seems puzzling to Weinreb, however. How could his maternal family of pious sages and scholars possibly have allowed their daughter to marry a simple man like his father, who had no leanings toward anything spiritual at all? Grandfather Jamenfeld could enlighten the boy on this matter also. David Weinreb may have been a simple businessman, but he was descended from a famous traveling preacher, the Maggid of Nadvirna, a town of great Hassidic dynasties. This teller of sacred stories possessed ancient texts with extremely difficult insights into the holy books, which can only have come from the Prophet Elijah himself. Even if these insights would never be accessible to Weinreb's father, his son might well be the chosen one to enter their mysteries.

Weinreb had another fantasy, stemming from those difficult years in Vienna. Surrounded as he was by people in great distress about losing loved ones in the war, he dreamed that he would take them by the hand and lead them into a beautiful garden, where they would meet their lost husbands and brothers again. Meanwhile, their benefactor, after creating this miracle, would disappear into the shadows. The women, crying tears of joy, would turn to him, but he would be gone.

2: Port Arthur/Lüshun

Port Arthur was once a quiet fishing village at the tip of the Liaodong peninsula, a kind of dagger aimed at China from Korea across the strait. The Chinese call it Lüshun, the Japanese, Ryojun. Westerners named it Port Arthur in the nineteenth century, after a British naval surveyor named William C. Arthur, who fetched up there during the Second Opium War. In the 1880s, the Qing imperial government commissioned the German arms manufacturer Krupp, which had already supplied the Chinese with big guns, to fortify the village as a naval base.

During the Sino-Japanese War in 1895, Japanese troops battling their way into Lüshun/Ryojun had found the heads of Japanese POWs displayed on spikes. This provoked an orgy of vengeful brutality, during which Imperial Japanese soldiers hacked, bombed, and shot thousands of Chinese to death, a macabre foretaste of what was to come several decades later in cities like Shanghai and, most notoriously, Nanjing.

When Prince Su's family was exiled in Lüshun/Ryojun, in a two-story redbrick mansion that had once been a Russian hotel, bits and pieces of classicist and baroque-style architecture were all that was left from the period of tsarist rule. The Russians would never have been in Lüshun at all if Japan had not been pressed by Western powers to relinquish its claim to the city after conquering it in the war against China. Russia had forced the Chinese government to lease the Liaodong peninsula with Port Arthur at its tip to the tsar. Still furious over this humiliation, the Japanese took back Port Arthur in 1904, in the Russo-Japanese War, at the cost of almost sixty thousand casualties on their own side, and more than half that number of Russians. The hilly khaki-colored landscape around the naval base was littered with the corpses of men mowed down by machine guns and howitzers. Once the siege was over, the Russian fleet sunk, and the Japanese victorious, the next aim was to expand Japanese influence over the rest of Manchuria, as well as Inner Mongolia. Japan coveted the land as a buffer against Russia, as a source of coal, iron, copper, tungsten, and other natural resources for its industry, and, eventually, as a *lebensraum* for Japanese farmers, teachers, soldiers, artists, businessmen, architects, engineers, prostitutes, spies, and a wide variety of dubious adventurers, eager to break out of the cramped and insular borders of the Japanese archipelago.

And so, Prince Su, once the family had settled down in the former Russian hotel in Lüshun, decided to give his thirty-eight children, born from his wife and concubines, not just a solid grounding in the Chinese classics, and such vigorous Manchu pastimes as horse riding, but also a strong dose of modern Japanese learning. There is a photograph of little Dongzhen/Yoshiko that must have been taken soon after the family's forced exile from Beijing. She looks solemn, dressed in a traditional Chinese embroidered silk robe. But people remembered seeing Prince Su's children going to school in Japanese uniforms. Japanese teachers were hired to instruct them in language, literature, and mathematics. The household was run like a Japanese army barracks: daily calisthenics, cold baths, runs up and down the local hills in the thick snow. Soon the older children were sent to the local Japanese school, invariably dressed in kimonos. They were instructed to bow to the Japanese emperor at the start of each day.

Life cannot have been easy for a family used to having servants take care of all their needs. They, too, like the Weinrebs in Vienna, had lost their status and clung to memories of an idealized past. National allegiances became complicated. Manchus were not only out of power but no longer a coherent or sovereign people. They were simply citizens of the Republic of China, to which they felt no loyalty. But Yoshiko recalls in her memoir how her father would try to turn misfortune into a virtue.

Fending for oneself, he said, would build character. This type of moral instruction typically took place in the dining hall, where all the siblings would gather after the gong was sounded. One uplifting story stuck in the young girl's mind, a tale that showed how deeply the Manchus had imbibed Chinese history and culture.

Prince Su reminded his children of the Han Emperor Gaozu (256– 195 BC), better known as Liu Bang, still worshipped by Chinese as a mythical martial hero. Gaozu, from a peasant family, was the leader of a Robin Hood–type gang of bandits, who peed into the hat of a cultivated mandarin to show his contempt for the foppish upper class. One day, during his campaign against the Qin Dynasty emperor, Gaozu was forced to live off the land, drinking from the river and eating barley, while surrounded by his formidable enemies. Yet he prevailed, defeated the Qin army, and founded the Han dynasty, the name of which is still invoked by Chinese ethnic nationalists to distinguish themselves from "minorities" in China such as the Manchus. If Prince Su's children could learn from Gaozu's spirit, he assured them, China would once again be theirs.

Prince Su and his extended family were closely guarded day and night by the Japanese military. The prince couldn't even go out fishing on his own. The Japanese liked to call this "protection," but it was protection of a particularly intrusive and oppressive kind, which would later be applied to the whole of Manchuria, when it became a puppet state, governed by powerless Chinese with grand titles under the firm watch of Japanese who had all the power.

In any event, Prince Su put up with this regime because he still thought his dream of reconquering China under the banner of the Qing might be possible with Japanese help. The northeastern Manchu and Mongolian parts of the former Qing empire were rather like the Baltic states after the Russian Revolution. Progressive princes, often educated in Japan, who had high hopes for Manchu and Mongolian independence, fought with other nobles who wished to remain part of China. Bolsheviks and White Russians battled each other in Outer Mongolia, which was then a theocratic Tibetan Buddhist state; and Japanese, Chinese, and Russians fought over these remnants of empire, sometimes with extremely bloody consequences.

Under Japanese protection, the house in Lüshun became a magnet for an assortment of plotters, gunrunners, and political schemers. One of the progressive Mongol nobles in Prince Su's orbit was Rungsangnoerhbu, or the Prince of Khallachin, who was married to Prince Su's sister. His Mongolian tribe, the Kharchin, had once enjoyed the traditional task of supplying the Manchu emperors with fermented mare's milk. The prince had been a staunch defender of the Qing government. But like his Manchu brother-in-law, he was a modernist who had picked up progressive ideas while studying in Japan. One was to establish schools for girls in Mongolia, with Japanese teachers to give them a modern education. He also set up the first Inner Mongolian newspaper and a proper postal system. This showed once again how Japan was both the source of modern progress and the breeding ground of brutal military expansionism that would soon engulf parts of Mongolia and Manchuria in the guise of pan-Asian idealism.

The name for Japanese adventurers who sought their fortunes on the wild frontiers of China was *tairiku ronin*, literally continental *ronin*. *Ronin* were the masterless samurai who had once roamed all over Japan, a bit like cowboys in American westerns, desperados with swords for hire. Manchuria was Japan's Wild West. One of those continental *ronin* was Kawashima Naniwa. Only five feet tall with a narrow bony face, he had been a timid, nervous child, easy prey for school bullies, when he grew up in Matsumoto, a provincial town high in the Japanese Alps. Born in 1865, Kawashima belonged to that class of former samurai who had lost their privileges in the Meiji Restoration of 1868, which formally did away with caste distinctions. Such men often resented the mercantile, Westernized ways of Meiji Japan, which struck them as effete, abject, and materialistic. They yearned for a feudal order, which was less a return to what Japan had once been than an Orientalized version of fascism.

Kawashima's hero and mentor was an officer named Fukushima Yasumasa, born in the same alpine region, who became a celebrated figure
in Japan for riding his horse from Berlin to Vladivostok. An even more
famous adventurer of this type was Doihara Kenji, an army officer who
learned to speak fluent Mandarin, as well as several Chinese dialects. As
one of the Japanese Imperial Army's China specialists, he spent much of
his military career in northern China and Manchuria. A burly rogue
with a Hitler moustache and a ready smile, Doihara cut a romantic figure and became known in the Western and Japanese press as Lawrence
of Manchuria. This might suggest that, like T. E. Lawrence, the famous
British fighter for Arab causes during World War I, he was a dreamer
who longed to liberate the native peoples. He was not. Doihara was an
agent of their oppression, as an assassin, a blackmailer, a terrorist plotter,
and a major operator in opium and prostitution rackets. Doihara would
be tried by the Tokyo War Crimes Tribunal and hanged as a war criminal in 1948.

Unlike Fukushima, who is said to have spoken ten languages, Kawashima
refused to learn English, or any other European language. Instead, he
studied Chinese, with every intention of achieving fame on the continent as a savior of Asia. After quitting his language school in Osaka,
Kawashima boarded a ship to Shanghai, where he quickly established a
reputation as a wild eccentric, prone to violent outrages. He often had to
be restrained from murdering hapless local guides or anyone else who
got on his nerves. In China, the timid youth now acted as a hard man.
Dressed up as a Chinese coolie, with a fake queue, but also with a samurai sword readily at hand, he went on spying trips with various Japanese
military companions, linking up with local warlords and gangsters who
might one day be useful to Japan. On one of these ventures, he fell off his
horse, which some blamed for his early deafness. Or perhaps the deafness was due to a bout of malaria, which he tried to ignore as he set off
on another trip into some inhospitable region of China.

Kawashima fell in with members of one of the most radical Japanese secret societies at that time, the Genyosha, or Black Ocean Society, a terrorist outfit formed by disaffected ex-samurai like Kawashima; it was led by the bearded ideologue Toyama Mitsuru, a gurulike figure who promoted the notion of a reinvigorated Asia under Japanese dominance. He later founded an equally extreme group, and named it the Black Dragon Society. The Genyosha, as well as its successor, attracted all kinds of shady characters, including mobsters and of course a fair number of continental *ronin*. Assassinating political enemies was a favored tactic of these hotheads, who believed that they represented the true Japanese (samurai) spirit. Toyama, himself connected to organized crime, had supported Sun Yat-sen's revolution, but his organization gradually developed an efficient continental spy network for the increasingly militaristic Japanese state, while making money out of prostitution, extortion, and other rackets.

During the Boxer Rebellion in 1900 against the foreign legations in Beijing, Kawashima finally managed to notch up a memorable feat, which has more than a whiff of legend. When foreign troops, led by a German field marshal, were about to bombard the Forbidden City and destroy its treasures if the Chinese refused to surrender, Kawashima, acting as the translator for the Japanese contingent, is said to have cried out: "Leave the Forbidden City to me!" Yelling in Chinese through the palace gates, Kawashima was then able to persuade the Qing imperial guards to come out peacefully. Prince Su was so impressed by the tiny Japanese man's fortitude that he asked to meet him.

Almost the same age, they struck up a friendship. In her memoir, Yoshiko recalls her father's passionate attachment to her future adoptive father, something that, in her words, "went far beyond personal interests." They were, she writes, "inspired by mutual feelings of love and sincerity, and became sworn brothers." Well, perhaps they did. But the feelings of Manchu-Japanese friendship were deeply entangled with politics, often of a sordid kind.

After the Boxer Rebellion, Prince Su asked Kawashima, who cannot have had any experience in such matters, to help organize a modern police force in Beijing. He may have assumed that his new friend, being Japanese, would be a master of all things modern. But the main thing that bound the two men was their shared ideal of Asia for the Asians. Decadent China had to be saved from itself. Japan would be the driving force. The abominable white powers would be kicked out. They could both drink to that.

After Prince Su's exile, Kawashima Naniwa became a regular visitor in Lüshun, staying there for long spells with his wife, Fuku, a sad and rather neglected figure who later fell into severe depressions. Kawashima was one of the plotters hovering around Su's household. Among other things, he was involved in smuggling arms to Mongolia to resist the Chinese republic. A popular fantasy among right-wing Japanese propagandists was that Mongolians and Manchus were racially and culturally closer to the Japanese than they were to the Chinese, which meant that China clearly had no legitimate claim on those areas. Kawashima may or may not have believed this. Possibly Prince Su did. But it doesn't really matter, for however much it was dosed with sentimental declarations of brotherhood, their alliance was largely opportunistic. The prince saw Manchurian independence as a stepping-stone to reconquering China; Kawashima's idea of pan-Asianism was to establish Japanese domination.

But it all came to nothing in the end. The Japanese government decided to support the Chinese republic, at least for a time. Kawashima was told by his old mentor Fukushima to back off from his Manchu-Mongolian interventions. He returned to Japan a deeply disappointed man. His dream of saving Asia had ended in failure.

And yet, Prince Su still extended his fraternal hand to the Japanese *ronin* in an extraordinary gesture. There is some dispute about when exactly this happened. In 1915? Or possibly a year earlier? In any case, one of the prince's sons had gone to visit Kawashima in Tokyo. He found him in a restless mood and obsessed with dreams of further plots in

Manchuria. His wife, Fuku, was suffering one of her bouts of depression. They were a childless couple, and they seemed terribly lonely.

If Yoshiko's memoir is to be trusted, which it surely isn't, the following scene then took place in the dining hall of the house in Lüshun. "Father dropped his head in deep thought. Then he looked up and said to me: 'Would you like to be Uncle Kawashima's child?' My brothers and sisters were stunned, but I instantly replied that I'd be happy to be his child. 'All right,' father said, 'if everyone agrees, you will be his daughter.'" Prince Su sent his friend a letter with the following words: "I am gifting you with a toy. How about it? I hope you will cherish her." The girl's mother wept silently.

The reasons for this peculiar gift never became entirely clear. Kawashima and Prince Su had murky financial ties. Money was still being channeled by Japanese operators to Qing loyalists. The prince's family received most of its income from a local open-air market with a dubious reputation for selling stolen goods. This "thieves' market" was managed by Kawashima, who was later accused by Prince Su's relatives of pocketing most of the proceeds himself. The prince might simply have wished to strengthen his ties with Japan to have another try at restoring the fortunes of the Qing Dynasty. But these dreams ended for good with his death in 1922. The manner of his death is disputed. According to a U.S. government report in 1945, he died by swallowing some kind of metal solution. Prince Su was buried with the full honors due to a Manchu prince. His fourth concubine, Yoshiko's mother, died soon after. Some say she committed suicide as well. Or she might have died from drugs meant to abort her eleventh child.

If Yoshiko ever resented being sent to Japan as a "gift," she did not say so in public. But her elder brother Xianli, quoted in Phyllis Birnbaum's fine biography of the princess, had a different account of this sinister event. In his memory, she refused to go to Japan and burst into tears.

So, at the age of six or seven, began her extraordinary story, as a toy, an object, to be passed on from one man to another. Not only did she soon learn how to embellish the facts of her own life, but she became a kind of canvas for others to project their fantasies on.

After arriving at the port of Shimonoseki, she was taken to a traditional inn, where she was made to change into a Japanese kimono and her hair was cut in the Japanese fashion, with a straight fringe just over the eyes. Even though she was never formally adopted, and her name was not included in the Kawashima family records, Dongzhen effectively became the daughter of Kawashima Naniwa and his wife, Fuku, whom she now had to address as "mama." There is a photograph of her, looking grave in her Japanese finery, clutching a Japanese fan. Scribbled on the left of the picture is her new name of Kawashima Yoshiko.

Three

Miracles

⌒⌒⌒

1: Berlin

Like Weinreb, Felix Kersten felt he was one of the chosen, though not quite in the same way, and certainly not based on ancient bloodlines.

After the Finnish Dr. Ekman told him that his fortune lay in his supple, big hands, Kersten acquired the techniques of Finnish massage therapy from a doctor named Kollander at a military hospital in Helsinki, where he earned a degree in 1921. Massage of the back and limbs to increase the blood circulation has a long history in Scandinavia, deeply embedded in the folk culture of Finland for example, along with sauna baths and self-flagellation with fresh birch twigs. Kersten was such a gifted masseur that he was soon asked by soldiers in Dr. Kollander's hospital to relieve their aching bodies. To make ends meet, Kersten worked as a dishwasher in restaurants. A big man, he also loaded freight on the docks of Helsinki. After getting his degree, he was advised by his teacher to continue his studies in Berlin, which had the best reputation in Europe for this type of therapy.

A country where all types of medical research and practices were highly prized, Germany was also a society of nature worshippers, mountain hikers, nude bathers, gymnasts, and other lovers of physical and spiritual fitness. One of the great proponents of modern German nationalism was Friedrich Ludwig Jahn (1778–1852), known as the Father of Gymnastics, the *Turnvater*. Gymnastic clubs all over Germany, as well as in German communities overseas, including the United States, were among the most favored conduits for promoting the healthy German "spirit."

But Germany between the two wars, when Kersten arrived in Berlin, was also a battered society, demoralized by defeat, a crashed economy, and extreme poverty. Clashes between the revolutionary left and the radical right erupted in street battles, with a lot of bloodshed on both sides. The German empire had fallen; Kaiser Wilhelm II had fled to Holland, where he plotted his comeback while sitting at his desk on a horse saddle; and inflation and revolution were constant threats. The twin symbols of Weimar-period Berlin were the prostitute and the blind or limbless veteran with a begging bowl. Kersten recalled that he got to know both the good and the bad sides of the German people. The latter would lead to Nazism, and Kersten always took the side of its victims. Or so he claimed after the war.

The social disruptions of Weimar Germany resulted not only in crime, corruption, bold artistic experimentation, cabarets, music halls, high suicide rates, and prostitution of all sexes, ages, and types but also in a taste for occult theories and exotic therapies. "In this period of tremendous political and economic uncertainty, hypnosis, mesmerism, clairvoyance, and every form of occultism flourished." The man who wrote this sentence, Wilhelm Wulff, was himself a professional astrologer who would later get to know Kersten well as a fellow member of Heinrich Himmler's court. (Himmler, like Hitler, needed to consult an astrologer to plot his next moves, frequently in battles against rivals in the Führer's entourage.)

Kersten was once again constrained to making a living washing dishes, but otherwise seemed to enjoy himself as a man about town. Lumbering, overweight, and pasty-faced, he was not physically attractive, but he was by all accounts easygoing, charming, a good-time Charlie, always ready for a bit of fun. One woman who was clearly smitten was several years older than him. Elisabeth Lüben lived with her widowed mother, a friend of Kersten's parents. Kersten was able to lodge at their comfortable house in Berlin, which took the rough edges off his rather penurious life. Relations with Elisabeth do not appear to have been sexual, even in the beginning. They were more familial. Her role, which continued for the rest of their lives, was a maternal one: she washed and mended his clothes, cooked his dinners, and generally doted on him. Elisabeth lived with Kersten as his caretaker and confidante even after he got married and had children. When he needed advice or solace, it was to Elisabeth that Kersten would turn.

Kersten's main teacher in Berlin was Dr. August Bier, a surgeon with various interesting achievements to his name. He was the first to anesthetize patients locally by injecting cocaine into their spinal cord. There was another reason for his fame. He helped to design the *Stahlhelm*, the German military helmet with its characteristic coal-shuttle shape protecting the back of the neck. Dr. Bier was also a keen proponent of German gymnastics, a lover of trees, and a practitioner of homeopathic cures that are now dismissed as quackery but were popular at the time.

Oddly, Kersten doesn't mention Bier in his memoir, even though he must have spoken about him to Joseph Kessel, his French biographer, who writes about him at some length. Kersten recalls other eminent professors instead, such as Otto Binswanger, a neurologist specializing in epilepsy and neurasthenia. One possible reason for this switch is that Bier became an enthusiastic Nazi and was showered with honors by Hitler, while Binswanger died safely in 1929, before all the trouble began.

Kersten's most important teacher was, however, allegedly not German at all, but a Chinese man named Dr. B. Ko. In Kersten's memoir, it was Binswanger who introduced him to Dr. Ko. In Kessel's account, it was Bier. Neither I nor others have managed to find any trace of Dr. Ko. His name is not in the Berlin telephone book of the period. This doesn't necessarily mean that he was an invention, just that his presence remains hard to pin down. Kersten's description of Dr. Ko may also be entirely accurate, but it does suggest some fantastical elements. He sounds a little bit too much like an Oriental sage in a prewar comic book.

When Westerners think of ancient Oriental wisdom, their fantasies often turn to Tibet, the land of flying lama priests and divine incarnations. Dr. Ko, in the story told to Kessel, was born in China, but raised in a Tibetan monastery, where he learned the arcane arts of Chinese and Tibetan healing, as well as the techniques of Tibetan massage passed on from generation to generation by Buddhist monks. Once he had mastered these skills to the satisfaction of his teachers, Ko was told to go west so he could acquaint Europeans with the wisdom of the East. He is said to have earned a medical doctorate in London before moving to Berlin after the Great War.

Even though Dr. Ko remains an elusive figure, the seeds of his Tibetan knowledge would have fallen on fertile ground in Weimar Berlin, where dabbling in Asian religions was in fashion, not just among health freaks and enthusiasts of mystical wellness but among certain Nazis as well. Madame Blavatsky's theosophy, positing that a "deeper reality" could be accessed through intuition and meditation, was much in favor at the time. She was a spiritualist born, like Kersten, in a Russian German family, who traveled in Asia in 1849, where according to her own possibly fictitious account she met the "Masters of Ancient Wisdom," who encouraged her to immerse herself in spiritual affairs and spend time with monks in Tibet.

Germany had long been a center of Sanskrit scholarship. But it was vulgarized in the 1920s and '30s by all kinds of peculiar seekers, including Heinrich Himmler, who is said to have always carried a copy of the Bhagavad Gita in his pocket. He appointed a Sanskrit professor named Walter Wüst to preside over Ahnenerbe, a kind of SS think tank that engaged in research on the Indian origins of the so-called Aryan race. It was from this kind of mumbo jumbo that the idea came to adapt the swastika, an ancient Hindu-Buddhist symbol, to the Nazi movement.

Himmler was considered to be a bit of a crank by some other Nazi leaders, but his interest in certain aspects of Hinduism—caste, sacred warriors, and so on—was not at all unusual. Yoga was commonly practiced in Germany between the wars. A German Australian occultist and yoga teacher named Ernst Issberner-Haldane promoted something called "Aryan yoga." A founding member of the so-called Swastika Circle, right-wing enthusiasts of the occult, Issberner was a ferocious antisemite who dabbled in esoteric groups favored by Himmler. Wilhelm Wulff was also a member of the Swastika Circle, and he became a student of Sanskrit to help his career in astrology. Himmler would later order Wulff to study Zen Buddhism as well, in the hope that the self-sacrificial Japanese warrior spirit could be transferred to the SS.

Dr. Ko, then, or at least Kersten's version of Dr. Ko, would not have been out of place at all in 1920s Berlin. The story goes that when Kersten was introduced to Dr. Ko, either by Binswanger or Bier, the Chinese masseur, in true "Oriental" fashion, said nothing but just kept smiling. Dr. Ko was not impressed by Kersten's demonstration of Finnish massage. The younger man had great promise, but he needed to learn again from scratch.

There is no reason to doubt Kersten's description of Dr. Ko's technique. It was a kind of *shiatsu*, based on pressing certain points in the body to relieve tension, after feeling for the nerves that were thought to be the cause of such ailments as migraine, stomach pains, or neurasthenia. But Kersten would have his readers know that for him to explain his skill would be like a poet or artist explaining the creation of a work of art. At the very least, it took an extraordinary sensitivity of the fingertips, with which Kersten appears to have been blessed.

Dr. Ko—in Kessel's retelling—realized the moment he saw Kersten that the astrological chart made up when Ko was still a Buddhist novice in Tibet had come true. The chart predicted that in 1922 he would meet a young man who knew nothing but could be taught. That young man turned out to be Kersten. He was chosen for this task. One of the things Dr. Ko taught his disciple was that probing the affected nerves under a person's skin was only the beginning. One had to enter the patient's body, as it were, which was only possible after intense concentration. "Manual therapy" Kersten called it, but it was also a spiritual discipline.

Kersten's apprenticeship with Dr. Ko allegedly came to an end as mysteriously as it began. After four years, during which he had been instructing Kersten in the ways of massage and life, feeding him the most exquisite Chinese dishes, Dr. Ko suddenly announced that he was returning to his monastery in Tibet, to prepare for his death, which would come in eight years. Dr. Ko knew this because it had been written in his horoscope. The Buddhist sage spoke of his death in complete serenity, smiling all the while.

2: Matsumoto

On her first day at school in Tokyo, Yoshiko must have made a peculiar impression on her classmates. They were dressed in drab, dark blue school uniforms. She turned up in a purple damask pleated silk garment tied with a large white ribbon. In those days, foreigners were even rarer in Japanese schools than they are now. Crowding around this extraordinary apparition, the children asked her which country she was from. Not knowing what to say, Yoshiko blurted out: "From my mother's tummy."

People still called her a *Chankoro*, a "Chink." And indeed, since her foster father chose not to enter her name in his family registry, she never became a Japanese citizen. Why Kawashima Naniwa neglected to complete this final act of adoption is unclear. Possibly he wanted to groom her as a pawn in his dream of Qing Dynasty restoration, and it would have been inopportune for her to become a Japanese citizen.

As an immigrant child, Yoshiko had several options to deal with abuse. She could try to conform to local customs and manners as much as possible, laying herself open to more ridicule for trying too hard or making trivial mistakes. Or she could play up the looks and attitudes of the exotic outsider, in the way Benjamin Disraeli, as the son of an immigrant, did when he posed as an aristocratic Jewish dandy flaunting his golden rings and velvet finery in dour Victorian Britain. Yoshiko's strategy would be a combination of both. The pose she chose to adopt was an outlandish imitation of the macho Japanese nationalists she encountered in her foster father's house. When things became too confusing, she would remember her Manchu father's words, instilled during those long lunchtime lectures in Lüshun: "You are neither Chinese, nor Japanese. You are to become the hinge between China and Japan."

One thing Yoshiko never forgot was her noble status. Japanese schoolchildren approached their teachers with the greatest deference, jumping to attention and bowing when they entered the classroom. The child Yoshiko treated the teachers as though they were waiters or servants, not *sensei*, but with a haughty "Hey, you . . . !"

No wonder she received most of her rudimentary education at home. Exposure to Japanese school discipline never agreed with her. "Home" for several years was Kawashima's rambling traditional wooden mansion in Tokyo, shaded by a row of sturdy oak trees. Yoshiko's home teacher was a remarkable woman named Akabane Matsue, who had gone on her own steam to study at Columbia University in New York. Back in Japan she specialized in tutoring students from various parts of Asia. Her progressive attitudes might have seemed odd in the milieu of the Kawashima household, frequented by ultranationalists. But again, modernism and radical nationalism were not always in contradiction. Members of the notorious Black Dragon Society, on whose fringes Kawashima Naniwa was now to be found, were aggressive chauvinists, aiming to bring Asia under one imperial Japanese roof. But they were enemies of Western colonialism. Japan would "liberate" and then "modernize" the backward Asians.

Kawashima and his friends were not in the mainstream of Japanese society. Tokyo, like Weimar Berlin, was going through its own frenzied, neon-lit jazz age. Modern girls (*moga*), with short, bobbed hair, red Clara Bow lips, and short skirts, and modern boys (*mobo*), sometimes called "Marx boys," in bow ties, white ducks and Harold Lloyd glasses, danced the Charleston to Fumio Nanri's Hot Peppers, read Nietzsche and Karl Marx, and met in cafés to discuss female emancipation. "Taisho democracy," the imperfect multiparty system named after the Taisho imperial reign (1912–1926), was more liberal than any time before or than the two decades that followed. The reactionary, often militaristic, emperor-worshipping politics of the 1930s were in part a nativist response to the free-spirited Taisho years. Adopting Western ways was seen by conservative intellectuals, as well as violent extremists, as a humiliation to be overcome. A plan by ultranationalists to assassinate Charlie Chaplin during his visit to Tokyo in 1932 made a certain zany sense in this regard.

Kawashima Naniwa had not yet given up on his plots to achieve Manchu-Mongolian independence from the Chinese republic; 1915 promised to be a propitious year. While Europeans were slaughtering one another in the cratered fields of Flanders, the Japanese bullied Yuan Shikai's quasi-imperial Chinese government into allowing Japan to take control of parts of northern China and Manchuria.

Encouraged by Kawashima, Prince Su gambled most of his considerable fortune on an anti-Chinese uprising in Mongolia and Manchuria. Japanese agents helped local activists smuggle arms and munitions into Inner Mongolia in crates of bean curd and pickled horseradish. Money came from sympathizers such as Baron Okura Kihachiro, an arms dealer and collector of Asian antiques, whose name still graces one of Tokyo's luxury hotels. Kawashima, meanwhile, was taking personal care of the sons of a pro-Japanese Mongolian general, by sponsoring their education in a Japanese military academy.

Yuan Shikai had himself crowned as the new Chinese emperor in December 1915. Unfortunately for him, his less than illustrious reign lasted no more than six months. He had too few friends and too many enemies, including Chinese republicans, southern Chinese warlords, the British, the Japanese, and many ordinary Chinese citizens. In June 1916, Yuan lost his throne and then swiftly died. Some said his kidneys gave out due to nervous prostration. Some claimed he died of shock. Some believed that darker forces were at work.

In any event, the semiclandestine movement to "help the Qing and fight Yuan" had lost its purpose. Japan no longer supported Manchu-Mongolian independence, even tacitly. Once again, the hopes of Prince Su and Kawashima for a revival of the Qing were dashed. Their sense of failure might have hastened Prince Su's own death six years later. The effect on Kawashima appears to have been similar to what happened to a number of Japanese continental dreamers: his enthusiasm for things Chinese started to curdle into contempt. To help stop the rot in China and kick out the white powers, Japan would have to resort to more forceful measures.

Perhaps in an effort to console Prince Su, or to sort out their complicated financial arrangements, Kawashima decided to board the ferry at Shimonoseki to visit his old comrade in Lüshun in the fall of 1916. Yoshiko traveled with him. Exactly what happened in Lüshun is uncertain. Yoshiko was apparently ushered into her father's presence, dressed in a kimono. She dutifully sang a Japanese military song and repeated phrases, no doubt coached by Kawashima and designed to please her father, about the glorious future of the Qing Dynasty. This, at any rate, is how her brother Xianli remembered the occasion. A more disturbing episode unfolded in the evening—still according to Xianli—when Yo-shiko, now dressed in her nightie, gave Kawashima a massage in the presence of her parents. Her mother wept and whispered to her husband that perhaps they should take their daughter back. Prince Su shook his head and said this was a "necessary sacrifice for the revival of the Qing."

Yoshiko's own account, which may or may not be true, omits any mention of this melancholy event, which is not surprising since her much-edited memoir was written for a Japanese readership in 1937, when the war with China had entered its most ferocious phase. Anything that reflected badly on a Japanese man in China, even a chancer like Kawashima, was unwelcome. What she does say, however, is revealing. She claims to have forgotten how to speak her native language. She felt like a stranger amid her siblings. Now she understood why *ihojin*, the Japanese word for alien, "was used as a kind of pronoun for loneliness." (Her Chinese would eventually come back to her; it was never perfect, but then neither was her Japanese.) By the time she began to feel at home again, Yoshiko writes, Kawashima whisked her back to Japan. This story was no doubt meant to elicit compassionate tears from her Japanese readers, but that doesn't mean the sentiment isn't true.

Kawashima, increasingly deaf and depressed, decided to move his household from Tokyo to the snowcapped mountains of his native Nagano Prefecture. It is a beautiful, rather remote place, lush and green in summer and snowbound in winter. The much renovated black-walled castle of Matsumoto can be seen from the many hot springs, whose sulphurous waters have all kinds of medicinal benefits. The Kawashima house, smelling of pine and cypress wood, was built on a mountain slope overlooking clear blue Nojiri Lake, which was filled with pleasure boats in the summer season.

Entering her teens, Yoshiko was by most accounts a lonely child, softly singing snatches of Chinese songs to herself and given to moods that shifted from clownishness to imperiousness. She was also noted for certain eccentricities. One was her habit of arriving at the local middle school riding her chestnut mare, which she would tether to a cherry blossom tree. The other was to adopt masculine speech, using words used only by boys or men, which was startling in a country where male and female speech is still quite distinct.

Yoshiko's attendance at school was spotty. She would come and go as she pleased. This may explain why a new headmaster decided it would be better for her to continue her studies at home. Yoshiko described this in her memoir as a typical example of anti-Chinese prejudice. No matter how much she acquired proper Japanese speech, customs, manners, and what was then extolled as the national "spirit," she was still treated as an *ihojin*. Whatever the reason, Yoshiko clearly didn't fit into the life of rural Japan.

Kawashima, whose wife was mostly absent, decided to take Yoshiko's education in hand and subjected her to a bullying military regime, not commonly inflicted on a teenage girl, including physical punishments. He also enlisted her as his secretary. Since he could barely hear what people were saying anymore, she would write everything down and pass him notes.

Their relationship was almost certainly exploitative, and possibly something even more twisted. Yoshiko shared his bedroom, which would not have been particularly unusual in a Japanese house, but some believe she was also forced to share his bed. She was eighteen in 1925, and he was sixty. Yoshiko's most painstaking biographer, Kamisaka Fuyuko, dismisses the suspicion of sexual abuse by pointing out that the age difference was too great. Her American biographer, Phyllis Birnbaum, is less naive. She considers the various accounts without coming to a conclusion. Since there is no clear proof either way, Birnbaum could hardly have done otherwise. But Yoshiko's brother, who was staying at Kawashima's house at the time, claimed that she broke down in tears one night and told him that her foster father had forced himself on her. Xianli also recalled a startling occasion back in Lüshun, when Kawashima is supposed to have said that since he was blessed with courage and Prince Su with benevolence, a child of his born by Yoshiko would combine both their fine qualities.

The most lurid account appears in a lightly fictionalized version of Yoshiko's life, written in 1932 by a boulevardier and connoisseur of Chinese low life named Muramatsu Shofu. He wrote his book, *The Beauty in Men's Clothes* (*Danso no reijin*), at Yoshiko's request, when they shared an apartment in Shanghai. It contains many tall tales but also supposedly quite a few true ones. His heroine, named Mariko in the novel, is raped by her foster father. And this is the version, true or false, that has been repeated in postwar Chinese movies and books about Yoshiko, portraying her as a victim of Japanese aggression as well as a traitor.

After Prince Su's death in 1922, Kawashima had become the official guardian of all Su's children. But he behaved as though he were more like the official head of the family, disposing of their money as he saw fit. Much of it had been wasted by Kawashima on various failed business ventures, including an attempt to use the local spring water in Matsumoto to manufacture a fizzy apple wine, which failed to find a market.

But most of Kawashima's time in his mountain home was spent on entertaining various aspiring continental *ronin* and louche right-wing ruffians with records of revolutionary violence. These were the kind of men that Yoshiko had grown up with ever since her time in Lüshun. They got drunk, sang rowdy army songs, and bragged of their violent exploits. One fierce anti-Communist youth had been involved in an assault on the former Japanese governor of Taiwan for being insufficiently bellicose toward the Russians. Another, named Iwata Ainosuke, had been linked to the fatal stabbing of a Japanese Foreign Ministry official for being soft on China. Iwata was president of the Patriotic Association, a terrorist group that would be responsible for the murder in 1930 of a liberal prime minister. Some of these young terrorists, including Iwata, had close connections with officers in the Japanese armed forces.

Yoshiko carried out her usual duty of writing down what was said on these occasions, so that Kawashima could follow what was going on. Even as she was engaged in this work, her adoptive father was terrified that she would get herself mixed up with one of his uncouth acolytes. He told her to stay away from them. But they didn't stay away from her. Caught between their rough advances and her foster father's violent rages, she attempted suicide at least twice. Once, she took an overdose of morphine. Phyllis Birnbaum relates that a suitor sucked the drug from her lips. The second occasion involved

Iwata, who proposed marriage. Feeling trapped once again, she said she'd rather die. Iwata later said he thought she was bluffing. He handed her his gun. She shot herself in the chest, but the attempt must have been half-hearted, since she appears to have survived without doing too much damage to herself.

There were other suitors. Yamaga Toru was a charming China enthusiast who would later become involved in the Japanese propaganda film industry in Manchuria, while operating as a secret police spy. He came to the house to practice his Chinese with Yoshiko. Gossip about a budding tenderness between the two was reported in the local paper. Kawashima was furious. Yamaga swiftly distanced himself.

Then Yoshiko did something radical. After having a "farewell to womanhood" photograph taken, dressed in a bright kimono, with her thick black hair arranged in traditional Japanese style, she shaved her head and borrowed her brother's school uniform. There is a photograph of her posing next to her foster father, who looks as though he is putting a brave face on things. She looks awkward, but also fairly pleased with herself, in her brother's garb and a military crew cut.

Why she did this is disputed. Always inclined to boyish language and pursuits, she may have considered herself transgender in today's terms. She certainly would have understood the concept of being nonbinary. Kamisaka, her Japanese biographer, thinks she was driven to it because of male abuse. Birnbaum quotes Yoshiko as saying: "I've had all this trouble because I'm a woman." But also as saying: "I was born with what the doctors call a tendency toward the third sex." In her memoir, Yoshiko blames her foster parent for wanting to keep her away from young men. As long as she was a tomboy riding horses and shooting guns, he was reassured. This doesn't sound wholly convincing.*

That there were serious tensions between Yoshiko and her foster father is obvious. But Kawashima did leave his mark. Birnbaum quotes him saying: "Yoshiko has an interest in matters like the problems in China and Asia and aspires to be like that mannish Western Joan of Arc." This is repeated in Yoshiko's own story. As well as finding it annoying to be a woman, she writes, "The dreamlike heroic feeling of restoring the Qing made me give up being a woman and to become a man."

Perhaps. The psychological grounds for sexual identity are complicated. Yoshiko admitted to having had childhood dreams of being an Asian Joan of Arc. After reading a book about the French heroine, she turned up at her school in Matsumoto and "started acting like Joan of Arc, telling everyone things like, 'If I had three thousand soldiers, I'd take China.'" But as an explanation for wanting a male identity (which was never permanent; there were times when she adopted a feminine role), this feels inadequate. The least one can say, however, is that as a masculine figure she became the perfect embodiment of dreams foisted on her by the patriarchs in her life.

---

*Still, it would be an anachronism to call her "they," so I will continue with the female pronoun as her other biographers have.

3: Scheveningen

Since the middle of the nineteenth century, Scheveningen, a suburb of The Hague, was a typical northern European seaside resort, not as grand as Ostend or Brighton, but more stylish than Ramsgate, say, or Dieppe. It has a wide esplanade for flaneurs, some more undressed than others, who don't mind braving the gusty North Sea winds; it has a pier with restaurants and arcades, built in 1959, after the first one, a lovely Indo art nouveau folly built in 1901, was destroyed by the Germans during the war. And it has the Kurhaus hotel, a Belle Epoque wedding cake of a building designed in 1884 by two German architects. Winston Churchill stayed there. A Rolling Stones concert in 1964 ended in a riot there. As a schoolboy, I suffered through the annual ball there, organized by our dance teacher who supervised our clumsy waltzing and fox-trotting in the mirrored ballroom.

For much of the year, the damp cloudy skies lend a rather bleak beauty to the ash-colored sea, but with luck a few stretches of fine weather brighten the summer. Before the war, especially during the 1920s and '30s, the Kurhaus was where German industrialists and aristocrats would spend their summers: Archduke Karl Alexander of Saxony-Weimar-Eisenach, or Max, Prince of Baden. Friedrich Weinreb found clients for his massage therapy in these circles, which was a reason for him to buy a house in Scheveningen.

There were other less glamorous parts of the town. On the picturesque side, fishermen still come and go in boats filled with North Sea herring. Well into the 1960s, their wives wore the traditional clothes of their community: stiff lace caps with silver clasps, pastel-colored woolen stoles, and long black skirts. Behind the waterfront, with its summer pavilions and fancy hotels, were cheaper streets with dingy bed-and-breakfast places, shady bars, and run-down establishments for long-term residents who couldn't afford much rent. Most fishing families used to live in tight little rows of small brick terraced houses, now quite chic. Just a bit farther back from the windswept dunes, where the Germans executed members of the resistance during the war, near the large redbrick prison, are suburban neighborhoods for the respectable middle and lower-middle classes: two-story homes whose rooms are rarely concealed by drawn curtains, even at night, so that ever-alert neighbors can observe, in typical Calvinist fashion, that nothing untoward is going on.

It was in such a neighborhood that the Weinreb family settled after they left Vienna in 1916. They were permitted to leave the tottering Austro-Hungarian empire because David Weinreb's health was too fragile for him to continue serving in the army: among other ailments, he suffered from a weak heart. A Dutch seaside resort and fishing village might seem an incongruous place for a family from Lwów to end up. In fact, they were joining what was already a relatively large Jewish community of about eleven hundred people, some of whom owned hotels or restaurants. Their families lived on a street best known for the later demolished Pavillon Riche, where fashionable people came to dance in the 1920s.

There were tailors from Kraków in Scheveningen, diamond dealers from Antwerp, rabbis from St. Petersburg, and kosher butchers and bakers who supplied hotels catering to Jewish guests, mostly from Germany. Many Jews had escaped the turbulence of war in Russia, and in Galicia and other parts of the Austro-Hungarian empire. Others had been forced to move to Holland from Antwerp during World War I because Belgium had decided to expel central European Jews who were officially citizens of enemy nations, such as Austria and Germany. In the 1930s, German and Austrian Jews would arrive as refugees from those same countries, now ruled by the Nazis.

The Jews of Scheveningen were both tight-knit and divided as a community. Tight-knit because most of them were foreigners living in a strange place. According to Weinreb, his parents could have had Gentile friends in Lwów or cosmopolitan Vienna, but they were stuck with fellow émigrés in Scheveningen, many of whom barely learned to speak Dutch and complained bitterly of having to do without the comforts and *Kultur* of German-speaking nations. Yiddish was spoken in some families, and German in others; the Yiddish speakers and German speakers rarely mixed, just as the Hassidic Jews wouldn't consort with liberal Jews, even though their synagogues were in the same former casino, albeit on different floors.

The Weinrebs were liberal, and the language spoken at home was still German. Like many Jews of their class from the Austro-Hungarian empire, they saw Holland as a temporary refuge. They still hoped to go home one day. Some people dreamed of a different return, to the holy land. Zionism was the secular faith of Jewish immigrants who pined for national belonging. Not only was there little desire to become Dutch, but aside from some diamond cutters who commuted between Amsterdam and Scheveningen, Dutch Jews didn't wish to have much to do with these *Ostjuden* either. Weinreb's parents were not Zionists. His mother never lost her trust in Emperor Franz Joseph, and his sickly father, who made a living representing German and Austrian companies, stuck to his faith in an enlightened universal brotherhood of man.

What marked out the young Weinreb, in his own account, which is factually unreliable but does reveal something of his disposition, was his superior intelligence and his alienation from his parents' circle of friends. He boasts of having been able to read and write when he was five, scribbling bulletins about the World War I battlefronts in France and central Europe. As a schoolboy in Scheveningen, he immersed himself in German philosophy, even as his schoolmates were still trying to master basic arithmetic. His mother, especially, was deeply impressed with her son's extraordinary precociousness, always comparing him with her father, Fischl, the pious sage from Wiznitz, and to his ancestors stretching back all the way to King David.

Except for one year at a private German-language school, which Weinreb found congenial, he was sent to Dutch schools, which he hated, ending in a high school whose curriculum was oriented toward science rather than the humanities, in preparation for studying engineering or economics. School bored him. His grades, to his parents' great dismay, were unimpressive. Weinreb's main complaint—indeed, if he is to be believed, a source of deep anguish—was the teachers' complete lack of interest in the deeper questions of life: Why are we here? and so on.

Weinreb's parents were secular but still wanted their child to have some basic knowledge of the culture of his forefathers. Even his Hebrew teachers were baffled, however, and then impatient, when the boy asked them questions about the meaning of life. To read Hebrew should be enough. One of his teachers was a Zionist who would soon move to Palestine. Another was a more traditional man with a beard who spoke mostly Yiddish and smelled of herring and onions. He, too, was unable to enlighten Weinreb on the deeper questions.

His parents' friends appalled Weinreb. They were, he later recalled, interested only in material things. The men talked about business, and the women about food or fashion. He recalls his disgust when he noticed how distressed these people were when the Great War finally ended. The war had been good for business, the women were able to buy pearls and fine furs, and now the good times were over. Some even wept.

Perhaps this was true, at least for some of his father's business friends. Perhaps it is an exaggeration. If so, it shows Weinreb's quasi-antisemitic contempt for the people he grew up with, people who claimed to believe in reason and universal values, or that practical problems need to be solved before we start fretting about issues best left to God—if He existed at all.

The twelve-year-old Weinreb rebelled by turning to the very thing his parents had left well behind: religious orthodoxy. The first signs of this had emerged in Vienna, when he picked up words of ancient wisdom from his grandfather. In Holland, Weinreb's inspiration came from one of his Hebrew teachers, a Lubavitcher Hassid from St. Petersburg named Monnoson. Not that Monnoson pretended to have any answers to Weinreb's philosophical questions. But Weinreb noted his teacher's respect for the sacred texts, how he handled the books as though they were holy icons, always making sure to place the Torah on top, over the psalms and the Talmud. Monnoson taught Weinreb that the words were hallowed and contained the keys to the mysteries of life, even though these would be revealed only to very few dedicated scholars— chosen ones, as it were.

Weinreb decided that reading the texts was not sufficient; one had to live the faith. He started going to the Hassidic synagogue, the one on a different floor from the liberal synagogue that his parents visited on high holy days. Not that the pious Jews had all the answers either. In Weinreb's view, the Hassidim were often weak, narrow-minded people. But he would stick with them nonetheless, even though their naivete was laughable. For at least, in Weinreb's words, they "lived with God . . . they knew about angels, good deeds, and sacrifice."

Weinreb's religious zeal shocked his parents and outraged many of their friends, as though he were betraying his own class, which in a way he was. One might also have assumed that he would have struck his classmates as an oddball, ripe for serious bullying. He hated school—his years of "martyrdom"—but asserts that his new religious habits were met with amused tolerance. He claims to have been good at sports, which would have helped, and that his superior intelligence enabled him to scrape through exams with very little effort. He was, of course, an oddity, among Jews as much as among Gentiles. He would cultivate this by aspiring to be a kind of guru, a miracle worker, a wonder rabbi of Scheveningen.

Like most forms of teenage rebellion, Weinreb's religiosity was clearly a way for a confused misfit to adopt an identity, not unlike Yoshiko's adoption of masculine ways. But it also jibed with certain currents in European culture that only grew stronger in the climate of disillusion and despair that followed a devastating world war. The fascination in Weimar Berlin—and not just there—for astrology, half-baked Hinduism, Oriental cults, and other flirtations with the irrational was felt everywhere, even by a muddled intelligent Jewish immigrant schoolboy growing up in a seaside resort in Holland.

One thing the young Weinreb had in common with Hitler (but also with Thomas Mann, lest one assumes that this concerns a specifically Nazi hobbyhorse) was an enchantment with Schopenhauer's philosophy. Of all the great nineteenth-century German thinkers, Arthur Schopenhauer was most open to Eastern religious and philosophical thoughts. His pessimism was especially congenial to people living in the ruins of war. But he also stressed the power of the human will. The reality of each individual is shaped by his or her volition. Why Hitler should be attracted to this idea is obvious. Weinreb was of course not a murderous dictator, but he was drawn to the notion of exercising power to manipulate reality. Weinreb's idea that human life is not only subject to mystical forces but also an act of imagination, and the view of his own life as a kind of Hassidic miracle tale, shows Schopenhauer's influence.

In the memoir of his childhood, and his Orthodox conversion, Weinreb tells an odd story, which might seem like a piece of meaningless name-dropping. It is in fact not so meaningless. One day in 1930, when Weinreb was twenty, and in a state of anguish about his failure to uncover the mystery of life, even among the Hassidim, he was taking a long solitary walk through Scheveningen. On this walk, he encountered an old man and a young girl. The old man asked him for directions in German. Soon they embarked on a literary discussion. The old man wanted to know whether Weinreb had read the symbolist plays of the Belgian writer Maurice Maeterlinck. Yes, Weinreb said, he had indeed. Did he wish to meet the great man? Yes, he would. The old man kindly took Weinreb by the hand and led him to the great man who was standing somewhere nearby.

Maeterlinck, whose most popular plays, such as *Pélleas et Mélisande*, showed a profound mystical bent, was a student of the occult. Schopenhauer had left his mark on him too. His attempt to grasp the meaning of life through symbolic representation is no longer fashionable, but it was highly influential in its time.

Weinreb's meeting with Maeterlinck in Scheveningen—if indeed it took place at all; there is no proof one way or the other—came as a revelation. Listening to the playwright talk, Weinreb felt he was now finally able to see a world that he had only intuited before. He became "conscious of a different reality in myself." Maeterlinck sensed that the young man understood him perfectly. He hadn't expected to visit the place where they met. But somehow, by some mystical force, Maeterlinck had been drawn to it, as though he knew he would meet a kindred spirit. Once again, just like in Vienna, where his special family legacy was revealed to him, Weinreb felt that he had been chosen.

Four

A LOW, DISHONEST DECADE

☲

1: Berlin

From about 1925, when Dr. Ko returned to Tibet to face his prophesied death in the peaceful confines of a Buddhist monastery, until 1940, when Hitler launched his blitzkrieg, Felix Kersten was the happiest of men. He had inherited a large clientele from his Chinese mentor, many of whom Kersten had already tended to as Dr. Ko's apprentice. Most of his patients were very rich men and women (but mostly men, it seems) who passed on the news of the Baltic wonder healer to friends and relations all over Europe. To get an appointment could take many months. Kersten himself relates that some people clamoring for his services came from as far away as India.

He was soon rich enough to move into a luxurious apartment in the plush Friedenau district of Berlin, which he furnished in the expensive overstuffed taste of the German well-to-do: a lot of mahogany and oak, crystal chandeliers, and Dutch old master landscapes. Kersten worked hard while his loyal companion, Elisabeth Lüben, took care of all his domestic needs, but he still had time to indulge in his two chief passions: rich food and fancy women, of all ages and types, married or unmarried.

A picture taken of Kersten around 1920 shows him in white tie, with a curly tuft sticking up from his large round head and the roguish sidelong grin of a vaudeville comedian. Several books mention a romantic attachment to Queen Marie of Romania, granddaughter of Queen Victoria, and wife of Ferdinand, the next-to-last king of Romania. Perhaps. But she was more than twenty years older than Kersten, and a grieving widow untouched by any hint of scandal. A more likely lover was Princess Maria of Romania, a society beauty, whose husband, Alexander I of Yugoslavia, was treated by Kersten before he was assassinated by a Bulgarian revolutionary in 1934. No matter. Suffice it to say that Kersten was very well connected.

One of Kersten's most important conduits into the world of dukes, barons, and princes was Duke Adolf Friedrich von Mecklenburg-Schwerin, also known as the African Duke. When Baltic German aristocrats tried in 1918 to set up the Grand Duchy of Livonia in Kersten's native country, the Duke of Mecklenburg was their choice to be head of state. A marvelous photograph shows the duke in all his splendor: white uniform, rows of medals, splendid Kaiser Wilhelm mustache. Alas, no one but the German kaiser chose to recognize this new entity, so the duke was never able to take up his post. Before this aborted venture he had been an African explorer and the last governor of Togoland, a German protectorate, hence his African Duke moniker. In later years, the duke became a pillar of the German Olympic Committee, one of those blazered worthies who held forth after long boozy dinners about the spirit of sportsmanship and fair play. The German Wikipedia entry on the duke describes his attitude to the Nazis as "open-minded." Because of his scientific interests in tropical countries, a genus of lizards, the *Adolfus*, was named after him.

In a slim book about his massage techniques, published in 1929, Kersten does not mention the duke by name but describes how an aristocratic patient suffered from such a weak heart that he could barely walk. After thirty sessions with Kersten, he was apparently fully fit again. The grateful duke then introduced Kersten to his brother, Prince Heinrich (or Hendrik in Dutch), the somewhat dim and sexually voracious husband of Queen Wilhelmina of the Netherlands. Prince Hendrik, a tall, burly gourmand like Kersten, was forever getting into embarrassing scrapes. He had mistresses all over the place. Stories were told, and continue to be told, of a police raid on a male brothel in The Hague that supposedly found him among the patrons. Even the youngest boy scouts, over whom the prince officially presided in the Netherlands, were said to be exposed to his roving hands. Perhaps these stories owe more to the prince's reputation than to any specific truth. Still, to keep him out of mischief, Queen Wilhelmina would often dispatch her wayward husband to the castle in Doorn where Kaiser Wilhelm II lived in exile after the German defeat in 1918. There, the frustrated kaiser would keep up his guests, including Prince Hendrik, day and night, subjecting them to his always long-winded views on Jewish conspiracies, the treachery of German republicans, and other pressing matters in world politics. But as long as the prince was with the kaiser, he couldn't disgrace the queen.

Prince Hendrik was so pleased with Kersten's ministrations that he made him his personal masseur. In a letter to Kersten, dated October 1928, the prince wrote that he felt "many years younger" because of Kersten's massages and would be happy to offer his personal references to anyone concerned. The queen, too, was pleased with the masseur, who soon became a trusted courtier to the Dutch royal family. He was even asked to accompany the prince on regular trips to Berlin, where, safely out of the queen's sight, they visited the capital's finest brothels together, when they weren't engaged in hunting and shooting.

Kersten claimed that he instantly felt at home in the Netherlands. He liked the flat green fields crisscrossed by narrow canals, he adored the royal family, he bought Dutch paintings, and he admired the lack of "provincial narrow-mindedness" that marked so many Germans. Holland, he wrote, reminded him of his native Estonia. Like the Baltic state, he said, it was on the cultural crossroads between Latin and Germanic civilizations. He wrote this to ingratiate himself with Dutch readers when he was under a cloud of suspicion in Sweden after the war. But there is no reason to doubt his affinity with the land of his paternal ancestors, even though they left five centuries ago. Identity can be a many-sided thing. Why shouldn't the Finnish citizen, born in the Baltics, whose first language was German, have felt an emotional bond to Holland too?

Kersten soon bought a fine house in Scheveningen on a leafy avenue lined with imposing art nouveau mansions, many of them bought with fortunes made in the colonial Dutch East Indies. Filled with the same kind of old master paintings and heavy furniture as his apartment in Berlin, the house was only a ten-minute walk to the more modest but perfectly respectable street of terraced houses where Friedrich Weinreb lived. But the two men lived in different worlds, which would never have overlapped. Kersten's Dutch contacts were rich industrialists, art dealers, generals, and aristocrats who did business and met one another in all the smart capitals and spa towns of Europe. Weinreb was still confined to a narrow milieu of Jewish immigrants.

Between 1928 and 1940, Holland was as much a base for Kersten's operations as Berlin. In both countries, as well as in other places, such as Rome, he specialized in a clientele of powerful people, whose pains, Kersten believed, were caused by the stress of overwork and too much ambition. In their desire for more wealth and power, they had lost touch with their "original psychic functions," in his words. There was nothing normal doctors could do to cure these psychic pains, which caused stomach cramps or intolerable headaches. Only Kersten knew how to relieve their agony. He was richly rewarded.

Neither Kersten nor anyone else who wrote about his life has very much to say about the politics of the 1930s, and how Hitler's rise to power affected him. In his own account, the dramatic events of 1933—when Hitler proclaimed the Third Reich, Jewish persecution began, the Gestapo asserted its sinister grip, and the first concentration camps were built—are mentioned only cursorily. Kersten was "not political," in the phrase used by so many Germans who feigned ignorance after Hitler's defeat. He never read newspapers. Life was good, the women were willing, the food was abundant, the money flowed, and the pace of his heady social life hadn't slackened. He was, in Joseph Kessel's words, "a gourmand of happiness."

Yet Kersten was aware of what was going on, even before 1933. As he later wrote, "A new power became visible. Its face was still veiled, but you could hear the marching in the street and the songs on the factory floor." Here is how Joseph Kessel describes the ambience Kersten was in: "Most of his patients—intellectuals and people from the upper class, as well as the simple people whom he treated for nothing—were afraid, ashamed or disgusted with Nazism. Kersten shared their sentiments. His instinct for justice, his deep natural goodness, his sense of tolerance, decency, and moderation, everything about him was disturbed, hurt, and outraged by the gross arrogance, the racial superstition, the police tyranny, the fanaticism for the Führer."

We should reserve hasty moral judgment even on a slippery figure like Kersten. But Kessel's account is almost certainly false. There is no evidence, even in his own memoir, that Kersten was especially hurt or outraged by the Nazis' power grab. He may not have liked it or deeply approved of it, but like most of his wealthy clients, he appears to have accommodated himself to it quite readily. He was, to say the least, like the Duke of Mecklenburg, open-minded.

For an "unpolitical" man, Kersten was, in fact, quite clear-eyed about the situation in Germany. He would explain in his memoir that the powerful industrialists and businessmen under his care conceded to the demands of the Nazi leadership because they feared the left more, and thought they would be able to bend Hitler to their will. He was surely right about that. But historians still argue about the extent to which the conservative German business elite was coerced by the Nazis to fall into line. In certain cases, they were. But some industrialists were more sympathetic to Nazism than they would later admit. And some, claiming to be "unpolitical" like Kersten, saw great business opportunities, even if they found the Führer's manners a bit rough and didn't believe all that nonsense about an Aryan master race.

On February 20, 1933, a secret meeting was convened at Hermann Göring's official residence in Berlin between two dozen German industrialists and Hitler. A number of these powerful men had already signed a petition the year before urging the old and increasingly feeble president, Paul von Hindenburg, to make Hitler chancellor of Germany. They were members of the so-called Keppler Circle, named after Wilhelm Keppler, who was was an early member of the Nazi party and one of Hitler's top economic advisers. In 1933, the circle became known as the Friends of Heinrich Himmler. The SS chief acted as the protector of sympathetic business leaders. They later donated money to some of his pet projects, such as eugenic research into ways to strengthen the "Aryan race."

At that fateful meeting, Hitler told the assembled businessmen that he would destroy the Marxist enemy and abolish democracy. He also assured them that private property would be protected (as long as it wasn't Jewish). But to facilitate this, the Nazis needed to win an absolute majority in the coming election. In Hitler's words: "We must first gain complete power if we are to totally crush the other side." Three million Reichsmarks (the equivalent of more than ten million dollars today) would be a useful contribution. Gustav Krupp, the arms and steel manufacturer, thanked the Führer. Göring said something to the effect of "reach for your wallets, gentlemen." Two million Reichsmarks were swiftly procured.

At least three people present at that meeting were patients of Kersten, and two of them were members of the Friends of Heinrich Himmler.

One was Friedrich Flick, a steel and coal magnate who was convicted for war crimes, including the use of slave labor from concentration camps, plunder of Jewish properties, and membership in the SS. Kersten describes this Friend of Himmler in his memoir as a thoroughly decent gentleman who hated the Nazis and was even in danger of being arrested by Himmler in 1940. An unlikely story, but Flick did pay Kersten the unusually high sum of twenty-five thousand marks a year for his massages.

Another Friend of Himmler and participant in the February 1933 meeting was August Rosterg, whose companies produced oil, gas, and potassium, which was used for bombs. The son of a miner, he became one of the richest German tycoons in the period between the two world wars.

Joseph Kessel tells a touching story about Kersten treating Rosterg for insomnia and ferocious attacks of migraine. Kersten charged him his usual fee of five thousand marks. Rosterg, in a fit of grateful generosity, slipped him a check for one hundred thousand marks. This extraordinary gesture enabled—still according to Kessel—Kersten to buy a fine but ramshackle estate named Hartzwalde in Brandenburg to the north of Berlin in 1934. Kersten explains in his memoir that he bought the property because he wasn't able to spend his German money abroad. At any rate, he completely renovated the place, had all the most up-to-date technology installed, and had furniture made in the rustic style "befitting this rural idyll." Hartzwalde would be his bucolic retreat until 1945. After 1940, prisoners (Jehovah's Witnesses) from the nearby Ravensbrück concentration camp made life even more pleasant by working the surrounding land. There is no evidence that Kersten treated them particularly harshly. He claims that he was their protector. This could be. In the Third Reich, everyone needed a protector.

August Rosterg loathed the power of trade unions and was terrified of Bolshevism. He was accused at the Nuremberg war crimes trials by Walter Funk, Hitler's minister for economic affairs, as one of the industrialists who was most sympathetic to the Nazis. Inmates from the

Buchenwald concentration camp were worked to death as slave workers for Rosterg's mining companies. But Kersten claims that Rosterg, "this *self-made* man," had had only one wish after the war broke out, and that was to escape from Nazi Germany, and that he, Kersten, help him to do so in 1944, when Rosterg moved to Sweden. There may be some truth to this. Kersten had good Swedish contacts. But the flight to Sweden might have had less to do with any antipathy to the Nazis than with a desire to leave a rapidly sinking ship. Rosterg died in 1945.

The most interesting figure in this group was Rosterg's friend and colleague in running the potassium syndicate, August Diehn, a man, in Joseph Kessel's words, "of great intellectual and moral stature." Kersten says Diehn was more than a patient and a close friend; he was like a father to him. He was, in Kersten's description, a well-traveled cosmopolitan, a German by birth and culture, but the type of man who felt perfectly at home in the highest society of London, New York, or Paris. He tried everything to stop Hitler from going to war, Kersten would claim.

Perhaps he did. But Diehn was already offering financial help to Hitler in 1931. He attended the meeting with Hitler in 1933 and was a member of a tight circle of industrialists who cooperated with the Propaganda Ministry under Joseph Goebbels. Diehn was given the equivalent rank of brigadier general in the SS. After 1940, Kersten says, Diehn advised his masseur to get out of Germany, but so long as he stayed, to exert his influence on Himmler and do as much good work as possible. Because Diehn died in 1942, there is no way of knowing whether he really said any such thing. The story does, of course, put Kersten himself in a better light.

Diehn is said to have been a bastard brother of Prince Hendrik. What the prince consort made of Hitler is unknown; he died in 1934. There are stories about his friendly relations in the late 1920s with the Thule Society, a group of antisemitic obscurantists who would dine regularly at a grand hotel in Munich to discuss racial theories. One of the mottos of this band of gentlemen was "Keep the blood pure." If the prince indeed took part in these creepy gatherings, it might have been more for the food and company than because of any deep interest in "ariosophical" ideas. Ideas were not really his thing.

Clearly, however, many of Kersten's clients from the European elites (Count Galeazzo Ciano, Mussolini's son-in-law and foreign minister of the fascist regime in Italy, was another one) were quite prepared to collaborate with the Nazis, either as believers or opportunists. Some might have held their social noses a little. (Ciano told Kersten that he loathed the Germans.) Once it became evident that the Third Reich was crumbling, such men swiftly plotted their next moves to adapt to the shifts of power. But one can safely assume that few of Kersten's closest associates were either ashamed or disgusted to be associated with the Nazi regime. Quite the contrary, in fact.

At some point it can behoove even an inveterate womanizer to get respectably married, and Kersten found himself a suitable wife in 1937. He was thirty-eight at the time. Whatever she might have hoped for, the ever-loyal Elisabeth Lüben was never considered for this role. The charming story, recounted by Kessel, goes that Kersten in a jovial mood had said that he might get married out of sheer ecstasy if he were ever offered a dish his mother used to prepare for him, which wasn't available anywhere in Berlin: *rassolnik*, a Russian soup with pickles, barley, and kidneys. One day, he and Elisabeth were invited for lunch at the home of a retired German colonel and his Baltic wife. They were joined by Irmgard Neuschaffer, the shy daughter of a family friend. She was young, in robust health, blonde, and her grandfather was chief forester to the Grand Duke of Hesse-Darmstadt. To Kersten's astonishment, they were served *rassolnik*. He asked Irmgard to marry him on the spot. Four months and several impassioned letters later, they were.

Toward the end of 1938, after German troops had entered Austria and Czechoslovakia, and after Kristallnacht, the Night of Broken Glass, when Brownshirts and gleeful mobs were unleashed on Jewish citizens and properties, Kersten's father figure, August Diehn, asked him for a favor. Would he be prepared to treat a special friend of his? He was a very powerful person who suffered from chronic stomach cramps. Again, there are slightly different versions of what followed. In Joseph Kessel's telling, Diehn was so anxious that he could barely utter this powerful man's name, which was, of course, Heinrich Himmler. According to Kessel, Diehn feared that Himmler was going to nationalize his industrial empire. There was in fact no evidence of this. Kersten mentions only that German industrialists had a "tense relationship" with Himmler.

That Diehn himself had any serious trouble with Himmler in 1939 is unlikely. But it is quite possible that he and other Friends of Himmler, including Rosterg, believed that Kersten, by relieving Himmler's cramps, might become a useful insider at the SS chief's court, and so advance their interests. Like hairdressers, court jesters, and bartenders, masseurs were in a position to become confidants of powerful people, especially if they were able to alleviate unbearable pain. Kersten explains this phenomenon well: "In the course of my practice I have found over and over that one gains the trust of men in leading positions that might seem exaggerated to outsiders. Because such leaders are always surrounded by self-interested people, they are systematically put on the defensive. But they can safely relax when they are treated by doctors who are used to seeing them in a vulnerable state."

And so Felix Kersten entered the grandiose office of Heinrich Himmler inside the palatial Gestapo headquarters on the Prinz Albrechtstrasse in Berlin for their first session of manual therapy.

2: Scheveningen

If anyone could be described as a plaything of choppy historical currents, it was a distant relative of mine named Fritz Kormis, whom I remember as a pale, lanky figure who made sardonic remarks about the vicissitudes of life in a thick German accent. Fritz was a sculptor whose bronze portrait medallions—of Churchill, Chaplin, King Edward VIII, and some of my uncles and aunts—were especially prized. Born in Frankfurt in 1897, Fritz was studying art at the Frankfurt Art School, where Max Beckmann was of one his teachers, when the great powers of Europe went to war. He was drafted into the Austro-Hungarian army to fight on the eastern front. Wounded and captured by the Russians, Fritz had a bad time as a POW in Siberia. "You learn a lot about your fellow man when you live in your underpants" is how he once described the grisly experience to me. He managed to escape by acquiring a false Swiss passport. If he ever told me how this was accomplished, I have forgotten. Back in Frankfurt, Fritz made a living by sculpting portraits, but then, in 1933, ill fortune caught up with him again. As Jews, he and his wife, Rachel, realized early on that there was no life for them in the Third Reich. So they moved to Holland.

They didn't stick around for very long. Fritz found the Dutch complacent and naive about the consequences of Hitler's rise in their neighboring country. They didn't think trouble would ever come to them. The Netherlands had managed to remain neutral in World War I and surely, in the unlikely event of a second one, would be able to do so again. Although Holland had an Asian empire in what is now Indonesia, where the colonial masters could behave with great brutality, the Dutch saw themselves as a peaceful nation of traders and shopkeepers. Why should anyone want to harm them?

And so, in 1934, Fritz and Rachel boarded the ferry at the Hook of Holland and joined their relatives in London, where Fritz became Fred and they lived for the rest of their lives near the Lord's Cricket Ground in St. John's Wood, with its sculpted images of sportsmen on the wall: "Meet me at the relief" was one of Fritz's instructions for a rendezvous.

Fritz was quite right. Holland would not turn out to be a safe refuge after the Germans invaded in 1940. Roughly thirty-five thousand Jews had fled there from Germany, Austria, and elsewhere in eastern Europe.

But already in the late 1930s, the Dutch government, like others in western Europe, decided that enough was enough and started sending refugees back into the arms of a regime that would soon want them dead. Other relatives of mine, a family name Schuster, were caught in occupied Holland. The Germans picked them up one by one. The severely ill youngest son, who was confined to a wheelchair, was the last to be taken away to be murdered.

German Jews were not universally popular in Holland, not among Gentiles, and not among Dutch Jews either. Even though they were forced to leave Germany after being persecuted, humiliated, and robbed of their properties, German Jews had the reputation of putting on airs: everything was better in Germany; the goose-feather down beds were more comfortable; and above all, Germany had its *Kultur*, which made Holland seem coarse and provincial in comparison.

Even the Dutch Nazis were *kleinstädtisch*, "small townish" in German eyes. No matter how much they tried to imitate the grandiose mannerisms and mass spectacles of their German comrades, the Dutch Nazis seemed a dowdy lot. The "Leader," Anton Mussert, was a small, plump, ruddy-faced engineer who looked more comical than menacing in his riding boots and absurd black uniforms. He may have been fanatical, corrupt, and power hungry, but he was not a natural killer. When Heinrich Himmler's SS purged rivals inside the Nazi ranks in 1934 by murdering the Brownshirt (SA) leaders at a Bavarian hotel and got rid of other political opponents on the same day by hacking them to death with axes, Mussert was so shocked by such "indecent behavior" that he refused to meet Himmler in the summer of 1935. Before he was shown the error of his ways during the German occupation, Mussert even allowed some Jews to become members of his Nazi movement, so long as they were true believers. No wonder Hitler always despised the Dutch Leader as nothing more than an irksome, petty bourgeois nationalist.

Friedrich Weinreb shared some of these views about the Dutch. But

Weinreb was catholic in his scorn. He despised most Jews, especially secular Jews, as well.

Reading the rather impenetrable memoir of his youth, one might get the impression that the young Weinreb was as impervious to political events as Felix Kersten, living just a few streets away from him. His interest mostly concerns his spiritual "journey" through the arcane mystical margins of Hassidic orthodoxy. This may reflect the time when the book was written, in the 1980s, when the author was making a good living in Switzerland as a spiritual guru instructing his followers in the secret codes contained in the Bible. We know he had a more practical side too.

After scraping through his high school exams, Weinreb enrolled in a business school in Rotterdam. He would have preferred to study philosophy or literature, but his father thought business would be a safer option, and though physically weak, his father usually got his way. Since there wasn't enough money to rent a room for him in Rotterdam, the young Weinreb commuted from the family home in Scheveningen. He was remembered by fellow students as a shabbily dressed young man who kept to himself.

Disaster struck in 1931, when Weinreb's father died of heart failure. When his mother died in the same year, Weinreb and his brother, Edmond, were left with no money. Edmond had to leave high school to take over his father's job as an agent for a German tobacco company. Friedrich was helped by his professor in Rotterdam to continue his business studies by getting a job at an economic research institute. Nothing much more is known about Edmond. Weinreb barely mentions him. They didn't appear to have got along well. Edmond became a Zionist, a course his elder brother despised. In 1942, Edmond was among the first Jews to be rounded up by the Germans. He died in Austria, at Mauthausen, one of the worst concentration camps, where the SS guards would toss exhausted prisoners down the deep stone quarries just for sport.

In his memoir, Weinreb depicts himself as a bit of a dreamer, a *luft-mensch,* a person whose mind is airborne. He was also, by his own account, deeply unhappy, because he had no one to talk to. Gentiles and secular Jews didn't understand his religious devotion and even made fun of it. The Orthodox in Scheveningen were narrow-minded and quarreled about the superficial rules of a religious life. Weinreb felt like a stranger everywhere.

Even people who wished him well, such as his professor Jan Tinbergen, who would later receive the first Nobel Prize in economics, grew exasperated with Weinreb. Tinbergen encouraged him to finish his PhD in Rotterdam. Weinreb kept putting it off, telling his professor that it was almost done. It was never done. The manuscript was stolen. The manuscript had been destroyed in a fire. The manuscript was inexplicably lost.

The only person who understood the brooding student was his maternal grandfather from Vienna, who stayed with the family in Scheveningen until he too was deported during the war, and murdered in Treblinka. Grandfather Fischl, according to his admiring grandson, understood that there was another more important reality than the material here and now, a reality that could not be analyzed by scientific methods or measured in economic statistics. Weinreb got a glimpse of this other reality when he embarked on a trip from Rotterdam to Vienna, and from there to Poland. Such a journey did indeed take place sometime in the mid-1930s. But the most extraordinary events on this trip might have existed only in his imagination. It doesn't matter. They tell us something about the fantasy life of a man who dealt in so many fantasies. It was that other, immeasurable reality that interested him, after all.

Weinreb felt very alone on the train slowly making its way to Warsaw, passing by small towns then still inhabited by many Jews, some of whom were dressed in black kaftans and fur hats. One of those small towns especially attracted Weinreb. Some superior force he couldn't explain told him to get off, but the conductor stood in his way, and the train resumed its trip to Warsaw. Then, for some unfathomable reason, the train reversed and stopped in the small town once more. This time, Weinreb managed to disembark. Looking for a place to stay, Weinreb was stopped by an excited figure in a dark suit. The town *rebbe* was waiting to see him. There had to be some mistake, thought Weinreb.

But it wasn't a mistake. The *rebbe* had always known that a young man, related to a mysterious visitor who had left behind a sheaf of secret religious documents many years ago, would come to see him, a young man from Holland and Vienna. The *rebbe* did not believe in magic. He wasn't a wonder rabbi. He just knew that heaven worked in mysterious ways. Gradually it all began to make sense to Weinreb: "I felt taken up in another world, just as though I had settled into a comfortable bed and glided into a dream."

The *rebbe* had waited for Weinreb so they could study the secrets of the Torah. Together, they would learn; Weinreb would become a *gelernter*. To be a *gelernter* is to be a scholar, not of economics or mathematics but of the ancient texts that contain the mysteries of the other reality. Weinreb still felt like a stranger in the world, but he no longer felt alone. The *rebbe* had given him a mission, as a *gelernter*. The spirit of Israel would bring the Jews out of exile and bring light where there was so much egotism and stupidity.

By Israel he didn't mean the country then named Palestine. Weinreb regarded Zionism as a stupid, even sinful, misunderstanding. In his ultra-orthodox view, a political state of Israel forged by human hands would be a form of blasphemy. Only the coming of the Messiah could lead people to a spiritual state of Israel.

Weinreb's struggle against human stupidity, which runs like a leitmotif through all his writings, was not just spiritual, however. He didn't only fancy himself as a *gelernter*; he was also *chochem*, or in Dutch Yiddish *goochem*, meaning clever. His earliest memory, back in Lwów, was of standing on a table surrounded by family members applauding something smart he had said. He was proud of being *goochem*. Much later, in Scheveningen, after he had become an Orthodox believer, he described friends and relatives of his parents, most of them Zionists who cared only for the material world, as "that vermin, those mockers, those idiots."

He would come to think the same way about the Nazis, who, needless to say, were the most stupid of all. Nazism was stupid. Weinreb's aim was to outsmart them, not as a *gelernter* but by being *goochem*.

Weinreb was not oblivious to political events at all. Even though historical events—Hitler's rise in 1933, the Nuremberg racial laws in 1935, Kristallnacht in 1938—don't feature in his books, Weinreb does mention refugees from Nazi Germany. Among them was a man named Rabinow, a *gelernter*, who was desperate for a job in Scheveningen, or anywhere else, as a religious teacher. But only Weinreb (he claims), who was still a poor student, was willing to help him.

As an economist, Weinreb wrote about practical matters that would become more and more pressing: how to feed a population in wartime, the consequences of the annexation of Austria in Hitler's Reich, and so on. Even as a member of a religious movement named Agudath Yisrael, now an ultraorthodox party in Israel, Weinreb was more than a *luftmensch*. Agudath Yisrael had been founded in Silesia in 1912 as an ultraorthodox answer to secular Zionism. The quest was for the Kingdom of God. Meanwhile, however, Jews had to run for their lives from the Nazis, and finding shelter was becoming more difficult by the day. Weinreb hoped to find empty places in South America, such as Colombia, Ecuador, or Peru, where Jews could live safely in their own religious communities. This solution, too, might seem more fantastical than realistic, but he saw better than most people what was coming.

In 1936, Weinreb married Esther Gutwirth, the daughter of Orthodox Jews who had moved to Scheveningen from Antwerp. They soon had three children. One would not survive the coming war.

3: Shanghai

The Japanese war in Asia began eight years before the German war in Europe, with the Japanese occupation of Manchuria in 1931.

The Japanese military incursion started with a fiction, a fraud that came to be known as the Mukden Incident. On the night of September 18, 1931, a Japanese army lieutenant placed a small amount of dynamite near the Japanese-owned South Manchurian Railway outside the city of Mukden, now Shenyang. The explosion hardly did any damage. It wasn't meant to. A train from Changchun, on its way to Dalian, passed over the broken rails minutes later with no trouble.

That was just how a group of Japanese Imperial Army colonels had planned it. They wanted to provoke a war in Manchuria that the government in Tokyo and most of the top army brass wished to avoid. All Japanese leaders, civilians as well as military, agreed on the importance of protecting and expanding Japan's interests in Manchuria. After securing the South Manchurian Railway in the Russo-Japanese War of 1905, Japan took control of the zone of land around the railway. This caused a serious conflict with the Chinese government, which saw itself as the natural ruler of Manchuria. But the Japanese government had hoped to get what it wanted through diplomacy, not violence. Middle-ranking army firebrands had more radical means in mind. The more prominent plotters became household names, celebrated in Japanese media at the time: Doihara Kenji, nicknamed Lawrence of Manchuria, the pugnacious continental racketeer; Ishiwara Kanji, a polyglot schemer with fanatical Buddhist beliefs (such people did, and do still exist); and Itagaki Seishiro, who went on to become a general and was eventually hanged as a war criminal.

The explosion was blamed on Chinese saboteurs, and the next day, Japanese troops attacked the poorly armed Chinese garrison led by the northeastern warlord Zhang Xueliang. A slim, dapper figure who looked as suave in elaborate military uniforms as in a tuxedo, Zhang was an excellent dancer and an opium addict. As the strongman of the northeast, he had allied himself with Chiang Kai-shek against the Japanese, which is why the Japanese needed to push him out. This was not simply a matter of vicious Japanese militarists stamping on a freedom-loving democrat. Known as the Young Marshal, Zhang was a tough warlord who was attracted to fascism, particularly in the Italian style. This didn't stop him from cuckolding Count Ciano, Felix Kersten's client in Rome, who was now stationed in Shanghai as the Italian consul. Ciano's wife, Edda, Mussolini's daughter, had a fling with Zhang. (Another admirer of Edda was Heinrich Himmler, who gave her an honorary SS rank in 1943. After her husband was executed in 1944 for attempting to oust Mussolini, Edda quickly moved on to have an affair with a Communist.)

Chiang Kai-shek, as well as the Young Marshal (who would eventually die at an advanced age in Honolulu, where he was known as Peter H. L. Chang), realized that their armies were no match for the Japanese force and decided to retreat from the northeast, whereupon the Kwantung Army, the Manchurian branch of the Japanese Imperial Army, egged on by a jingoistic press in Japan, occupied every major city and town in Manchuria. The civilian Japanese government, and even Emperor Hirohito himself, were taken aback by this raw aggression by insubordinate officers, but they too, like the Chinese leaders, recognized force majeure and soon fell into line.

Kawashima Yoshiko was living in Shanghai at the time of the Mukden Incident. She decided that life with her adoptive father in Japan was intolerable and tried her luck on the Chinese mainland. But before moving to Shanghai, she had become, in her own words, "a most peculiar wife." Her husband was a tall, handsome Mongolian named Ganjurjab. They had been married in a splendid ceremony at the Yamato Hotel in Lüshun with all the most senior officers of the Kwantung Army in attendance. About this Manchu-Mongolian match in 1927, there are as many versions as there are about everything else in her life story. Yoshiko later claimed that she was forced to marry the Mongolian and gave in only after he promised that there would be no question of physical intimacy. She was not like other women, she explained. But she would go along with their fictional relationship for the sake of the cause so close to the hearts of both her fathers: Manchu-Mongolian independence. Others, including her brother Xianli, have said that she was actually quite fond of Ganjurjab, whom she had known since they were both at school in Tokyo, and was perfectly happy to marry him. Whether she could find any happiness living with his family in the freezing Mongolian plains is another matter.

The marriage suited the Japanese perfectly in any case. Ganjurjab was a graduate of the main Japanese military academy. His father was a general who fought on the Japanese side against the Chinese Nationalists. Whether Yoshiko was forced to marry him, or whether she chose to do so to escape the clutches of her abusive foster father, will never be known. The latter is at least plausible, for when Kawashima Naniwa took on Yoshiko's younger sister as his new helpmate, Yoshiko warned her against him.

Perhaps inevitably, the marriage didn't last long. Yoshiko found life at a feudal Mongolian court, where every move was scrutinized by her suspicious mother-in-law, hard to bear. Bored to distraction, she wandered around the local villages at night, where she claims to have become a figure of legend: "These Mongols," she wrote, "liked to make up stories, and they made up a drama about me that even surpassed those created by the author of *Arabian Nights*." This clearly pleased her. She encouraged people to make up stories about her. This was her way of feeling chosen, as a figure of legend.

One story that was made up by Muramatsu Shofu, author of Yoshiko's fictionalized biography, *The Beauty in Men's Clothes*, concerned a trip made by the young married couple through the Mongolian desert, when they were attacked by Chinese "bandits." Yoshiko, or her fictional alter ego named Mariko, showing immense courage, managed to fight them off with her gun but still sustained a bullet wound in her left shoulder. This bullet wound would reappear in subsequent stories about her. It was as much a fantasy as were her martial exploits as the Manchu Joan of Arc.

Alas, things had gone wrong with the Manchu-Mongolian match already on the morning after the wedding night, when there was no speck of blood on the white wedding bed cushion, which had to be shown according to Mongol custom as the sign of an auspicious union. Three years after the grand wedding reception in Lüshun, Yoshiko made her escape to Dalian, the larger port city next to Lüshun, where she titillated the local Japanese gossip columnists by turning up in all the most fashionable dance halls, often in the company of dashing Japanese officers. The couple got divorced. In Yoshiko's words: "My husband and I were free once more, having reached a mutual Manchu-Mongolian understanding."

Ganjurjab's life did not end well. He was imprisoned after the war as a traitor by the Chinese Communists. During the Cultural Revolution, more than sixteen thousand Mongolians were lynched and tortured to death for being the "heirs of Genghis Khan." Ganjurjab had indeed been a keen worshipper at the shrine of Genghis Khan. The Mongol warrior cult had been encouraged by the Japanese, who compared it to their samurai tradition, in contrast to China's effete and decadent civilization. The Chinese Communists later regretted the mass killing of Mongolians. Like much else that happened during the Cultural Revolution, it had been an unfortunate "mistake."

One of the fictions of Japanese propaganda on the Chinese mainland was that the Japanese would protect and promote the independence of Manchus and Mongolians against illegitimate Chinese rulers, hence Yoshiko's marriage, hence also the wider political events that followed in which Yoshiko was more than peripherally involved.

Having taken the vast territory between Korea, Russia, and China by force, the next Japanese step was to create another fiction: the founding of the newly independent state of Manchukuo, literally Country of the

Manchus. The head of this state would be the last Qing emperor of China, Puyi, now living in the Japanese concession in Tianjin. Under the benevolent patronage of imperial Japan, Manchukuo would be not only independent (a fiction) but also the most modern, most progressive (partly true) model of multiethnic, multicultural, and multireligious harmony (almost total fiction).

After having been evicted from the Forbidden City in Beijing, Puyi had been living the life of an expatriate playboy in Tianjin, with his elegant and thoroughly bored and frustrated wife, Wanrong, a high-ranking Manchu aristocrat, whom foreigners called Elizabeth. Puyi liked to play tennis, or dance at the Astor House Hotel and then dine at the Tianjin Country Club (as a guest only, for Chinese were not acceptable as members). Always impeccably dressed, in tweed plus fours for golf, or in English suits and a pink carnation when lounging about town, Puyi was a regular feature of the society columns in the expatriate press of Tianjin.

Wanrong/Elizabeth was well educated, spoke fluent English, and played the piano very nicely, but she was miserable in an unconsummated marriage with a husband who was feckless and most probably gay. Life at the Jing Garden House, with its stifling protocol, obsequious but irksome eunuch retainers, and endless visits by Japanese officials and other dullards of an international but provincial high society, became intolerable. She found relief in opium smoking as well as morphine injections. Quite when the empress first met Yoshiko is unclear, but she was amused by her. That Yoshiko would play a role in the next stage of Wanrong's life is beyond dispute. Everything else about Yoshiko's part is enveloped in the thick fog of her legend.

Puyi did not need all that much persuading by Japanese Kwantung Army officers to take up his position as Manchukuo's reigning head, or, as it would soon transpire, figurehead. Yoshiko, in her own telling, did her best to assist the Japanese in this enterprise. That is why, again in her account, she was rushing to Tianjin from Shanghai on the Blue Express, a French-made luxury train. The Japanese officers who pressed Puyi to comply were some of the same men who plotted the Mukden Incident. One of them was a particularly sinister figure named Amakasu Masahiko. A balding man with spectacles, he looked like a bank clerk, or indeed a bit like Heinrich Himmler. He was in fact a murderer. Amakasu was briefly under a cloud for beating two anarchists and a six-year-old boy to death after the Tokyo earthquake in 1923, and stuffing their bodies down a well, but he soon went on to bigger things on the continent, where he ran the opium business for Lawrence of Manchuria.

To help Puyi make up his mind, Amakasu and Doihara staged a few spectacular assassination plots in Tianjin, supposedly instigated by Chinese "terrorists." The official story, repeated in Yoshiko's memoir, was that Chiang Kai-shek's Nationalists had sent terrorists to Tianjin to whip up anti-Japanese feelings. On one occasion the former emperor of China received a fruit basket filled with hand grenades placed among the peaches and pomegranates. The Japanese told Puyi that he would be much safer under their protection in Manchukuo.

Perhaps it was fear for his life that prompted him, or maybe it was the illusion that the restoration of the Manchu throne in the land of his ancestors would lead to a full revival of the Qing Dynasty in China, but Puyi finally agreed to be transported by boat from Tianjin to Manchukuo. He dithered about whether he should wear his dove-gray Prince of Wales suit, or whether something else might be more suitable. His minders wrapped him in a Japanese general's greatcoat.

To create a diversion, Doihara (Lawrence) paid local Chinese thugs to start shooting their revolvers in the streets of the Chinese quarter. This is when, in her version of the story, Yoshiko popped up, dressed in a man's suit and hunting cap. Whoever wrote her memoir (her own Japanese was not up to it) reached for the effect of a cheap detective novel. Yoshiko drove Puyi "at breakneck speed" through the dark streets of Tianjin with the headlights turned off, braving machine gun bullets and Chinese patrols. After skidding to a halt on the waterfront, Yoshiko made sure Puyi was safely bundled onto a Japanese steamboat bound for the northeast, where he would be put up under Japanese guard in the former house of Yoshiko's late father, Prince Su.

This is a pure invention. Yoshiko was nowhere near Tianjin when Puyi was smuggled out of the city. Somewhat closer to the truth is the story told by Muramatsu Shofu in *The Beauty in Men's Clothes*. Here, too, the heroine (Mariko) in a dark suit and hunting cap drives her illustrious passenger through the wild streets of Tianjin. But it was Wanrong, not her husband, who left Tianjin a few days after Puyi. In Muramatsu's book, there was a last-minute hitch, when Wanrong realized she had left her beloved Italian toy dog behind, so they had to turn back to retrieve it. Who knows whether this detail was really true? Muramatsu's account was written in 1932, the same year it all happened. In Yoshiko's own book, written five years later, she lifted the story from the novel almost verbatim and switched the characters around from Wanrong to Puyi.

We don't even know for sure that she was really the intrepid driver in the hunting cap. But Yoshiko *was* dispatched to Tianjin by the Japanese secret police in Shanghai to persuade the reluctant empress to follow her husband to Manchukuo. That Yoshiko helped the Japanese in these shenanigans is not just an invention. Why she did so is less clear. She may have been deluded by the idea of a Qing Dynasty restoration, like Puyi himself. She certainly saw the Chinese as unsympathetic to the Manchu cause—true of both the Nationalists and the Communists—and often referred to herself as the Manchu Joan of Arc. Or perhaps she was just trying to live up to her fantasies of being a hero in men's clothes.

The problem with trying to separate fact from fiction in Yoshiko's life is that her own mythomania, widely publicized in the Japanese press, and further embellished in Muramatsu's novel, written at her own behest, was suffused with Japanese propaganda. There is no doubt that the Japanese tried to use her status as a Manchu princess to dress up their military invasions in China as a noble liberation of Manchus and Mongols from wicked Chinese warlords, and ultimately of all Asians from wicked Western imperialists.

Tired of the provincial limitations of Dalian, Yoshiko had moved to Shanghai in 1931, where she cut a swath through the ballrooms and nightclubs, dancing in male evening clothes. There she was, winning the first prize in a waltzing competition at the Astor House, and there, networking at the Cathay Hotel on the Bund with agents and political fixers from all sides: Chinese, Russian, Japanese. She often stayed up all night, with a small entourage of female servants, tipping generously from thick wads of money, living it up with Russian courtesans, Chinese taxi dancers, and Japanese army officers at places like the Bluebird on Xizang Road. Staying at an apartment filled with dolls and pictures of Japanese beauties, she liked to be woken in the morning by her servant to the music of Beethoven's *Moonlight Sonata*, followed by some jazz. To soak up the atmosphere for his book, Muramatsu lived with Yoshiko for several months, while staving off her sexual advances, or so he said.

His novel is at least artful. Yoshiko's own story of her time in Shanghai reads like a very clumsy piece of pulp fiction. It revolves around an invented nightclub named the Romanshi, short for Russia, Manchuria, and China, the native countries of the club's three owners, whose utterances are like cartoon versions of Japanese propaganda. The White Russian hates Communists, the Manchurian hates the Chinese Nationalists, and the Chinese man hates the warlords. They are joined by an upstanding Japanese who renounced his old leftist ideals. All agree that Japan is the only nation that can bring peace and prosperity to Asia.

Precisely when or how Yoshiko became an active spy for the Japanese is unclear. After the war, she denied that she ever had been a spy, repudiating the stories that she herself and her Shanghai chronicler had put about so assiduously before. No one denies, however, that she had a passionate relationship (certainly on his side) with a Japanese spymaster and military plotter named Tanaka Ryukichi.

A mentally unstable man with a history of volatile romantic relationships, one almost resulting in a double suicide, Tanaka looked like a caricature of a Japanese war criminal: stocky, bullnecked, moonfaced, with a tight little mouth and little suspicious eyes. While giving testimony after the war at the Tokyo War Crimes Tribunal, Tanaka was called "the Monster" in an American magazine. Muramatsu called him "somewhat crazy" and tried to stay out of his way. In his view, Tanaka was the source of those thick wads of cash that Yoshiko carried around with her. He also claims to have witnessed the two of them in situations with the Monster as a masochist, groveling at the cross-dressing dominatrix's feet, while she bawled him out for some infraction.

Tanaka was proud to be seen around town with a Manchu princess, which might explain his readiness to indulge her whims. But he also saw her as a useful agent for the Japanese. Yoshiko was paid to brush up on her Chinese and learn English, so she might make better use of her many social contacts in Shanghai to furnish the Japanese with secret information. Like most mythomaniacs, Yoshiko liked to claim intimate acquaintance with powerful people. In some cases, this was quite true. The dance halls of Shanghai were a convenient stage for her social skills. She supposedly informed on several senior figures in the Chinese Nationalist Party. When the Chinese leaders became aware of these leaks, Yoshiko helped some of her sources to get out of Shanghai. These feats earned her another sobriquet in Japanese military and media circles: the Mata Hari of the Orient.

Details about Yoshiko's spying remain fuzzy. But most people who have studied her life assume she had a serious hand in a disgraceful episode known as the Shanghai Incident. This happened in 1932, four months after the Mukden Incident. A telegram arrived on Tanaka's desk one day from the Kwantung Army headquarters. Things were going well in Manchuria, it said, but as might be expected, the Mukden Incident had attracted unwelcome international criticism and was provoking anti-Japanese protest in China. It was time to do something about this. The independence of Manchukuo would be greatly helped if world attention could be diverted, by a splashy incident in Shanghai for example.

This much is known: On January 18, a group of militant Japanese

Buddhist monks, beating drums in a provocative march through a Chinese working-class area, was attacked by a mob near the Sanyou towel factory, which had the reputation of being a Communist stronghold. Two monks were badly wounded; one died. Groups of Japanese militiamen then torched the factory in retaliation. Chinese in other parts of the city erupted in demonstrations and called for a boycott of Japanese products. The Japanese issued an ultimatum to the Shanghai Municipal Council: full compensation for damage to Japanese properties, a public condemnation of Chinese violence, and active steps to stop further anti-Japanese agitation. The council agreed. But ten days later, ostensibly to protect the safety of Japanese citizens, dense Chinese residential areas were heavily bombed by planes from a Japanese aircraft carrier in the bay, while foreign residents watched from the balconies of their offices and hotels on the Bund. It was the first instance of terror bombing, a strategy that would escalate first in China, then in Europe, and finally with the atom bombing of two Japanese cities in 1945. Thousands of Japanese troops invaded the city. Chiang Kai-shek's army fought back. More Japanese troops landed. A truce was eventually called, but the second Sino-Japanese War had begun in earnest.

Less well-known is that Yoshiko was supposedly sent to the Sanyou towel factory by her Japanese masters to stir up the workers against the marching monks. And that it was she who paid the Japanese militias to burn down the factory, causing many people to die. The problem with this story is that the erratic Tanaka was the only source. He bragged in his postwar memoir that Yoshiko had become the perfect spy, infiltrating Chinese army positions on the outskirts of town and feeding secret information to the Japanese. Muramatsu claimed after the war that the spy stories were all made up to sell Yoshiko's legend to the public.

But it is also in Muramatsu's book that we read a plausible account of Yoshiko's motives. Of course, plausibility does not make it necessarily true. These are the words of the main character: "I'm not just a spy. . . .

I'm not Japanese. I'm a Manchu. [As far as fighting Chiang Kai-shek is concerned] I'm on the Japanese side. When our interests coincide, I will work for Japan. I don't like being thought of as a Japanese spy." Mariko, her fictionalized alter ego, said that. Yoshiko might conceivably have said it too.

Some of the Shanghai events are recorded in Yoshiko's own memoir, but in a passive and oddly evasive voice: anti-Japanese elements attacked the monks; anti-Japanese rioters ran amok; the Japanese had no choice but to restore order with maximum force. But she remembers with pride how she managed to mingle with Chinese soldiers and militiamen. And she was quick to note that Chinese warlords posed the biggest threat, not just to Manchukuo independence, but to peace in China proper. All she herself wanted was peace. Even though she was a Manchu, the blood of China ran through her veins, and her soul was infused with the Japanese spirit. These sentiments were greatly admired by the Russian, Manchu, Chinese, and Japanese friends at the Romanshi Club described in her memoir. They were in awe of her extraordinary courage and ingenuity.

The rest is pure Shanghai pulp fiction. Her friends are kidnapped by Chinese gangsters with machine guns and dark glasses. Yoshiko then manages to get them released. Du Yuesheng, or "Big-Eared Du," the king of the Shanghai underworld, duly makes an appearance, as he does in every tale of old Shanghai. Du, leader of the Green Gang, which controlled prostitution, gambling, and protection rackets, was real enough. His grand Western-style mansion in the French concession, where he lived with dozens of concubines, still exists as a hotel. A staunch conservative, like most gang bosses, and a Chinese patriot of a kind, Du was a close ally of Chiang Kai-shek. Everyone was terrified of him, but not Yoshiko, who confronts Big-Eared Du in his own home and tells him to stop resisting the Japanese in Shanghai, so that peace and order can return to the city. Impressed by her courage and sincerity, the tough gangster boss meekly promises to do as she says.

This is an unlikely story. What is incontestably true is that the bloody Shanghai Incident, reported in newspapers all over the world, distracted international attention from the other "incident," in Mukden. Manchuria was now firmly in Japanese hands. The founding of Manchukuo, the Japanese puppet state, would follow. And Yoshiko had played her part in it.

Five

Crossing the Line

We like lists because we don't want to die.

Umberto Eco

1: Scheveningen

One of Friedrich Weinreb's most ardent defenders after the war compared him to Till Eulenspiegel, the medieval German prankster, who exposes human greed and other vices through a series of highly improper practical jokes. W. H. Auden once wrote that inflicting practical jokes on people is a way of playing God: the joker manipulates his victim without the victim realizing what is going on. When did Weinreb choose to play God?

The Germans invaded the Netherlands on May 10, 1940. Nazi occupation, though humiliating and deeply resented, did not seem so bad to most Dutch people in the beginning. German soldiers generally behaved reasonably well, or they kept out of sight. Unlike people in Poland and other parts of central and eastern Europe, the Dutch were to be treated as a fraternal Germanic race. Even the Jews were left alone, at first, so as not to cause undue alarm. The Hungarian filmmaker Péter Forgács found footage from home movies shot by a Dutch Jewish family in the first two years of the war. He used them in an extraordinary documentary called

The Maelstrom (1997). Nothing, but absolutely nothing, in these happy scenes of birthdays, bar mitzvah parties, and weddings, shows any hint of what was about to happen to the smiling men, women, and children featured in the films; almost all of them were choked to death in gas chambers very soon after the movies abruptly stopped in 1942.

Because many Dutch Jews—the better-off more than the poor, of course—were quite well integrated into the general population, the first thing the Germans had to do was separate them, ghettoize them, make them distinct enough so that deportation and murder could be managed with a minimum of fuss. The drip-drip of measures and decrees was so gradual that most people, including the Jews themselves, still couldn't imagine the dreadful consequences. Weinreb, through his close contacts in the 1930s with eastern European and German Jewish refugees, was less deluded than most. Obviously, he couldn't predict Auschwitz or Treblinka. Treblinka didn't even exist in 1940. But he was never naive about Nazi intentions.

With the Dutch government in exile in London, the Netherlands was ruled as a German Nazi police state under *Reichskommissar* Arthur Seyss-Inquart, a former Viennese lawyer. Seyss-Inquart was highly if narrowly intelligent. With his thick glasses and pronounced limp, he seemed an unimposing figure, more a legal bureaucrat than a murderous thug. People who liked him thought he had typical Viennese charm. He was in fact fanatically devoted to Hitler and a ferocious antisemite who shared Himmler's crackpot beliefs that Aryan racial purity might be traced to Tibetan origins. He, too, like the Jewish family in Forgács's film, was keen on home movies. In one well-known clip, shown in *The Maelstrom*, the *Reichskommissar* can be seen playing tennis with Himmler, even as the Jewish subjects of their own home movies were being deported in cattle cars to "the east." But during the first year of occupation, Seyss-Inquart never once mentioned the Jews in a public speech.

The initial measure against Jews seemed so innocuous that it made people even more complacent. From July 1940, Jews were no longer allowed to take part in civil air defense units. Since most Jews would have had no interest in defending the skies against Allied aircraft, this cannot have been a great blow. But it was the first small step toward total segregation.

Then came an order to no longer employ Jews or half-Jews in government jobs. Then all civil servants were told to sign a form declaring whether they were "Aryans." Then all remaining Jews in the civil service, including judges and university professors, were thrown out of their jobs. Weinreb lost his position at the economic research institute in Rotterdam at the end of 1941. There was some protest here and there. Rudolph Cleveringa, a law professor at Leyden University, made a famous speech in defense of his purged colleague, the distinguished legal scholar Eduard Meijers ("this noble and true son of our people"—the Dutch people, that is). Cleveringa had already packed his bags in preparation for his inevitable arrest. However, the Dutch Supreme Court did not utter a word of protest when its Jewish president, Lodewijk Visser, was dismissed. Jews were ordered to move to designated "Jewish areas" in Amsterdam (there never had been an official ghetto in Holland). Jews were no longer allowed to shop in "Aryan" stores, visit cinemas, parks, swimming pools, or anywhere else with signs that read NO JEWS ALLOWED. Unemployed Jews were sent to work in labor camps. In April 1942, all Jews had to wear the yellow Star of David with the word *Jood* written in black letters on the upper left of their garments—noncompliance would lead to arrest and deportation. The rest, from the German point of view, was easy, so easy that Adolf Eichmann, the top Nazi bureaucrat in charge of the Jewish genocide, is supposed to have remarked that the swift expulsion of Dutch Jews was "a pleasure to behold."

One reason the machinery of persecution operated almost without a hitch was that the Netherlands was a very well-organized society of generally law-abiding citizens, who had had almost no recent experience of civil disobedience, unlike the French, or even the Belgians. The idea that authorities could be acting with deliberate malice, let alone embarking on a program of mass murder, was unimaginable. Typical was this statement by the chief rabbi of Amsterdam in May 1940: "Above all, we should stay calm and follow the demands of the authorities with dignity. We must show that we are loyal citizens by obeying all the regulations." Every rule that pulled the noose a little tighter was like another administrative measure, a bureaucratic nuisance people just had to put up with, involving piles of documents, stamps, signatures, lists, and endless queueing in front of desks manned by bored officials hunched over their clattering typewriters. Some of the most heartbreaking photographs of the first stages of the murder of Dutch Jews are not the blurry images of men being kicked viciously by uniformed men in boots as they lie facedown in the streets of Amsterdam: worse, in a way, are the pictures of anxious men and women, trying to look cheerful, as they wait their turn to have documents stamped that would turn out to be their death warrants.

The prime and much-criticized symbol of civic compliance was the so-called Jewish Council. Everywhere they went to carry out their murderous program, from Amsterdam to Minsk, the Germans ordered the establishment of a Jewish Council, to take the administrative weight off their shoulders and carry out their odious demands. It was the Jewish Council that distributed the Stars of David, the Jewish Council that advised unemployed men to sign up for hard labor, and the Jewish Council that made up the lists of people to be sent on their way to the death camps in Poland. Most men who served in these councils were respectable, well-meaning pillars of their communities—professors, doctors, rabbis, accountants, lawyers. Some were Zionists, some not, some religious, and some not. It is easy to condemn them in retrospect for doing the Nazis' work, or at least making it easier for the German occupiers. But they often believed that by doing so, they might mitigate the harshness of persecution, or at least ease some of the suffering. Some, but certainly not all, thought of protecting their own families first—almost always in vain. They were of course put into an impossible position. Powerless to stop the systematic killing, with very few exceptions they ended up being murdered themselves.

Weinreb despised the obedient Dutch authorities, including the Amsterdam police who actively helped the Germans round up Jews from their homes. He despised the Jews who refused to recognize the danger they were in. He despised the non-Jewish citizens who carried on with their lives as though there was nothing amiss, averting their eyes from unpleasantness, such as the lines of Jewish families, pale with fright, laden with suitcases, being pushed onto trams and trains bound for who knows where. Soccer games continued to take place on Sunday afternoons. The cafés were filled with laughing, chattering customers. Theaters and cabarets still drew crowds, albeit without some of the popular Jewish performers.

But above all, Weinreb despised the Jewish Council. This was partly a matter of class resentment, the eastern European immigrant's bitterness about what was often seen, not always without reason, as the haughty detachment of the local Jewish elite. There is a great deal of ranting in Weinreb's memoirs against the "stupid kiss-asses," the "power-hungry" snobs who "were so shocked by the occupation that they sought compensation by identifying themselves with the German police, with the powerful."

This is unfair, but it sums up exactly what Weinreb claimed he was standing up against. He would be cleverer than the stupid Nazis and the equally stupid Jewish Council, and the mass of foolish Dutch citizens. The time had come to let go of the old norms, of respect for laws and regulations. He learned how difficult it was to persuade people to do something "illegal." Most, he realized, "choose to remain legal to the death." The Jewish Council, he argued, was typical of a Dutch bureaucratic mentality. People simply didn't have the imagination to resist. In the topsy-turvy world of Nazi occupation, everything—rules, regulations, laws, news, information—was a dangerous sham. The thing to be, the thing Weinreb aspired to be, was an "administrative guerrilla." The only right response to persecution was to break the rules and even to lie through your teeth. Or as he put it: "To tell the truth could be ruinous under certain circumstances, and to fill in forms accurately was foolish."

Weinreb's perception was accurate. He was right about the vulnerability of law-abiding people in the face of an utterly ruthless enemy. But his career as an administrative guerrilla, of trying to outfox the Germans by appearing to play their own game, by making up imaginary lists of Jews who would be exempted from deportation, started before the Jewish Council existed and the deportations began. And he began his activities by foxing his fellow Jews.

The problem with Weinreb, as with Kersten and Kawashima Yoshiko, is that his fantasies tend to overwhelm what really happened. (At more than a thousand pages, his memoir is indeed overwhelming.) In his case, however, we know quite a lot, because of an exhaustive report on Weinreb's wartime operations, published in 1976 by the Dutch National Institute for War Documentation (now the NIOD Institute for War, Holocaust and Genocide Studies), as well as a thorough study of the Weinreb case and its aftermath written by Regina Grüters in 1997.

Quite how Weinreb got started is still lost in the Scheveningen fog. In his own story, he was approached by a young Jewish acquaintance named Stiel, who was called up for duty in a forced labor camp. This was supposed to have happened in late 1941. Weinreb was sought after for advice, because he was an educated man, an economist, and a pious Jew. This is when Weinreb, by his own account, became an administrative guerrilla. He called the local labor office, mimicking the barking manner of a Nazi official, and said that Mr. Stiel could not be sent to a labor camp because the German military specifically forbade it. Stiel, he said, had access to money abroad. Sufficiently cowed, the official on the other end of the line told Weinreb to send him the relevant documents that made the exemption from labor official. Weinreb later claimed that this gave him the idea of making up official-sounding lists of Jews who would not only be spared from deportation but would also be allowed, in exchange for undisclosed sums of money to be remitted by rich Jews abroad, to board special trains to France, and from there to the safety of Switzerland or Portugal. The scheme had a very high-ranking sponsor:

Herbert Joachim von Schumann, *Generalleutnant* in the German army. Weinreb had met the general by chance in The Hague, where he had saved his benefactor's life by dragging him away at the very last minute from an onrushing tram. This story alternated with another one, which attributed General von Schumann's generous help to his appreciation of Weinreb's excellent research on wartime economics. As proof of the general's backing, Weinreb even had an official letter from von Schumann, embossed with an impressive-looking Wehrmacht letterhead.

That General von Schumann was a complete invention, and his letter faked by Weinreb, does not prove that the story of his beginnings as a trickster was false. More of a problem is the timing. No one was called up for forced labor until the beginning of 1942. There was no reason for Stiel to ask for help in 1941, not to avoid going to a forced labor camp at any rate. The compilers of the official report on Weinreb concluded that the story of Weinreb's calls to the labor office were imaginary as well. This doesn't mean, of course, that all was still fine in the second year of Nazi occupation.

An escalation of Jewish persecution had begun in the first months of 1941. Like the Shanghai Incident, it began with a deliberate provocation. Even though most people in the Jewish neighborhoods of Amsterdam were much too frightened and powerless to act, the Nazis warned of Jewish riots. When black-shirted Dutch thugs from the collaborationist militia attacked Jews at random, for a bit of fun, smashing windows of Jewish shops, beating up defenseless people in the streets, a few young Jewish men decided to fight back and one of the black-shirted militiamen died of his wounds. This was the excuse the Germans wanted. More than three hundred Jewish men were rounded up, beaten, and humiliated in ways that Nazis liked to call "sport," and sent to Buchenwald and then to the even more notorious camp of Mauthausen. They all died horribly, some in early experiments with poison gas. One of the dead was Weinreb's brother, Edmond, who had been arrested for an unknown reason the year before. Long before people had heard of

Auschwitz, Mauthausen was the name that struck the greatest terror in Jewish hearts.

Partly in protest against the deportations, the Communist Party organized a general strike on February 25, 1941. Factories, docks, trams, trains, all came to a halt, first in Amsterdam, then in nearby towns. The February strike made Jews feel they were not abandoned. In the words of the Israeli historian Tom Segev, who was told the story as a child, this act of Dutch defiance was like a small flickering candle in a world of utter darkness. The Germans crushed the strike with great brutality in two days. But it gave the Netherlands a reputation for brave resistance, which Israelis are unwilling to question to this day. When Queen Beatrix, in a speech to Israel's parliament, the Knesset, in 1995, said that Dutch people who actively helped the Jews were exceptions, this was not particularly well received.

After the February strike there was no longer any pretense about German intentions. Seyss-Inquart first mentioned the "Jewish problem" in public at the venerable Concertgebouw, home of the Amsterdam philharmonic orchestra. "To us," he said, "Jews aren't Dutch. They are enemies with whom neither a truce, nor peace is possible. We will hit them where we can, and those who stand with them will bear the consequences." The Jewish Council was established in the same month. The yellow star had to be worn from May onward. But Anne Frank and her family had not yet gone into hiding. Few people had. Mass deportations to "the east" started a year later.

Weinreb began telling people about his magical lists, backed by General von Schumann, well before that. In exchange for one hundred guilders per person, a considerable sum in those days, and more from those who could afford it, he promised to put people on the trains to safety—three trains to be exact. Children under eighteen could go for free, and so, in principle, could people who lacked sufficient money to buy their freedom. In fact, only a few people ended up on the lists without paying. In time, as thousands of Jews applied, Weinreb ended up with 350,000 guilders, roughly equivalent to three million dollars today. How these funds were administered by Weinreb and his helpers is opaque. A great deal of cash was piled up in a fruit bowl in Weinreb's living room. Some of it might have been used to help people evade arrest and go into hiding, as Weinreb alleged. Certainly not all of it.

Weinreb was not the only one engaged in making up lists of people who might be spared a violent death. The threat of deportation offered rich opportunities to a variety of local gangsters who promised to smuggle people out of the country in exchange for cash, properties, or jewelry. Once the transaction had been successfully concluded, the criminals made yet more money by handing their victims over to the Nazi police.

Having absolute power over helpless people did not invariably lead to criminal abuse. Lives were sometimes saved by men who tried to do some good. A German lawyer named Hans Georg Calmeyer oversaw "Jewish affairs" in the occupation government. It was up to him to decide whether someone was wholly or only partly Jewish, which could mean the difference between life and death. He apparently turned a blind eye to many documents that were patently false. But he also did his administrative duty in other cases, where he sent people to their deaths. Some still regard him as a hero. He is remembered at Yad Vashem, the Holocaust memorial in Jerusalem, as a "righteous man among nations." But he was also an important cog in the machinery of systematic murder. Weinreb was not such a cog. His power over other people's fate was a fantasy.

A lot of time, energy, and ingenuity went into making his list to freedom appear plausible. Weinreb asked his "clients" to fill in elaborate forms—always more forms—and supply passport photographs. Strict rules decreed what clothes to take (nightshirts, no pajamas). He also insisted that people get medical examinations. Weinreb himself maintained that these examinations were performed at the request of the people who begged to be on his lists. They assumed that clean bills of health were normally required for emigration. The first examinations were done by a medical student named Van Lier. More and more, however, Weinreb himself took over this duty. He claimed to have been a qualified doctor who had completed his degree in Vienna. He even had a letter from a medical professor to prove it. The degree and the letter were as fictional as the promised trains and the German general.

Weinreb subjected the men to cursory inspections. But the women had to undergo more thorough, often painful gynecological examinations, involving a lot of probing and useless injections. Keen to recruit young women, supposedly as nurses and teachers to accompany the children on lucky convoys to safety abroad, Weinreb even opened a special list for young women, all of whom needed to be examined, either in Weinreb's own house or at various addresses in The Hague, Rotterdam, or Amsterdam.

Weinreb got into trouble many years later for similar practices, this time involving female students of his religious instruction. He even admitted that he was not an ordinary man, intellectually, philosophically, spiritually, or indeed sexually. But to reduce Weinreb's schemes to financial greed or sexual abuse would be too simple. Something else was at work too. He was not only *goochem*, clever, and a *gelernter*, a devout scholar, but he would be a *macher*, a fixer, a man who gets things done, a man with the right connections. There is no reason to disbelieve him when he writes about his new role as a *macher*: "It was as if I had broken through that ghastly passivity, that sense in the most ordinary human matters that things were 'impossible.' I felt that I was now at war. And battle is liberating."

And yet all he was offering people was an illusion. There were no trains, there was no escape. Weinreb admitted in an interview in 1976: "All promises were soap bubbles. You couldn't do anything else but sell soap bubbles. The only truth in those days was that the Germans wanted to destroy the Jews. The question was how long it would take before the soap bubble burst."

Some people distrusted Weinreb and distanced themselves from him. But many were extremely grateful. Weinreb wallowed in their gratitude. He related one woman saying to him: "You are a *malech* [angel]. You will be rewarded." He was greeted by people with tears in their eyes, calling him a miracle worker. People—still according to Weinreb—sent their wives to him and encouraged them to do anything—"up to the farthest limits of respectability"—to persuade him to put them on his lists. This may have been true. By the summer of 1942, even Jews who had hoped things would not turn out too badly recognized the mortal danger they were in.

Weinreb later defended his fraudulent scheme by claiming that by offering people hope, even if it was a mere soap bubble, he gave them a little more time to save themselves, either by going into hiding or by holding out until Germany was defeated. There are people who believe that their lives were saved by being on Weinreb's lists. But they are few. Of the roughly 4,000 Jews on his lists, just a handful survived the war. Of the more than 140,000 Jews living in the Netherlands in 1940, only about 30,000 were still alive five years later. Weinreb was right that Dutch Gentiles, whether out of indifference, complacency, fear, or malice, did too little to help their Jewish compatriots, let alone foreign refugees, but this doesn't mean that his lists did anything more than sell vain hope in return for money, undeserved gratitude, sexual favors, and a false reputation as a *macher* and a miracle worker.

One remarkable indication of Weinreb's trickster psychology lies in his mention of others who offered hope to his clients. When Weinreb's brother, Edmond, was arrested in late 1940, and was held in the prison in Scheveningen before being deported to Germany, Weinreb asked a respectable lawyer in The Hague for help. The lawyer promised that he would, for the hefty sum of five hundred guilders (equivalent to about four thousand dollars today). Weinreb relates that he paid the man promptly. Alas, promises were just promises. Nothing happened. The brother was doomed. Here is Weinreb's description of another futile meeting, this time with the owner of a bakery:

Yet another meeting, again the big stories about German contacts, more promises and then silence. For nothing I was subjected to his tales about his enormous influence, and how he could wind the Germans round his little finger. I have met such people several times during the war, men who took visible pleasure in telling big stories and offering promises . . . who loved the impression they thought they were making on others. They weren't even *thinking* of carrying out their promises. They didn't even have a clue how to do so. All they did was dream of being in a position of power, and in those days that meant having "important relations with high-ranking Germans."

This story of the baker is a perfect example of what Freudians call "projection." Weinreb could not have given a more concise, more accurate description of himself. The most astonishing thing is that he didn't seem to realize it. Perhaps, as so often, the mythomaniac was deluded by his own myth. As he put it: "It takes so little to give a person courage and self-confidence. I began to believe in the power of my letters myself."

So Weinreb initiated his lists and quickly gathered a few dozen takers, and there is no doubt that by the summer of 1942 many people were knocking on his door in despair. To give his list extra plausibility, Weinreb used the same technique as many fraudsters before or since: the promise of exclusivity, of being one of the chosen ones. This is how the New York broker Bernie Madoff created confidence in the 1980s, when he tricked his marks into investing their money in a Ponzi scheme. As a prominent figure in the Jewish community of New York and Miami, he exuded trustworthiness and respectability. That he turned down prospective clients, who begged to be included, added to his air of probity. Weinreb observes in his memoir that people regarded inclusion on his list as a "status symbol," which provoked envy. He, too, turned some people down, which may, in some cases, have saved their lives.

Like Madoff, Weinreb began by taking on people who were close to him, mostly eastern European Jewish immigrants in Scheveningen and The Hague. Many had looked up to him, proud to have a *gelernter* in their midst. But some knew him a little too well. A fellow member of the ultraorthodox Agudath Yisrael saw through him early on, after Weinreb had boasted in the late 1930s of being in close touch with government ministers and members of the royal family. An inevitable result of a scheme in high demand, however exclusive, is that word gets around. Even as more and more people were desperate to be on Weinreb's lists, word reached dangerous places, such as the dreaded Sicherheitsdienst, or SD, the security arm of the SS, whose office and torture chambers were in a villa designed in the 1920s by an admirer of Frank Lloyd Wright. The Villa Windekind, as it is called, was on the same street as Felix Kersten's house, and in walking distance of Weinreb's more modest abode.* On September 11, 1942, Weinreb was arrested.

2: Berlin

Felix Kersten must have had an extraordinary capacity for putting up with boredom. After he agreed to take Himmler on as a patient, Kersten was pressed to spend time with the SS chief and his wife and daughter at Gmund am Tegernsee, their lakeside country retreat in Bavaria. There, Himmler, the relaxed family man in his white knee socks and *lederhosen*, would hold forth at lunch and dinner on all his pet subjects, including his

---

*The house was designed by Dirk Roosenburg, grandfather of the famous Dutch architect Rem Koolhaas. The original owner, François van 't Sant, a former chief of police, was a louche figure who used the house to provide prostitutes for Felix Kersten's royal client Prince Hendrik, the husband of Queen Wilhelmina.

self-identification with Henry the Fowler, the tenth-century king who fought the Danes, the Slavs, and the Magyars and is often viewed as the first German monarch. Kersten said Himmler was "imbued with that typically German weakness: an extraordinary capacity for creating illusions." By all accounts, including Kersten's, Himmler had all the charm of a pedantic petit bourgeois German schoolmaster, whose vulgar prejudices echoed those held in thousands of provincial beer halls. Kersten recounts some of them at tedious length.

Public health was one of Himmler's hobbyhorses. Modern medical doctors and other so-called experts were all wrong. Not scientific research or medicine, but natural remedies would keep the German people healthy. He was especially taken by the hot- and cold-water bath cures devised by a nineteenth-century Bavarian priest named Sebastian Kneipp. Himmler was also a great bore about diet. He had a peculiar passion for natural honey. Finnish sauna baths were another enthusiasm that he wished to take up on the national level. There is an unforgettable description by the Italian journalist Curzio Malaparte of Himmler taking a sauna bath in Lapland surrounded by naked SS officers: "He stood before us, the big toes of his flat feet oddly thrust upward, his short arms dangling. Little streams of perspiration gushed like little fountains from the tips of his fingers. Around his flabby breasts grew two little circles of hair, two haloes of blond hair; perspiration gushed like milk from his nipples." When his SS men started thrashing him with twigs in the prescribed Finnish manner, Himmler ran away, squealing into the forest of birch trees.

Then there were his diatribes against homosexuals, whom he vowed to eradicate "root and branch" because they were "a danger to the national health." During one of his conversations with Kersten on this topic in 1940, Himmler even wished to nominate his masseur as his "special adviser on homosexual matters." The Hitler Youth, Himmler said, had already devised a program to counter unhealthy sexual tendencies, "but nothing yet [had] been done to reach a fundamental solution to the problem." Happily, Kersten managed to wriggle out of this assignment.

Himmler's views on Jewish and Masonic conspiracies were as clichéd and dreary as they were mad. "High-grade Masons," he opined, were "identical with the inner circle of the Elders of Zion. Thus, the Jewish rulers of the world have used Masonry as a camouflage for their own international power." He believed that "the Jewish empire" drained all other nations of their wealth, strength, and influence. Kersten pretends in his memoirs that he argued with Himmler's opinions on Jews and other mortal enemies of the healthy German race. Since Kersten professed to have no interest in political affairs, and Himmler was not one to tolerate opposition on such vital matters, this is somewhat doubtful. But here is an example of the kind of exchanges they supposedly had:

Kersten: You take your arguments from a time that lies seven centuries away. Science and world commerce have long ago transformed your field of ideas into something quite different. . . .

Himmler: I'll answer you quite simply. Despite world science and commerce, it disgusts me when I see a Jew strolling on the Bavarian mountains in *lederhosen*. I don't go about in a caftan and ringlets. In terms of racial feeling, there are two different worlds.

This was by no means an exceptional feeling in Germany, or indeed many other parts of Europe. Even Himmler's notions of breeding a superior Aryan race, as though human beings were dogs or chickens, were, if a little extreme, not entirely beyond the pale of medical opinion in his time; eugenics, after all, had supporters in many countries, including the United States, even among people who were not Nazi sympathizers at all. More eccentric were Himmler's views, as reported by Kersten, on blood sports—eccentric, that is, for a German who prided himself on his tough manly qualities. Himmler hated hunting animals—"those poor creatures, sitting there at the edge of the forest, innocent and without a care. How can you take pleasure, my dear Kersten, in killing them?"

Himmler was just one of Kersten's many powerful patients before the war broke out, first in Poland, on September 1, 1939, and then, more fatefully for Kersten, in Holland on May 10, 1940. Joseph Kessel reports that both Elisabeth Lüben, Kersten's faithful companion, and his wife, Irmgard, strongly advised Kersten to distance himself from Himmler after the invasion of Poland. They may have. In any case, he didn't. A more serious dilemma faced him after the Dutch surrender. Himmler told Kersten not to go back to his home in The Hague. Kersten was supposedly warned by Himmler that the Dutch Nazis would target him because of his well-known connections with the Dutch royal family. He might even be assassinated. Since Anton Mussert, the Dutch Nazi leader, refused to criticize Queen Wilhelmina and her family, even after they fled to London, and Kersten would not have ranked high, if at all, on the Dutch Nazis' enemy list, this is an unlikely story.

Various explanations have been advanced, by Kersten himself as well as others, for his agreement to be at Himmler's disposal as his personal masseur. Kersten and his family were trapped in Germany and obedience was his only option; a refusal would have resulted in arrest and concentration camp. But there is no evidence that this threat was ever real. Since he was a Finnish citizen, and Finland was not an enemy of Germany at that stage, Kersten could have moved there to be out of Himmler's way. When he asked the Finnish embassy in Berlin for advice, Kersten was apparently encouraged to stay close to Himmler and pass on useful information to the Finns. This could well be true. But the most plausible reason for Kersten's compliance is the most banal. He was enjoying a good life in Berlin and at Hartzwalde, his country estate. Even though he claimed that Himmler never paid him money, Kersten was well rewarded by his other German patients, including the industrialist Friedrich Flick and some of the top Nazi leaders. Karl Wolff,

Himmler's chief of personal staff, said after the war that Kersten was actually paid up to fifty thousand marks a year by Himmler himself. Kersten had made a career out of relieving the pains of the richest and most powerful people wherever he was; in Nazi Germany, these happened to be people like Himmler, the foreign minister Joachim von Ribbentrop, the gauleiter and Labor Front leader Robert Ley, and the deputy Nazi leader Rudolf Hess, all of whom submitted to his healing hands.

Much of Kersten's wartime archive—letters, notes, diaries—was lost at the end of the war. Almost all his documents now at hand are copies. He also rewrote his diaries in Stockholm after the war and he almost certainly faked some of the letters he ostensibly wrote to Himmler and others. So, it is hard to know what is true. But a copy of one of the letters helped to convince people after the war that Kersten had been a heroic figure on the side of the anti-Nazi resistance from the start. Himmler had offered Kersten a rank in the SS, as *Standartenführer*, but, naturally, only after he had made sure of his racial purity. Documents show that Kersten cooperated fully in this investigation, advising Himmler on contacts who could vouch for Kersten's clean Aryan family record. This was in May 1939, a few months before the invasion of Poland. But the letter that appears to demonstrate Kersten's anti-Nazi bona fides was written on May 11, 1940, the day after the invasion of the Netherlands. Kersten wrote to Himmler that he wouldn't have anything to do with any political organization, either the SS or any other Nazi institution. He was a Finnish patriot and felt a deep connection with the Dutch people; Holland was his second home. Therefore, he could only continue to treat Himmler as a private patient.

If he really wrote such a letter, it is contradicted by another letter, written in August 1942 to the Finnish foreign minister. Kersten explained that he had been asked by Himmler to join the military branch of the SS, the Waffen SS, and he wanted to know whether he would lose his Finnish passport if he were to do so. A week later, a letter from the foreign minister reassured him that he would remain a Finnish citizen even if he should choose to wear a German officer's uniform.

Kersten did not join the Waffen SS or wear a German uniform. Every wartime photograph shows his ample frame dressed in a smart suit or a white doctor's coat. The fact that he never joined the Nazi party was indeed a reason for other top Nazis, such as Reinhard Heydrich, the Gestapo chief and architect of the Final Solution, to distrust him. There were other reasons too.

Like all despotic empires, Hitler's regime was a congeries of rival courts, which were themselves nests of spying, backstabbing, and ferocious bureaucratic infighting. No one trusted anyone. Every snippet of information on rivals for power was valuable. Everyone, from Hitler down, had to be constantly on their guard against traitors. This venomous atmosphere is beautifully dramatized in Shakespeare's *Richard III*, with its escalating acts of treachery and political murder. It might explain why members of such courts so often suffer from chronic headaches, insomnia, or stomach cramps—afflictions often linked to mental stress. Li Zhisui, Chairman Mao's personal physician, identified similar ailments in Mao's court as "a peculiarly communist disease, the result of being trapped in a system of no escape."

It isn't a Communist disease, of course: it is the disease of any dictatorship. Hitler suffered from stomach pains and bowel problems. Ribbentrop had terrible headaches, as well as stomach cramps. Robert Ley was always drunk and had a pancreatic disorder. Rudolf Hess suffered from stomachaches and gallbladder pains. Hess, surrounded by a rich assortment of quacks, soothsayers, and astrologers, would lie in his bed with a huge magnet suspended over his head, which he hoped would draw the pains from his body. Himmler was keen for Kersten to continue his treatment of all of them, and even to massage Hitler. For whatever reason, Kersten claims to have refused to tend to the Führer himself.

But Himmler didn't tell Kersten to massage the other Nazis out of kindness or humane concern. As a mere masseur, who had the full confidence of the Reichsführer SS, Kersten was the perfect spy. His role was to find out what the other Nazi bosses were thinking, so Himmler could use that information against them if or when it suited him. Himmler couldn't stand Ribbentrop. He despised Ley. He had contempt for Hess. He didn't even fully trust Heydrich, his odious chief deputy. And he trusted the thuggish Ernst Kaltenbrunner, Heydrich's successor, even less.

This made Kersten, as well as his colleagues offering spiritual and medical services, into courtiers who were used, as in Shakespeare's plays about tyrannical kings, to serve the interests of their bosses against powerful rivals. Kersten may not have been "political," but he prided himself on his skills as a networker, a flatterer, an intriguer, a man of influence, a *macher*. This was a very dangerous environment in which to be an intriguer. But Kersten knew that as long as he was useful to him, he had Himmler's protection.

He needed this protection after Rudolf Hess, a mentally unstable man at the best of times, decided in May 1941 to fly to Scotland on his own in a two-seater aircraft. His madcap idea was to persuade the Duke of Hamilton, a fellow aviation enthusiast, to press King George VI to make peace with Hitler. The mission failed, of course. The Duke of Hamilton, whom Hess had never met, was not against the war, as Hess had believed. And the king was in no position to make such a deal, even if he had wanted to. But Hess's flight caused a great stir among the Nazi leadership. Heydrich ordered the arrest of the astrologers, who were blamed for influencing Hess, including Wilhelm Wulff, whom Kersten would later bring back into Himmler's orbit. And Heydrich was about to arrest Kersten too, when Himmler intervened.

Kersten always claimed that he had several allies inside Himmler's court, which is entirely possible. The main ones were Rudolf Brandt, Himmler's private secretary; Walter Schellenberg, Himmler's intelligence chief; and SS General Gottlob Berger. Each may indeed have helped Kersten in his various schemes, out of self-interest, if for no other reason. But just as Kersten exaggerated, or even invented the anti-Nazi credentials of his prewar German patients, he continued, after the war, to paint his SS allies in oddly rosy colors. General Berger was one of the "moderates" in the SS, whose rugged exterior concealed "a good heart." Not only was Schellenberg a decent man, but he felt ashamed of the Nazi excesses he had been unable to prevent. Even if he had tried to do so, he would have been arrested himself. And Brandt was an "idealist" with a "passion for his job" who felt deeply disillusioned by the "corruption in the Nazi party and the SS" and tried hard "to break away from the system."

General Berger, the man with the "good heart," was in fact a fierce antisemite and had been a brutal storm trooper before taking charge of the Waffen SS. He was responsible, among other things, for mass murder on the eastern front and kidnapping fifty thousand eastern European children as slaves. One of his closest associates was Oskar Dirlewanger, a psychopath who led a murder unit of ex-convicts and was one of the worst butchers of Jews and other civilians in Poland and Belarus. Berger was convicted as a war criminal after the war. Dirlewanger died in a POW camp, mercifully for him, for he would surely have been hanged.

Rudolf Brandt, the "idealist," was hanged in 1948 for war crimes and crimes against humanity. A member of Ahnenerbe, Himmler's think tank on racial purity, Brandt was responsible for the administration of frightful medical experiments on concentration camp inmates. He was also involved in a "research" project that involved the murder of eighty-six Russian Jews, whose skeletons were sent as "specimens" to an SS doctor in Strasbourg. Dachau was one of the camps where experiments on prisoners took place. The American reporter Martha Gellhorn spoke in 1945 to a Polish doctor who had been a prisoner there. He said, "The Germans made here some unusual experiments. . . . They wished to see how long an aviator could go without oxygen, how high in the sky he could go. So, they had a closed car from which they pumped the oxygen. It is a quick death. . . . It does not take more than fifteen minutes, but it is a hard death. They killed not so many people, only eight hundred in that experiment."

Brandt, a weedy little man with spectacles, was a loyal member of Himmler's staff until the end. He was much prized for his shorthand skills. Walter Schellenberg described him in an affidavit taken during the Nuremberg trials as a human typewriter.

Schellenberg himself was the most complicated of Kersten's three best friends in the SS. A smooth operator with a gentle smile rather than a swaggering thug, Schellenberg was nonetheless a convinced Nazi who climbed up the ranks of the SS. He established his reputation for ruthless action in the so-called Venlo Incident. In November 1939, pretending to be a German officer opposed to Hitler, Schellenberg started negotiations with two British intelligence agents in neutral Holland, until one day, on the orders of Heydrich, the agents were kidnapped by SS men and sent to concentration camps in Germany. Schellenberg convinced Hitler that the agents, in league with Dutch intelligence, had masterminded a plot to assassinate the Führer. This served as a pretext to invade the Netherlands. And yet Kersten insisted that Schellenberg was a "respectable man" who had a "fierce longing to escape the tentacles of the Nazi system."

If so, Schellenberg disguised his longing well. He was trusted by both Heydrich and Himmler, and he played a leading role in many tasks taken up by the SS. In 1941, he managed to organize vital logistical support from the German army in Poland and the Baltic states to help the death squads (*Einsatzgruppen*) in their murder sprees against the Jews.

Quite why Kersten continued to insist that these men were decent types who didn't like what the Nazis were doing any more than he did, isn't immediately clear. They were certainly involved in attempts to make secret deals with the Allies when German defeat began to look inevitable, deals of which Himmler was aware. It is most likely that the plotters, including Kersten himself, had a mutual interest in hiding inconvenient aspects of their past.

Unlike Brandt, Schellenberg, or Berger, Kersten cannot be held responsible for mass murder. At the very least, however, he made life a great deal easier for the chief mass murderer. The summer and fall of 1940 were spent following Himmler around on his travels through Europe, often confined to the SS chief's luxurious private railway train, listening to his endless monologues about racial purity and the search for an Aryan religion that would replace Christianity. Since Himmler relied entirely on his masseur to relieve his stomach pains, Kersten's position as his main confidant became ever more settled. He was able to take advantage of this by helping certain people. For instance, Kersten's client and benefactor August Rosterg, the industrialist, asked for his intervention when one of his employees, a former Social Democrat, was arrested for being politically unsound. This, according to Kersten, was his first foray into this peculiar form of manipulation, in every sense of the word. Kersten sometimes asked Himmler for a special favor. Himmler, wracked with pain, would have agreed to almost anything apart from showing any leniency toward the Jews—for that was a matter of principle. But the release of Rosterg's employee was not a problem, if Kersten could make the pain go away.

In March 1941, Kersten was finally granted permission to visit the Netherlands to sell his house and wrap up his personal affairs. One of Kersten's proudest boasts after the war was his pipeline to Dutch resistance figures, who communicated with him by mail sent to Kersten's own secure mailbox in Himmler's private mailroom. Kersten pretended that this was a discreet way to stay in touch with his many girlfriends. Himmler, "a man of the world," understood. And so, no one was allowed to pry.

Kersten did indeed have contacts in Holland, but they were hardly members of the resistance. His main informant was a certain Jacob Nieuwenhuis, a dubious figure who joined the Dutch Nazi party (NSB) before the war in the Dutch East Indies (now Indonesia). Kersten encouraged Nieuwenhuis to stick closely to the NSB in occupied Holland. How useful Nieuwenhuis really was as a source of information is impossible to tell. Evidently a rather clumsy man, he fell afoul of everyone in due course: the Dutch Nazis as well as the Germans, who suspected him of being a spy. Kersten helped him get away to Sweden near the end of the war. There were some official hurdles to overcome: the Dutch embassy in Stockholm wanted nothing to do with a Nazi collaborator.

Another shady contact in The Hague was a fine arts dealer named Charles Bignell, head of the auction house Van Marle and Bignell. Kersten recounts in his memoir how he managed to get Himmler to release Bignell from a Gestapo prison, where he had been locked up on suspicion of being in the resistance. The head of the SS in the Netherlands was a hulking brute named Hanns Rauter. Kersten, so we learn from his account, humiliated Rauter by getting Himmler on the phone to overturn his subordinate's action against the alleged resistance man, Bignell.

I had heard of Bignell during my childhood in The Hague. His grandson, a schoolyard bully, was my contemporary at primary school. Although Bignell was still a considerable presence in The Hague society, there were discreet whispers about his tarnished reputation—only whispers, to be sure, because most people in society preferred to keep quiet about past unpleasantness. Bignell was, after all, a gentleman. The truth about Bignell was squalid. He had done very nicely during the occupation by auctioning artworks looted from Jewish owners. He sold fine art and other treasures to German Nazis, but also to Felix Kersten, who remained a client until his death in 1960. Bignell's contacts with the German authorities were excellent. Far from being a resister, he was given a five-year prison sentence after the war as a collaborator.

Like Rosterg, Diehn, and Nieuwenhuis, Bignell was yet another member of Kersten's vast circle of smart clients and acquaintances who rode the menacing waves of their era to their own profit and needed to cleanse their reputations after the Reich came tumbling down. Ever the courtier, this explains Kersten's rosy accounts of his old contacts: a kind of loyalty, perhaps, but a very self-serving one.

The story that contributed more than any other to Kersten's postwar status as a heroic friend of the anti-Nazi resistance, and to his acclaim in the Netherlands in particular, is also the most spectacular: his single-handed feat of saving the entire Dutch population from being deported to Poland in 1941.

Since the initial German policy in the occupied Netherlands was to treat the Dutch as fellow Aryans, and to avoid doing anything to upset the locals unduly, Joseph Kessel's description of Holland in the first year of the war could not be more wrong. He writes that letters received by Kersten revealed a "nightmare" of "deportations," "famine," "torture," and "summary arrests." All these things would happen in time, but not yet in 1940. Kersten himself relates that Himmler regarded the Dutch as a fraternal people. Himmler also admired the British upper class, by the way, as did Hitler, whose favorite film for private screenings in Berlin was *The Lives of a Bengal Lancer*, starring Gary Cooper, about doughty British colonial officers fighting off rebellious natives. In other pages of his memoir, Kersten recalls that Himmler expressed very different sentiments; that the Dutch and the British always had been archenemies of the Reich. Perhaps, in this case, we should attribute the confusion to Himmler, and not to his masseur.

It is true, though, that after the February strike in 1941, the Germans felt "betrayed" by their fellow Aryans, and they were preparing to get a little rougher. This is when Kersten claims to have heard of the vengeful plan to deport the Dutch population to Poland. There are no documents to prove that this was ever the case, only Kersten's word for it, backed up in vague and often contradictory statements made after the war by several former SS men, including Rudolf Brandt, who had an interest in currying favor with one of the few witnesses who would vouch for their good character at their war crimes trials.

Various versions of the story have been put forward by Kersten in his memoirs, notes, and interviews, and by Kessel, his admiring French biographer, who, as so often, presents the case in the most dramatic form. Kessel writes that on March 1, Kersten was tucking into a rich cream cake at the SS officers mess in Berlin when he saw Reinhard Heydrich and Hanns Rauter stride into the room, serenely ignoring the clicking of heels, the raised arms, and the *Heil Hitlers!* that greeted them. Kersten overheard the ensuing conversation, which apparently horrified him. Rauter complained about Dutch scoundrels who had thrown stones at two of his men. But, he said, they would soon be taught a lesson they wouldn't forget. Heydrich's thin lips showed a hint of mirth. They will freeze to death in Poland, he chuckled. Hitler had just issued instructions for a mass deportation.

In a state of shock, Kersten asked Brandt for more information. At the risk of his life, Brandt showed Kersten a top-secret document about the imminent expulsion of the Dutch and Flemish populations to Poland. Since the treacherous Dutch continued to resist, their punishment had to be merciless. Three million men would be forced to march to Poland through Germany. The rest of the roughly nine million people would be transported by train and ship, and then plunked amid the icy lakes and dark woods near Lublin. Dutch Jews would be transported to the east as well, but certain measures would make sure that they would never reach their destination. Kersten himself relates in his memoir that this extraordinary project would be announced by Hitler on his birthday. (In fact, Hitler was never in the habit of making public announcements on his birthday.)

Kersten tells more or less the same story in his Dutch-language memoir, minus the cream cakes and the conversation between Heydrich and Rauter. In an interview with the Dutch war historian Loe de Jong in 1947, Kersten admitted that he couldn't hear a word of what the two SS officers were saying. (In fact, he couldn't have seen Rauter in Berlin at all, since the SS man was in Holland at the time.) Other accounts, including Brandt's, mention a plan to deport only a portion of the Dutch population. In a "Memorandum about My Helpful Acts in the Years 1940–1945," drawn up in Stockholm in June 1945, Kersten doesn't even mention the deportation plan. He only added the story in a supplement to the memorandum, written three months later.

But the tale gets even wilder. Kersten realized that only he could save his beloved Dutch people. He did everything to convince Himmler of the folly of his plan. Himmler absolutely refused to budge. The Dutch were damned traitors, he said. It was Hitler's decision anyway, and how could he possibly go against the word of the Führer? Everything was set to go. Loyal German farmers would be settled in the Netherlands to work the vacant Dutch soil. Following Himmler around Germany and the Balkans on his special train, Kersten couldn't stop fretting about the catastrophic fate awaiting the people of his second home. Life became intolerable. He couldn't sleep. He pleaded and pleaded, but Himmler held firm.

Fortunately for the Dutch people, Kersten had one ace up his sleeve. Himmler's stomach was giving him even more agony than usual. No wonder, Kersten said: he was grossly overworked. Transporting nine million people from one country to another would be a vast enterprise. And this while the Waffen SS was being reorganized, and the German armies were mobilizing—Kersten had already heard rumors of an imminent invasion of the Soviet Union. If Himmler persisted in doing all these things at the same time, his health would collapse, and even Kersten's hands would no longer be able to work their magic. Surely the Dutch deportation could wait until after the war was successfully concluded. Himmler, who could no longer bear his pain, finally agreed in desperation to speak to Hitler. ("I'll do anything you like," Himmler cried, "only stop these stomachaches.") Kersten gave him a soothing massage. The cramps subsided. Hitler relented. The deportations would be postponed. Kersten celebrated this miracle by placing a bowl of flowers picked from his country garden in front of a photograph of Queen Wilhelmina and her husband, Kersten's old patient and companion, Prince Hendrik.

This amazing story of how the Finnish masseur saved the Dutch people added the greatest luster to Kersten's legend (and resulted in a prestigious Dutch decoration after the war, pinned to his lapel by Prince Bernhard, Queen Wilhelmina's German-born son-in-law—who himself preferred to keep quiet about his prewar stint in an SS horse brigade; but that's another story). Kersten's heroic tale was repeated in every book and article written about him since, including glowing tributes from historians, such as the famous British scholar of Hitler's Reich, Hugh Trevor-Roper. Then, in 1972, after an exhaustive investigation, Loe de Jong concluded that the story was full of holes. No documentary evidence for the Dutch deportation plan exists. The places and dates in Kersten's notes made after the war are full of errors. Even Brandt, who was keen to support Kersten, couldn't remember what was in the secret document he supposedly showed him in 1941. It is in any case highly unlikely that such a logistical nightmare would have been seriously considered, just when Germany was about to launch a massive invasion of the Soviet Union. Kersten may have based his tale on rumors about other plans that were mooted at various times, about resettling some Dutch farmers in Ukraine, or on Arthur Seyss-Inquart's threat after the February strike in 1941 to take "harsh measures" against Dutch resisters.

De Jong conceded that Kersten may indeed have done some people favors by exploiting Himmler's cramps. Kersten might have persuaded Himmler to commute the death sentences of a Dutch general accused of spying and of a Dutch industrialist's daughter for being in the resistance. But De Jong's conclusion on Kersten's role as the savior of the Dutch population in 1941 couldn't be clearer or more succinct: Kersten had made the whole thing up. It was just another one of his stories.

Six

BEAUTIFUL STORIES

1: Shinkyo

Kawashima Yoshiko was still in Shanghai in 1932, the first year of the new Manchukuo republic, living the high life in dance halls and cabarets, throwing money around with great panache, while working steadily on her own legend. Some of her entirely imaginary stories, about heroic feats as a flying ace, her fictional status as the last Chinese emperor's daughter, and her near-death experience after being shot during the fighting in Shanghai, found their way into the book of a gullible American visitor, Willa Lou Woods, an exchange student from Wenatchee, Washington, with a taste for Eastern exoticism. The book of self-inventions was entitled *Princess Jin, the Joan of Arc of the Orient.*

Yoshiko's domestic arrangements were complicated and increasingly fraught. She was still in a sadomasochistic relationship with Tanaka Ryukichi, the Japanese army officer who kept her on his payroll in exchange for spying and sexual favors. Without Tanaka, Yoshiko's lavish spending would have come swiftly to an end. At the same time, a young Japanese woman named Chizuko served as Yoshiko's companion and all-purpose retainer. Yoshiko liked to call her "my beautiful wife." There is a photograph, reproduced in Phyllis Birnbaum's biography, of Yoshiko visiting her adoptive father in Japan. Her hair is cropped short. To her left sits Chizuko, birdlike and diffident, almost a child, dressed in a flowery Chinese silk garment.

Even though Yoshiko, through Tanaka, had been useful to the Japanese military in Shanghai, she was also causing them problems. Her rows with Tanaka were often violent. Yoshiko's verbal abuse usually ended in his abasement. But on at least one occasion, Tanaka ordered for her to be killed, before kneeling to her in abject apology, tears streaming down his plump cheeks. Yoshiko was not always a benign gossip, and Tanaka was especially annoyed when his erotic tangle with the princess was recounted in lurid detail in *The Beauty in Men's Clothes*, Muramatsu Shofu's fictionalized biography.

Yoshiko had friends in the Japanese Imperial Navy, whom she turned against Tanaka. Rivalry between the Japanese armed forces could be lethal. Legendary stories, known as *bidan*, literally meaning beautiful tales about heroic feats, played an important part in this. They were taken very seriously by soldiers and sailors. Such stories were part of their corporate identities, as it were. Yoshiko told a rear admiral about Tanaka's attempt to disparage the navy's role in the Shanghai Incident of January 1932, when the navy bombed the city after Yoshiko allegedly helped to stir up a Chinese rebellion. The navy was especially proud of a beautiful story about three brave naval officers who had died in a suicide-bomb attack on the Chinese enemy. After their valiant deaths, they were officially deified as "warrior gods." Yoshiko told her navy friend that Tanaka dismissed the naval *bidan* and said the explosion had been a stupid accident. The rear admiral was so enraged that he ordered his men to kill Tanaka. Only Tanaka's groveling apology saved his life.

Yoshiko's presence in Shanghai had clearly become impossible. She was told by the Japanese military authorities to move to Manchukuo in the summer of 1932, where she could be more useful and was less likely to get into mischief. The Kwantung Army leadership decided she should be employed as head of the ladies-in-waiting at Puyi's court in exile, where the last Chinese emperor was fuming because the Japanese still refused to give him his imperial title; he had to be content with Chief Executive of the Manchukuo Republic. To his intense annoyance, he would be addressed as Your Excellency and not as Your Imperial Majesty. Yoshiko didn't last even a month in her new position. Wanrong (Elizabeth) was happy to be reunited with her old friend, but Puyi couldn't stand her. Yoshiko didn't return to Shanghai, however. Instead, her own *bidan* became part of the beautiful story of Manchukuo.

Almost nothing in Manchukuo, stretching from Russia in the north to the Korean peninsula in the south, was as it seemed. It was a phony republic, founded in March 1932, and a phony empire, founded two years later with the grand yet somehow tawdry inauguration of Puyi as the emperor. Manchukuo was neither an independent state nor an empire, but a Japanese colony. The Chinese today call it *wei Manzhou*, "fake Manchuria." It wasn't governed by the emperor and his Manchu courtiers, some of whom had served him as a child emperor in Beijing, or by the Chinese members of his State Council, despite their highfalutin titles, but by Japanese "vice-ministers" and officers of the Japanese Kwantung Army. The imperial palace was not a palace at all, but a former office for administering taxes on salt. The national flag of Manchukuo was yellow with bands of black, white, red, and blue, signifying the "five races"—Manchu (yellow), Mongol (white), Han Chinese (blue), Japanese (red), and Korean (black)—who lived in perfect harmony and equality. There never was perfect harmony, or indeed anything remotely like equality. The Japanese, as the Asian *Herrenvolk*, lorded it over the small number of Manchus, Mongols, and Koreans, and the much larger number of Han Chinese. Manchukuo, despite patches of striking modernity— the fastest express train in Asia, among other feats of technology, and the best, most modern movie studio—was a brutal place, where local workers, who were little more than slaves, extracted coal, iron, and other raw materials for Japanese industry often in appalling conditions, and Chinese peasants were robbed of their land to make way for Japanese immigrants. Much of the country to the east of Mongolia was flat, hot in summer and frozen hard under thick layers of snow in winter. Compared with the cramped conditions of Japan, however, the landscape gave off a sense of infinite space and grandeur. Until not so long ago, many older Japanese still recalled the acacia trees in Dalian and the ice-skating rinks in Harbin with deep nostalgia.

After his arrival in Manchuria at the end of 1931, poor Puyi, holed up in Yoshiko's former family home in Lüshun, as well as in a variety of Japanese railway hotels, was very bored: gone were the ballroom parties in the foreign concessions in Tianjin and cocktails around the tennis court. Wanrong, whose "tiny hands," in the words of two British admirers, were "quite shell-like in their loveliness," spent much of her time in a haze of opium, provided by her Japanese minders.

So Puyi was full of hope in March 1932, when he was told to move with his courtiers to the new republic's capital, a dreary sprawl that used to be—and is once again—called Changchun but was renamed Hsinking, or Shinkyo in Japanese, meaning new capital. Fully expecting a rise in his official status, Puyi and his entourage boarded the Asia Express, the sleek fully air-conditioned pride of the South Manchurian Railway Company, and they were met at Shinkyo station by a fleet of black bulletproof limousines that sped them through the empty boulevards of the brand-new town center, still smelling of plaster and paint.

Boredom descended once more over Puyi's existence; he could barely stroll beyond the empty swimming pool of his compound without being told to return to his quarters by Japanese guards. He had to wait two long years for his promotion from chief executive to emperor. The two British admirers of Elizabeth's hands wrote about that illustrious occasion in their typical upbeat style: "It was indeed with a fine understanding of Chinese character that the Japanese planned the enthronement of Puyi as Emperor of Manchukuo. The ceremony, which took place on March 1, 1934, was carried out with every attention to ancient tradition."

Well, yes and no. Puyi still thought he would be restored to the full pomp of the Great Qing Emperor. He envisaged himself sitting on the throne dressed in his old yellow silk imperial robes, elaborately embroidered with five-clawed dragons. This would vindicate his collaboration with the Japanese. But Itagaki Seishiro, then vice chief of staff of the Kwantung Army, informed him that it would not be appropriate. Puyi was to wear the uniform of the commander in chief of the armed forces of Manchukuo. Photographs of the event show the hapless Puyi in dark glasses dressed like a nineteenth-century toy soldier in a blue double-breasted coat down to his knees, festooned with a gallery of large silver and gold medals, his narrow shoulders weighed down by heavy gilt epaulets, and a tall helmet with pale feathers streaming down the back of his small head. Around him are his courtiers and cabinet ministers, dressed in formal mandarin robes, and many Japanese officials in silk top hats flanked by military officers in mud-colored Kwantung Army uniforms. Puyi was driven down the main street of Shinkyo in an open car, his slim figure dwarfed by the bullish Japanese "ambassador," General Hishikari Takashi, as cheering schoolchildren waved Japanese and Manchukuo flags.

The Japanese did make one concession to Puyi. In the early morning before the official ceremony, he was allowed to wear his dragon robe to honor his ancestors in a sacrificial ritual at the makeshift Temple of Heaven, especially constructed for the occasion. While the emperor knelt in prayer facing the sun, the throat of a white bullock was cut by a priest and Japanese war planes came roaring overhead.

There was an air of Gilbert and Sullivan's *Mikado* about the enthronement of Puyi: the flimsy stage setting of the Temple of Heaven, the Ruritanian uniforms, the Manchukuo soldiers riding by on tiny donkeys, and the rituals performed amid smirking Japanese officers. After the ceremony was concluded, the emperor returned to his "palace," where buglers announced the arrival of Prince Chichibu, the Japanese emperor's brother, followed by General Hishikari and Colonel Itagaki, both in full-dress uniforms with plumed helmets. Wanrong was absent from the occasion. Her sad countenance can still be seen in the old salt palace, now the Museum of the Puppet Empire, where she lives on as a wax model with her opium paraphernalia at hand.

One oddity of all this quasi-traditional theater was its setting. Shinkyo still had some messy Chinese quarters on its outskirts, but the new city in the center was designed by Japanese urban planners and engineers as a showcase of modernity—like the vaunted Asia Express. Public hygiene was an obsession of Manchukuo technocrats. Shinkyo was the first city in Asia with flushing toilets in all-new residential houses and office buildings—something virtually unheard-of in most parts of Japan, let alone China. Even though the Japanese insisted that Manchukuo was an independent state and not a colony, they were still eager to show Western imperial powers that the Japanese empire was in no way inferior to theirs.

Modernity in Asia still meant Westernization, even in a colony that was self-consciously "Asian." Shinkyo looked more European than much of Tokyo. The urban model was Haussmann's Paris, with its wide boulevards, geometric street patterns, and pompous municipal architecture. The large number of parks, tree-lined streets, ponds, shrubbery, and a well-stocked zoo were inspired by British ideas on the Garden City. And so were the standard two-story, red-roofed homes, which looked as though they had been transplanted from a suburb of Manchester or Baltimore.

Since the Manchukuo emperor's native subjects had very few rights,

Manchukuo was a perfect spot for Japanese engineers, architects, industrialists, entrepreneurs, urban planners, filmmakers, sociologists, and even socialist dreamers of noncapitalist, multiracial equality to engage in experiments that rules, regulations, and public opinion would have impeded in Japan. Manchukuo was not only a place where adventurers like Yoshiko's adoptive father, Kawashima Naniwa, could act out their fantasies, but also a magnet for hundreds of thousands of Japanese who wanted a taste of life outside their own narrow archipelago, in a country that was excitingly exotic, yet safely under Japanese control.

To cover brute force under the guise of high ideals, one more theatrical flourish was necessary, a Manchukuo *bidan*, as it were. Japanese mass media loved stories about intrepid pioneers, death-defying warriors, and patriotic swashbucklers engaged in building a new Asia for the Asians, freed from the corrupt and racist Western imperialists. This appealed as much to Marxist intellectuals in Japan as it did to far-right Kwantung Army officers. To this end, the Japanese newspapers outdid one another with beautiful stories of derring-do on the wild Asian continent. This is where Yoshiko enters the stage once more, in one of her most flamboyant roles. She would lend her aristocratic Chinese glamor to the Japanese colonial enterprise by acting as the largely fictional heroine in a series of beautiful tales in Manchukuo. The legend of Shanghai's Mata Hari now evolved into Manchukuo's Joan of Arc.

Once again, there are various versions. Her own story first: Yoshiko was living in Shinkyo, above a furniture store, with her companion Chizuko and a Chinese servant. Quite where she found the money to keep her going in her accustomed style, still visiting fancy nightspots with names like Café Baron or Salon Tokyo, isn't entirely clear. Colonel Itagaki was one obvious person for the occasional touch. And she had formed a new liaison with one of the most interesting Japanese military officers in Manchukuo: General Tada Hayao, senior adviser to the Kwantung Army. His task was to build a Manchukuo army. Tada was unusual in that he was not only an expert on Chinese affairs but sympathetic to the Chinese.

He was apparently a true believer in "harmony of the five races." It behooved the most powerful race, he said, to be humble and consider the position of the weaker peoples. He later clashed with more chauvinistic Japanese military leaders, and after the attack on Pearl Harbor in 1941 his army career was pretty much over.

Tada, a trim man with the sensitive features of a Kabuki actor specializing in female roles, was in his fifties when he met Yoshiko. Her connections with Manchu royalty may well have appealed to his Sinophile snobbery. Yoshiko's brother Xianli found their passionate encounters embarrassing. Even in his own house, he reported, they lost all restraint. But then Xianli was often a little censorious of his notorious sister. Who knows how much passion there was on Yoshiko's side? But she needed the money and the proximity to Japanese power.

The Kwantung Army was in control of the main cities along the South Manchurian Railway line. But Chinese "bandits" were still an unruly presence in the countryside, and a few rebellious warlords were causing trouble in the border regions of Manchukuo. One of these was Su Bingwen, the Chinese Nationalist commander of a mountainous part of Inner Mongolia. When the Kwantung Army made aggressive moves to sweep out the rebels, General Su joined forces with another Chinese general and decided to make a stand against the Japanese in the city of Qiqihar, a provincial outpost with a gigantic railway hotel, built under the Qing Dynasty as a military bulwark against Russian incursions. General Su's troops took more than two hundred Japanese civilians as hostages.

General Su refused to set his hostages free. He even refused to negotiate. In Yoshiko's telling of the story, she decided that she alone could affect a breakthrough. She would use her connections to fix matters. Like Weinreb and Kersten, she fancied her talents as a *macher*. The general was no stranger to her. They had dined together in Mukden on several occasions. That he had become a "mutineer" and would have to be put down with force was unbearable to her. After all, she claimed, they had the same Manchu blood running through their veins. Yoshiko didn't want money for her help. She didn't care about her personal safety. All she wanted was the chance to persuade Su to give up his rebellion and recognize "the dawn of Manchukuo." This, she thought, was about "the future of peace in Asia." She begged General Tada to let her parachute into Qiqihar. All she needed was the use of a plane.

Tada was skeptical at first. Surely this wasn't a woman's job. But her "will was unshakable," and she was allowed to practice parachute jumps. All was set to go. But just then an old nervous condition flared up. Yoshiko could barely move her legs. And General Su showed no sign of being open to persuasion anyway. Sadly, her parachute adventure had to be called off.

This is not the way it was reported in the Japanese press, however. Pictures appeared of Yoshiko, looking splendid in her khaki uniform and goggles, as though she had just jumped out of a plane. Stories were written about her intrepid efforts to thwart the rebellion against the benevolent government of Manchukuo. Joan of Arc's name was evoked in almost every article written about the affair. This was Yoshiko's first appearance in a Manchukuo *bidan*.

What really happened was more prosaic. Rather than Yoshiko begging her lover to let her parachute into enemy territory, it is more likely that Tada asked her to contact General Su, though not by parachuting in. A diplomatic effort from her would look so much better than a show of Japanese force, especially since Japan's expansion into Manchuria had attracted a great deal of international criticism. A hero of royal Manchu blood on their side was just what the Japanese needed. Tada may also have had an erotic interest in dressing his lover up in uniforms, in which case he was simply encouraging her own predilections. But Yoshiko's part was purely for show. When negotiations failed, the Japanese 14th Division launched an attack on the rebel stronghold. General Su was forced to flee across the border to the Soviet Union. The remaining rebel soldiers moved farther south to Jehol, or Rehe in Chinese, setting the scene for another Japanese "pacification" campaign, and another *bidan* with Yoshiko in a starring role, dressed this time in riding britches, high black leather boots, Sam Browne belt, and a fur hat.

The main city of Jehol is now called Chengde, in the northern Chinese province of Hebei. Prettily set in a valley filled with Buddhist pagodas and an impressive Tibetan monastery, Jehol was where Chinese emperors would stay during the hunting season. Their lodge, in a lovely park well stocked with deer, later became the headquarters of a brutal warlord named Tang Yulin, who commanded the region in the 1920s as governor for the Chinese Nationalist government. There is a famous photograph of Tang, a burly, mustachioed figure cradling a rifle on his knee while riding a ferocious-looking tiger. Immensely corrupt and very rich, Tang spent part of his time in a Renaissance Italian–style mansion in Tianjin, close to where Puyi stayed before his move to Manchuria. Tang made a fortune by heavily taxing his Mongolian subjects and peddling precious antiques to foreigners in China. But most of his wealth came from selling opium, which was Jehol's main crop. General Tang's army, Yoshiko claims in her memoir, ran not on food but on opium.

The Japanese had had their eyes on Inner Mongolia for a long time. Now was their chance to take it. The Kwantung Army decided to expand Manchukuo's borders to include opium-rich Jehol. Tang made brave statements about fighting the Japanese to the death. But despite being hampered by snowstorms and high mountain passes, the Japanese were far too strong for Tang's troops, most of whom were lightly armed with guns, grenades, and traditional Chinese swords. The Japanese had bombers and tanks. While some of Tang's officers quickly went over to the Japanese, Tang commandeered his army trucks to transport his treasures and fled south. He died peacefully in 1937, in his Italianate mansion in Tianjin, surrounded by his collection of Chinese fine art.

Yoshiko's own *bidan* of how she got involved in the Battle of Jehol is recorded in her memoir. One wintry day in 1933, a young man turned up at her apartment in Shinkyo. His name was Fang Yongchang, a Manchu brigand who had once commanded thousands of men. He told her a most peculiar story. His boss had been a well-known gangster and war-lord named Zhang Zongchang, also known as the Dogmeat General. General Zhang, whose harem of concubines was so large that he gave them numbers instead of names, was an opium addict and a rabble-rouser who fought for the Chinese Nationalists, then against the Chinese Nationalists, and finally found refuge in Japan, where he repaired with some of his mistresses to a hot spring resort and killed one of Yoshiko's brothers with a revolver. An accident, Yoshiko writes. A row over a woman is more likely. According to Fang, General Zhang and his retainers had felt bad about the killing. Three years later, in 1932, the Dogmeat General himself was shot dead in China by one of his many enemies. His gang was now without a boss. Fang begged Yoshiko to be their leader. They would submit themselves to atone for the murder of her brother. She would no longer be Kawashima Yoshiko, but Commander Jin Dongzhen.

A ceremony was held to formalize her command in a squalid hotel in the Chinese quarter of Mukden. In the presence of a Japanese reporter for a monthly magazine, Fang insisted on kowtowing three times before Commander Jin, who was dressed for the occasion in a fantasy army uniform that made her look, in the reporter's words, like "a soldier in a Chinese opera." Twenty-eight "officers" of her new volunteer corps, to be called the National Army, the Peaceful Nation Army, or the Jehol Self-Defense Force, stood by. They were actually a bunch of desperados dressed in raggedy Chinese outfits, some missing fingers, others with hideously scarred faces. Kneeling at the tips of Yoshiko's black riding boots, the men swore to die for Commander Jin and for the sake of peace in Asia. Commander Jin declined to join them for what promised to be a rowdy drinking party at the railway hotel.

Word of the Peaceful Nation Army soon got around. Thirty-odd men—still in Yoshiko's telling—grew to about three thousand. If she is to be believed, money from various patriotic Chinese societies (loyal to the Qing, one assumes) started pouring in, as well as essential matériel, including trucks, uniforms, and camels. Commander Jin and her ragtag corps could not be ignored by the Kwantung Army high command any longer, and, in Yoshiko's words: "My volunteer corps and I were allowed to take on our assigned roles in battle."

Quite what those roles were, and how, if at all, they were fulfilled, is not mentioned in Yoshiko's account. There is no clear evidence that her National Army took part in any fighting at all, even though she spoke in interviews about being wounded in action once again. She wrote an article for the leading Japanese woman's magazine, *Fujin Koron*, recounting how she led her troops to battle, seen off by adoring crowds, how her soldiers fought bravely on the front lines, and how all she thought about was the happiness of the people of Jehol. Her love for Japan, and for her native land, was also warmly declared. If she saw a contradiction, she certainly didn't say so. But there was at least one truthful sentence in her story: "I was running all over Jehol, but I am embarrassed to say that the propaganda value was ten times more important than anything I actually did."

She was surely right. But the truth barely mattered. What was important to the Japanese was the legend, the *bidan*. There she was, in the publication *Asahi Shimbun* on February 22, 1933, sitting like a hardened warrior in her male military uniform and riding boots, leaning on her long samurai sword. Kawashima Yoshiko, "the beauty in men's clothes" was ready to "go to battle" as commander of the National Army, "doing everything to assist a general who is doing his best to unify the Manchu armed forces."

The general was of course Tada Hayao, Yoshiko's lover, who was much more likely than some vague Chinese patriotic societies to have supplied her private army with money. This glowing report of Yoshiko's gallantry appeared on the same page as a much smaller notice about the death at a Tokyo police station of the famous leftist author Kobayashi Takiji, who died after being tortured by the dreaded Special Police as a political dissident. This detail went unmentioned.

Yoshiko's star in the Japanese media rose to an even greater height with the publication in 1933 of Muramatsu's fictional biography. She was now a popular guest on radio shows, promoting the Manchukuo cause and burnishing her exotic legend as a singer of popular songs, some of them written herself with passages in garbled Mongolian, bearing such titles as "Bells of the Caravan" and "Mongolian Song." She did moderate her paeans to the Japanese liberation of her country a little later with unwelcome remarks about the poverty of Manchurian peasants and their rough treatment by Japanese ruffians. Perhaps she felt the sting of residual feelings of guilt. But if so, this came much too late. The legend had been set. She had become the product of her own *bidan*. Her indulgent biographer Kamisaka Fuyuko observes that she was just a puppet dancing to the strings of her Japanese masters. If so, the puppet was usually more than willing to dance.

2: The Hague

The SD, the SS security service, would issue a yearly report on how things were going in the occupied countries. These detailed annual reports, written in numbing bureaucratese, were for a limited number of eyes only. Heinrich Himmler read them carefully.

The 1942 SD document on the Netherlands was able to report considerable progress. The Jewish Council had been established to help the German authorities in their efforts to "evacuate" the Jews. The SD had taken charge of the Westerbork concentration camp not far from the German border. Westerbork was officially a transit camp (*Durchgangslager*). Forty-two trains left Westerbork between July and the end of 1942, transporting 38,606 Jews to the death camps in Poland. "Understandably," the report continued, there had been some resistance from Jews to these measures. More irksome, however, "was the uncomprehending and Jew-friendly attitude of the average Dutch citizen that impeded our Jewish actions." Still, "despite these difficulties, the removal of Jews [the word *entjudung* is used here, "de-Jewing," as though it were a variation of delousing] has proceeded without pause and friction. Of the original population of 140,000 Jews, about 50,000 have left the country by evacuation or emigration. Thousands more are held in camps run by the SD. The collection of sick Jews from their homes and hospitals, planned for the first few months of 1943, has been prepared."

"Evacuation," "emigration," "collection": these were the SS functionaries' carefully typed words for mass murder.

Friedrich Weinreb was arrested by the SD in September 1942, two months after the deportations began (the first roundups in The Hague were in August). Three days later he was free again, something that was almost unheard-of. Once a Jew fell into the hands of the SD, there was usually no way of escaping from the bureaucracy of murder. Precisely what happened during those few days will never be known for sure. We have an idea of what probably happened. And we have Weinreb's version of a *bidan*.

Here is how Weinreb described his beautiful story, beginning on the eve of Rosh Hashanah, the Jewish New Year. Weinreb and his secretary Coen de Vries, whom Weinreb describes as a bit of a dolt, were taken to the large prison in Scheveningen. Many members of the Dutch resistance were held there before being executed in the dunes nearby, hence the patriotic nickname Orange Hotel, after the royal House of Orange. The following day, Weinreb was taken to Villa Windekind, the notorious SD office, whose cellars now functioned as torture chambers. His interrogator was Fritz Koch, a tall man with puffy cheeks and a slack mouth, more like a pasty-faced accountant than a torturer, but doubtless no stranger to sessions of "enhanced interrogation" (*verschärfte Vernehmung*).

Weinreb wasn't tortured. Koch was surprisingly affable, possibly because of Weinreb's assumed connection with an important German general. General von Schumann, thought Weinreb, was not just a figment of his rich imagination. In fact, "it wasn't even me who created him. Call it what you will. But I think God had made the general and delivered him to me."

Koch told Weinreb that a young Jewish woman, Bep Turksma, had been caught in a cinema with fake identity papers. Turksma told her SD interrogators that Weinreb had been the source of these documents. She also mentioned Weinreb's list, which included her name. Worse, she spoke about von Schumann, thus implicating the general in a serious case of fraud. What could Weinreb tell Koch to cast further light on the matter? Weinreb replied that this was clearly a case of calumny. How could he, a simple Jew, possibly implicate a German general in such a shabby affair?

Koch agreed that this was indeed hard to imagine. This Turksma woman clearly had blabbed nonsense in desperation. There was no hint of menace in the SD man's voice. Indeed, he seemed to respect Weinreb for his fine mind. It was such a pleasure, he said, to speak to a scholarly man who could put matters in a broader context. They even exchanged notes on their respective families. Koch pulled out pictures of his children in Germany, and he shed a tear thinking how much he missed them. But it wouldn't do to be soft. Duty came before private sentiments. He liked Weinreb so much that he could hardly believe this big, stocky man was a Jew.

There had indeed been a young Jewish woman named Bep Turksma. But she wasn't arrested in a cinema. And she hadn't betrayed Weinreb. Her name was never on his list. She didn't even know him. Her arrest just happened to coincide with his, providing a useful story for the SD, or for Weinreb, or both, to account for his brief incarceration. A conclusive explanation for Weinreb's arrest has never been given. Some speculated that his contacts with the SD had already been going on for some time. Again, there is no proof.

Turksma's own story is remarkable. Contrary to Weinreb's account, she wasn't arrested because she was Jewish, but for being a member of the student resistance. After a stint in the Orange Hotel and Villa

Windekind, where unlike Weinreb she was beaten savagely, she was taken to the Westerbork camp. Working in the camp as a night nurse, she escaped, went into hiding for a while, but soon made her way through Belgium and France with the help of two Michelin maps, hoping to reach England. Twice she was caught; first in France, where she was locked up in a French concentration camp, from which she managed to flee, and then, after a grueling trip across the Pyrenees, in Spain. But she finally made it to London, where she worked for the Dutch government in exile. Her brother was gassed in Auschwitz and her mother in Sobibór.

After the war, Turksma worked in obscurity as a secretary at various Dutch embassies. Weinreb's mention of her "betrayal" in the first volume of his memoirs in 1969 was the first time her name appeared in public. Her efforts to clear her name from this smear caused her extreme distress. She was finally exonerated only in 1976, when the official *Weinreb Report* was produced by the National Institute for War Documentation.

Weinreb feared that the General von Schumann story was unlikely to survive even the most cursory scrutiny. And so it turned out. Inquiries had been made in Berlin. There was no General von Schumann. Nonetheless, God's gift of the imaginary general continued to protect Weinreb for the time being. For Koch jumped to a peculiar conclusion. Clearly there was someone, possibly in the German army, who not only was sabotaging important measures against the Jews but had also set up a scheme for shaking down Jews for money. Weinreb was obviously an honorable man who was being used by these pernicious racketeers. The SD would soon get to the bottom of this, with Weinreb's help.

Rivalry between the SS and the German army may have played a part in Koch's assumptions. Officers of the Wehrmacht were often suspected of being less than sound in their loyalty to the Nazi cause. Koch was quite aware of criminals, Dutch and German, who promised protection in exchange for money, only to betray their victims to the Germans for more cash. The German authorities had no scruples about fleecing the Jews, but they didn't approve of freelance rackets outside their control.

Order was of the essence, and the German authorities wanted to monopolize the extortion of Jewish wealth.

In any event, Weinreb felt rather pleased with his ingenuity. But now he had to come up quickly with a plausible elaboration of his fantasy story to stave off further danger. He had seen General von Schumann only once, he told Koch. He even recalled that the general, or the impostor posing as him, had worn the Iron Cross. "The scoundrel!" exclaimed Koch. "But surely not the Knight's Cross?" Weinreb assured the policeman that it hadn't been the Knight's Cross. That really would have been too much. Weinreb had to think fast. He added more characters to his story. Even though he knew nothing of the general's whereabouts, he had been in regular touch with two go-betweens, he said, a German named von Rath and a Dutch aristocrat by the name of Six, a descendant of the famous Six family, whose notable ancestor had been painted by Rembrandt. Perhaps to give him an aristocratic air, Weinreb added a small detail: Six was always heavily perfumed. Well, thought Koch, the SD would soon roll up this gang of criminals, saboteurs, and homosexuals. Weinreb was free to go but should report to Koch every week, and set up his contacts for a swift arrest. Meanwhile, Koch would make sure Weinreb and his family would be protected from any anti-Jewish measures.

Not all of this was made up. Since the SD set him free, there clearly had been an understanding that Weinreb would help Koch round up the imaginary gang. There was another favor, however, which he doesn't mention in his book. By continuing to work on his list of people to be exempted from deportation, Weinreb could help the German police flush out Jews who had gone into hiding. There is no evidence that this ruse worked, and Weinreb always insisted that he advised people to find a place of refuge—to "dive," or *onderduiken* in the Dutch expression. This raises the question why Weinreb himself made no attempt to hide with his family. Why didn't he make the necessary dive?

None of his explanations make complete sense. Going into hiding would imperil his secretary, Coen de Vries, he said. But De Vries was soon freed as well. (He was arrested again in 1943 and was killed with his family in the Sobibór extermination camp.) Weinreb also claimed that he couldn't hide because he needed to protect the people on his list. Since the list was a fantasy and there was nothing Weinreb could do to protect them, this too is an unlikely story. Weinreb stressed the difficulties of hiding with Gentiles. Trying to dive with more than one person was extremely hard, he said. Jews who went into hiding were often robbed of their money and valuables, not infrequently raped as well, and then betrayed to the Germans. The chance of diving successfully until the Germans were defeated was almost impossible. It almost always turned out to be a trap. And yet, he also claimed to have saved many lives by helping people to hide.

A more credible explanation for Weinreb's decision to carry on was his belief that he could master the situation and deceive the German SD through his brilliant cunning. As long as he could string Koch along with his fantasies, he felt protected by the German police. Indeed, he recalled the months that followed his arrest and swift release as "a glorious time." This is a very strange way to describe the period in which so many Dutch Jews were forced into "evacuation" from which only a tiny number returned. Still, whatever one may think of Weinreb's fantastic schemes, it must never be forgotten that he was always in mortal danger himself, and not for being a fraudster, but for the simple fact that he was born a Jew.

Weinreb's description of the German "measures" is actually of great interest. About himself, he lied, exaggerated, and spun endless myths, but his fine eye for detail, and especially for the peculiar atmosphere at the time, continues to lend an air of truth to his account. One everyday scene out of many: Gawkers gather round a house in the center of The Hague on a cold November day. SD agents are dragging a sick old man in his pajamas by his feet down the stairs. He is screaming in pain. A brutal-looking figure with a glass eye pulls him across the sidewalk. The gawkers give him some room. A priest passes by and tells the crowd to go home. There is nothing to see, he says. But no one makes a move. Weinreb hears some women giggling. "Well," he recalls with his customary note of sarcasm, "those pajamas were a funny sight. In that busy street, on a winter afternoon."

Weinreb may well have talked himself out of extreme danger in Villa Windekind. But to continue working on his lists, he had to retain the trust of Jews who were desperate enough to spend their last savings to be included. There had to be a credible explanation for Weinreb's arrest, and his miraculous release. This is where his account of telling tall tales became a tall tale in itself.

Far from raising suspicion, at least in the minds of most people in his vicinity, Weinreb's release was met with enormous relief. That Weinreb was freed so quickly was read as proof that General von Schumann's scheme had the full backing of the SD. A childhood friend, Herbert Kruskal, later described how Weinreb's house in Scheveningen was besieged by people begging to be on his list. Even more than before, they regarded him as a miracle worker.

Talking to Kruskal, Weinreb couldn't help exaggerating the importance of his brief time in prison. Even inside the Orange Hotel, he was a *macher*. He had been in touch with some of the highest German authorities, he said. Ferdinand aus der Fünten himself, the top SS official in charge of Jewish deportations, had come down all the way from Amsterdam to interrogate him.

Even though Weinreb continued to use the Madoff trick of turning people down to make his list seem more exclusive, it soon swelled. Thousands pinned their hopes on him. He took more and more money from Jews who appeared to be able to afford it, ostensibly to help poorer Jews escape, as though he were a kind of Robin Hood. Some paid royally to jump the queue. Again, how much of this money ended up in Weinreb's own pockets, and how much was spent on helping the needy, remains a mystery. Promises were made about not one, but three trains that would leave for the south in December. Careful instructions were given, departure times were announced, and secret meetings were held to discuss living arrangements in Portugal and Spain. Young women were carefully selected to take care of the children, some after being subjected to Weinreb's amateur medical checkups. Seat numbers had been allocated. But all these arrangements ended in crushing disappointment when last-minute "technical hitches" prevented the lifesaving trains from leaving the station. Weinreb was also able to point out, quite correctly, that escape through Vichy France ceased to be an option after the Germans occupied the whole of France on November 11, 1942. But, of course, the trains had never been anything else but a mirage in Weinreb's imagination to begin with.

Not everyone was taken in by Weinreb. His sister-in-law, Lili Gutwirth, who was staying at his house for a time, smelled a rat and told people not to trust him. This caused great rows in the Weinreb household. He threatened to have Gutwirth arrested by the Germans and accused her of stealing money. She was caught later—though apparently not because of Weinreb—and murdered in a death camp. Weinreb also told a German Jewish refugee named I. G. Lange about a meeting with General von Schumann in a smart Amsterdam hotel. The general was supposedly outraged that Weinreb had been refused entry to the hotel for the obvious reason that he was a Jew. Weinreb was delighted to report, however, that the general had given Hauptsturmführer Aus der Fünten a good piece of his mind. Having had his doubts already about the veracity of Weinreb's claims, Lange made some inquiries. Naturally, the hotel had never heard of any General von Schumann.

Still, the believers vastly outnumbered the doubters. The question was how long Weinreb could continue to spin Koch along. They had weekly meetings at Villa Windekind, and Weinreb was carefully watched. Somehow, all attempts to trap von Schumann's helpers Six and Von Rath ended in failure. There was always some reason for delay. Weinreb's deception of the SD was hailed by his postwar admirers as a particularly crafty piece of passive resistance, especially since he claimed to have helped Jews in hiding with money and fake ration books. Whether Weinreb was really responsible for enabling dozens of people to go underground—a feat he contrasts favorably to the cowardly, abject, treacherous behavior of the snobs in the Jewish Council—is questionable. But he probably helped some people. He was even arrested briefly, in December 1942, for carrying illegal documents, but a phone call to Koch got him off the hook.

In at least two instances, Weinreb kept Koch happy by betraying members of the resistance. One man, named Ringeling, was an accountant who had offered Weinreb blank identity papers. The other, Van Walt van Praag, had once supplied Weinreb with false documents. Ringeling was arrested by the SD in his office during a meeting with Weinreb. In the case of Van Walt van Praag, the SD were already inside Weinreb's home and grabbed him as he walked out the door.

Weinreb's shenanigans couldn't go on like this forever—more betrayals would have caused suspicion—yet he had to give the SD something substantial. He thought of another ploy to make the Germans believe in his beautiful tale for a little while longer.

Weinreb was fond of old Jewish stories. One was the famous tale of Judah Loew ben Bezalel, the sixteenth-century rabbi of Prague, who created a figurine from clay. This figurine, or Golem, was brought to life through a variety of arcane rituals that involved a piece of paper with the name of God slipped into its mouth. The Golem, a constructive as well as destructive figure, would help to ward off pogroms against the Jews of Prague. In some versions of the story, the Golem ran out of control and went on a rampage like Frankenstein's monster. Finally subdued by his creator, his clay body was stored in the attic of the rabbi's synagogue. According to a wartime legend, a Nazi officer went to look for the body during the occupation of Prague. In his attempt to kill the Golem in the attic, the Nazi died for reasons that were never cleared up.

Weinreb would create his own Golem. A character in his own invented story would be made to appear real, a person of flesh and blood.

Someone was needed who could pose as the aristocratic Six, be arrested by the SD, confirm that he too had been duped by the reprehensible German gang, and then be released, or so it was hoped, winning Weinreb more time. To find a candidate for such a perilous role, Weinreb turned to the world of petty, and sometimes not so petty, criminals, from which the German occupiers recruited many of their most brutal collaborators. Thieves, black marketeers, extortionists were paid for hunting down hidden Jews. Some were also employed to do the dirty work in Gestapo prisons, and other places where Jews, Communists, and resistance members were tortured.

Criminality was of course a fluid concept in the upside-down world of Nazi occupation. Professional criminals who helped the Germans murder innocent civilians were acting "legally," in Nazi terms, while the resistance had to subvert the laws of the occupiers, by acts of sabotage, creating false documents, printing illegal newspapers, and so on. In rare cases, the resistance was helped by the criminal class. Subterfuge, false identities, and infiltration of the enemy were methods used both by the Nazis and those who resisted them. One of the great classics of postwar Dutch literature, *The Darkroom of Damocles* (*De donkere kamer van Damokles*) (1958), is a novel about just that: resistance heroes and Nazi collaborators who change identities; nothing is unambiguous. The author, W. F. Hermans, would one day play a major part in the story of Friedrich Weinreb.

Weinreb always insisted that Jews had to act illegally to survive. And he was right. That, apart from the chip on his shoulder about upper-class Jewish snobbery, is why he had such contempt for the Jewish Council; they stuck to the rules, at their and every Jew's peril. So Weinreb made up his own rules, which were not necessarily any less perilous, at least for some people. He had to find "a being that I would make myself and who would obey my instructions blindly. Only a Golem could play Six. Only a Golem would do as I say."

Through a friendly art dealer, Weinreb met a small-time crook named Sottens who dabbled in art forgeries and helped the resistance with fake identity papers. He lived in an attic on a dark, insalubrious street in Amsterdam, near the dockyards. Weinreb bamboozled Sottens with his usual fictions. Someone was needed to distract the Germans from a General von Schumann by posing as one of his helpers, the Dutch aristocrat Six. "Six" would have to spend some time in prison, but there were advantages to this, since he would be well paid and not be forced to work in Germany, as other Dutchmen between the ages of eighteen and thirty-five were. His job inside would be to follow Weinreb's careful instructions and send the Germans on a wild goose chase by mentioning a few imaginary members of the general's gang. That way the general would be able to continue his good work.

The crook, who never doubted General von Schumann's existence, praised Weinreb for his extraordinary ingenuity: "You thought all that up yourself? Even our boys wouldn't have come up with that. A brilliant scheme, I must say." He thought he knew just the right person for the job.

Hendrik Kotte was a burglar who had been arrested before the war on several occasions for robbery and perjury. A seedy ex-jailbird with a florid nose, Kotte did not have the air of a typical aristocrat, but for the very generous sum of ten thousand guilders, he was prepared to take on the task. The risks did not appear to worry him. In Weinreb's description, he "sat there, like a puppet. If I had to find someone to act as the Golem in a film, this would be the man I'd choose. He wouldn't even have to act." Kotte spoke in a strangely muffled tone, as though he were exchanging confidences in a prison yard.

Weinreb would travel to Sottens's squalid attic in Amsterdam three or four times a week to transform his Golem from a petty crook into an aristocrat. He taught Kotte upper-class manners and how to speak in a posh accent—why Weinreb should have been an expert in these matters is obscure; his acquaintance with the Dutch upper class was probably greater than Kotte's, but not by much. And the transformation of his Golem may not have been quite as successful as he later remembered. They would stage mock interrogations, with Weinreb taking the role of

Koch. Intricate stories were rehearsed about the workings of General von Schumann's outfit. After several weeks, Weinreb was almost satisfied that Kotte could pass for a polished gentleman.

But there was something about the charade that spooked him, as though Weinreb felt uneasy about being caught in the web of his own confection. Once again, there is no way of telling whether he was being truthful, but Weinreb's description of his own anxiety is arresting: "I was frightened for a reason I couldn't explain, as though I were in a haunted house, and felt a cold draught despite all windows and doors being closed. Was this fear about my own Golem idea? . . . Why was I afraid? Wasn't *I* in control of the Golem? I created him in that role, didn't I? I inspired him."

The theatrical trap had been carefully set with the SD. Weinreb would meet Six at a tram stop in the center of The Hague, and Koch's men would make a swift arrest. On the first occasion something went wrong. Kotte failed to turn up. He had gotten cold feet. Once more, Weinreb had to travel to Amsterdam to reassure him that everything would be fine. As soon as the SD realized that he too had been a victim of Wehrmacht racketeers, they would surely let him go.

The second time, things went according to plan. Kotte was dressed in a fine suit, with silk socks, a pocket handkerchief, and royally, perhaps too royally, sprayed with perfume. The SD agents swooped down on the two men at the tram stop. Both were taken to prison. Kotte was separated from Weinreb for interrogation. And Koch, beaming with satisfaction, said: "Congratulations, Weinreb, that was really superb." And then, still in Weinreb's words, Koch "trembled with emotion. His voice shook. And I saw drops of sweat run down his forehead."

Koch may have been as dim as Weinreb said. But not that dim. Even the most obtuse Gestapo officer would soon have realized that the petty Dutch crook was not the patrician descendant of a grandee painted by Rembrandt. On January 19, 1943, Weinreb arrived at the SD office for one of his regular meetings with Koch, which usually passed so pleasantly. But not on this occasion. Koch grabbed him by the lapels of his jacket and shouted: "The theater is over now!" Weinreb was arrested.

A week after his arrest, Weinreb's wife and children were sent to Westerbork, on the way to an almost certain death. After ten months in prison, Kotte was first deported to a Nazi concentration camp in the Netherlands. This camp, bad enough, was Vught. In 1944, he was sent to Dachau, which was worse. He died there in January 1945.

Seven

THE SHOOTING PARTY

◓⊖◓

1: Himmler's Train

On October 26, 1941, the guests of Joachim von Ribbentrop, Nazi Germany's foreign minister, shot 2,400 pheasants, 260 hares, 20 crows, and 1 roebuck. The landscape around Ribbentrop's castle, a gift from Hitler in 1939, was beautiful as in a German Romantic painting: dark blue lakes, dense forests, misty mountains. The company was illustrious. Himmler was of the party, but he expressed his usual distaste for killing innocent living creatures. Felix Kersten took part with gusto. So did Count Galeazzo Ciano, Mussolini's son-in-law, Italy's foreign minister, and Kersten's former patient.

There was little love lost between Ribbentrop and Himmler. The foreign minister couldn't understand why the head of the SS kept missing the pheasants streaking overhead. "He ought to show what he can do," sneered Ribbentrop, "but probably his humanitarian feelings stand in the way." Still, he approved of his Italian colleague's prowess with the gun. "Isn't this shoot symbolic?" Ribbentrop exclaimed to Ciano. "As we combine to shoot down the pheasants, so we'll also combine to down the enemies of Germany!"

This scene is described in Kersten's memoir. It may have happened in this way. There is no way of knowing.

Well-known, and meticulously documented, is what happened three months later, on January 20, 1942, in a pleasant villa in the neoclassical style on the Wannsee outside Berlin, where a number of top Nazi functionaries gathered to discuss the logistical problems involved in the plan to exterminate all the Jews of Europe. Adolf Eichmann, the SS official in charge of solving these problems, had prepared the briefs with care. He later testified that the gentlemen attending the conference had used robust language without bureaucratic euphemisms. This may have been true of informal conversations over glasses of brandy in front of the marble fireplace, but not of the official minutes kept by Eichmann. Reinhard Heydrich, chairman of the conference, told the assembled company: "As previously authorized by the Führer, emigration has now been replaced by the evacuation of the Jews to the east as a further solution." This was, however, only a step toward "the final solution of the Jewish question." Heydrich called Himmler the next day to keep him abreast of the proceedings.

How much did Himmler's masseur and supposed confidant know about this, and what did he make of what he knew? As usual in the shifty stories of Felix Kersten, his fascinating but flattering biographer Joseph Kessel gives the most fanciful account. On November 11, 1941, two months before that fateful meeting at the Wannsee Villa, Himmler was in terrible distress. He moaned to his masseur that nobody could help him. Kersten implored his patient to unburden himself. All right, said Himmler, since Kersten was his only friend, he would take him into his confidence.

Here was the thing that so depressed Himmler: Hitler was convinced that there could be no peace on earth as long as the Jewish people existed. I see, said Kersten, and what of it? Himmler's pale, slender hands rested immobile, as though they were frozen by some paralyzing dread.

"And so," he said, "he has instructed me to eradicate that race completely and forever."

Horrified, Kersten asked Himmler to consider what the world would think of Germany if such an abomination were carried out. Himmler replied that "it is the curse of greatness to have to step on dead bodies." How could Himmler do such a thing in good conscience? Himmler repeated that it was a direct order from the Führer. He had reacted "like an idiot" at first, assuring Hitler that he and his SS were prepared to die for him, but "please not to ask me to embark on this mission." Hitler, in a screaming rage, grabbed Himmler by the collar and called him a traitor. Himmler could barely breathe as he recounted this terrible ordeal to Kersten. His looked miserable, like a "dog after a beating," and he implored him to understand his situation.

Kersten was devastated: Hitler was clearly insane. But what could Kersten do? He had managed to save the Dutch population from being deported to Poland. But such miracles cannot simply be repeated. Even if he continued to take advantage of Himmler's stomach cramps, even if the withdrawal of his ministrations were to make Himmler incapable of carrying out this monstrous plan, Hitler would surely find someone else to do it. Since Kersten could do nothing to save the collective murder of the Jews, he would do his best to save as many people as he could.

If this version, written by a former member of the French resistance and a Jew himself, were true, Himmler would still be a man with some moral scruples, Hitler would be solely responsible for the genocide, Kersten would be a man fighting for the right cause, and his continued care for the master of the Final Solution excusable.

In his own memoir, Kersten maintains that Himmler never wanted to kill the Jews, but just to "evacuate" them—to Madagascar, for example. To the idea that the Holocaust was exclusively Hitler's mad idea, Kersten adds the untenable theory that the original plan actually came from Joseph Goebbels, the minister of propaganda. It was Goebbels who ordered the burning of synagogues and persecution of Jews on Kristall-nacht in 1938. In Himmler's opinion, according to Kersten, Goebbels had convinced Hitler that all Jews had to be killed. And it was Goebbels who persuaded Hitler to entrust the SS with this unpleasant but neces-sary task. Himmler supposedly declared that he was "very indignant about this," but that "there was nothing I could do."

The reason Kersten would have his readers believe this story is also the reason he maintained that most SS officers he knew were as dis-gusted by the killings as he was, and that the men in Himmler's entou-rage, such as SS General Gottlob Berger and Himmler's private secretary, Rudolf Brandt, were upstanding "idealists" with "good hearts." It makes his own complicity, which was never murderous, a great deal less egre-gious. He was a good man, surrounded by other basically decent men, who were forced to carry out the orders of a lunatic. In a way, one might say that Berger and the others were also victims of the crazy Führer, even, at a slight stretch, Himmler himself.

The known facts throw a rather different light on Himmler's activities back in the spring of 1941, many months before the shooting party at Ribbentrop's estate, and his subsequent "confession" to Kersten. In the course of that year Himmler was rushing around conquered areas of Po-land, the Soviet Union, and the Baltic states on his private armored train, organizing death squads to annihilate suspected Communists, partisans, and Jews. Himmler instructed these special troops made up of various SS police units that all Jews were by definition partisans. Countless numbers of people were tortured to death or hanged, but more often they were shot over pits, which they had to dig themselves, by these special-ized killers who were either drunk, or happy in their work, or too afraid to defy their superior officers. As Christopher Browning showed in his brilliant book *Ordinary Men*, most of them were conformists; they re-fused to stand out from their peers.

Quite apart from Himmler's own feelings about the Jews, which he didn't hide from his masseur, his zealous leadership in murdering them was also part of his effort to assert the authority of his SS. His men, and his men alone, should be in charge of the destruction of the Jewish race. The army was quite welcome to help, of course, which it did, but Himmler would give the orders.

One of his main henchmen in the slaughter was a bespectacled Prussian officer named Erich von dem Bach-Zelewski. He led the death squads in 1941, had helped set up Auschwitz as a concentration camp the year before, and butchered up to two hundred thousand Poles in the Warsaw Uprising in 1944 (he did, however, save the preserved heart of Frédéric Chopin from a memorial to the composer and later returned it "to the Polish people" as a sign of his generosity). In a testimony after the war, Bach-Zelewski said that Himmler had told him at a meeting in June 1941 that thirty million people in the Soviet Union needed to be killed to create the proper *lebensraum* for the superior Nordic races to be able to spread their wings.

In July 1941, after a meeting with Bach-Zelewski in Belarus, Himmler gave the following order to the SS: "All [male] Jews must be shot. Drive all females into the swamps." (When the swamps proved to be too shallow, the women were shot.) After another meeting with the same functionary in Riga, Jews were murdered all over Latvia. That November, around the time that he allegedly told Kersten how much he loathed his task, Himmler witnessed the shooting of Jewish men, women, and children in Minsk, an event that was recorded on film by Walter Frentz ("Hitler's cameraman"). Himmler not only watched the proceedings with interest but instructed the killers to shoot people who still showed signs of life as they twitched in a pile of bodies in the ditch that was their mass grave. He noted in his diary: "Dined on the train. Newsreel and film of Minsk."

And all this happened before the murder of the Jews was even finalized at the Wannsee Conference in 1942. Countless academic papers and books have been written about the question of responsibility for the Holocaust. Was it Hitler who made the decision to eliminate Jews from this earth? If so, he left no written order. Was it Hitler's loyal satraps who knew what Hitler wanted and were they "working towards the Führer," in the phrase coined by Ian Kershaw, the eminent British historian? Was their "working towards the Führer" based on ideological fanaticism or a bureaucratic scramble for influence and authority? Or a combination of both? That Himmler was by no means squeamish should be apparent from a statement he made a few years later to generals of the Wehrmacht (not even his own trusted SS): "I did not consider myself justified—as far as Jewish women and children are concerned—in allowing children to grow up to be the avengers who kill our fathers and our grandchildren. I would have seen that as cowardly. As a result, the issue was solved uncompromisingly."

And what was Kersten doing during those months when Himmler was riding his train hither and thither through the conquered territories? He was traveling with the stressed Reichsführer SS to ensure his comfort and relieve his pain. These soothing sessions normally took place in the morning, so Himmler could start his day refreshed. Life was not too uncomfortable in Himmler's temporary headquarters in East Prussia. The train had a decent restaurant. And a cinema was set up for Himmler and his men. According to Joseph Kessel, these privileged few were able to enjoy banned Hollywood movies, as well as duller German fare. Because of his bulk, Kersten couldn't fit himself into the narrow wooden seats, so a special outsized seat was constructed for him. The rest of the time, he was out gathering mushrooms in the surrounding forest, which he sent to his country seat in Hartzwalde after having them dried in a bread oven.

Mushroom picking and movies may have kept Kersten busy, but for a man in such close physical proximity to Himmler to have heard nothing of what his boss was up to in the summer and fall of 1941 seems highly improbable. Either Kersten lied about it after the war, or he must have been pathologically obtuse. Kersten maintains in his memoirs that ordinary Germans had no idea of what was going on, and that he was no exception. But ordinary Germans did not travel around eastern Europe on Himmler's private train.

Friedrich Kellner was a fairly ordinary German; a middle-ranking official in the town of Laubach in Hessen. A former Social Democrat who hated the Nazis, Kellner kept a wartime diary, later published as *My Opposition*. October 28, 1941: "A soldier on leave here said that he personally witnessed a terrible atrocity in occupied Poland. He watched as naked Jewish men and women were placed in front of a long deep ditch and, upon the order of the SS, were shot by Ukrainians in the back of their heads, and they fell into the ditch. The ditch was filled in as screams were coming from it."

This atrocity occurred two days before the shooting party at Ribbentrop's, when Himmler expressed his aversion to killing pheasants.

And what of the concentration camps that had been built in Germany as early as 1933? Dachau, near Munich, already had such a frightening reputation in Germany long before the war that a song circulated that went: "Dear God, make me dumb / so that I won't go to Dachau . . . If I'm deaf, dumb and blind, I'll be Adolf's favorite child."

Kersten is certain to have known about one concentration camp at least, because it was located very near his country house in Brandenburg. Ravensbrück was constructed for female prisoners in 1938 on Himmler's orders. Of the more than 130,000 women who passed through the camp between 1939 and the end of the war, about 50,000 were killed or died in miserable conditions. A little more than 1 percent of the inmates was made up of Jehovah's Witnesses. Their "crime" was a refusal to join the Nazi movement and to take up arms for their country. They were citizens of God's kingdom, and they lived according to His laws. Even the camp guards were impressed by the strength of their faith, which no amount of terror could shake. Jehovah's Witnesses had a reputation for total honesty and obedience, which is why they could be trusted to work as farmhands and domestic helpers outside the camp; they would never run away.

This is how, in July 1942, Kersten acquired ten Jehovah's Witnesses to work on his estate. He later asked for more, including men. If Wilhelm Wulff, whom Kersten later brought in as Himmler's personal astrologer, is to be believed, Kersten did this entirely out of self-interest; the prisoners provided slave labor. Wulff called Kersten's Hartzwalde estate a "branch" of Ravensbrück concentration camp. But Wulff was probably biased. He didn't like Kersten, whom he described as a selfish operator with "greedy little eyes," obsessed with money and power. Wulff was fonder of Irmgard, Kersten's wife, but his story that she hated Himmler because he had once ordered his men to strip the Jehovah's Witnesses and have them whipped for fun doesn't sound right either. Himmler was, after all, a fastidious mass murderer.

Kersten always maintained that he treated his slave laborers with extraordinary kindness, kept them out of the camp, and turned his own estate into "a refuge for the oppressed and the persecuted." Joseph Kessel goes even further, writing that Hartzwalde was a paradise for the prisoners and Kersten a "messenger from the angels" sent to deliver them from hell. It is quite possible that Kersten and his wife did treat the Jehovah's Witnesses decently, even as they profited from their labor. As the more famous story of Oskar Schindler revealed, opportunism did not exclude compassion. There can be little doubt that life in Hartzwalde would have been preferable to misery in Ravensbrück.

Kersten claims to have received the first intimations of the cruel conditions in Himmler's camps from the prisoners on his estate. This is hard to believe, but not out of the question. Like many people in Germany, Kersten might have preferred not to know about things that were distressing. But in an interview with a Dutch government research committee after the war, Kersten told a slightly different story. He had heard about what went on the concentration camps in 1942, when SS officers, whom Kersten plied with drinks, told him all about it. Even Himmler's own secretary, Brandt, hadn't known. It was he, Kersten, who had to enlighten him. This, I think, is out of the question.

In any case, he decided, according to his own account, to confront

Himmler directly. Were the stories he had heard true, Kersten asked, about torture and other abuses in the camps? He had picked a moment of vulnerability, when the Reichsführer SS was suffering from a particularly bad case of cramps. Himmler tried to laugh it off and told his masseur to ignore enemy propaganda: "We Germans are not as bad as that." Kersten insisted that he had been shown horrific photographs at the Finnish embassy. This was an invention. He didn't wish to implicate his workers in spreading rumors. Himmler stiffened at the mention of photographs and admitted that there might have been some excesses. After his conversation with Himmler, Kersten tried to find out more from other SS officers, almost all of whom were as disturbed as he was, but they blamed everything on Hitler. Of course, this is not what he told the Dutch research committee.

Again, Joseph Kessel, either repeating Kersten's story, or making it up himself, lays it on much thicker. Himmler supposedly said that Kersten, with his "Finnish mentality" and the "intellectual habits" instilled from his "Dutch democracy," wouldn't understand the necessity for harsh discipline. At any rate, he said, "you know perfectly well that I'm incapable of harming anyone with my own hands." Himmler then took a document from his wallet. It contained Hitler's signature, and his name embossed in gold. The text certified that Hitler would take full responsibility for any orders to exterminate the Jews and other prisoners in the camps. Once more, one marvels at the gullibility of a former member of the resistance—Kessel, that is. But perhaps he was neither gullible nor naive, but simply on to a good story, implausible though it was.

Even as Kersten was hearing about the horrors of Nazi rule for the first time, he was still supposedly in close touch with the Dutch resistance through secret missives sent through Himmler's personal post box. If this were true, his obliviousness to what went on in the camps becomes even harder to explain. As we know from Weinreb's memoirs, in Holland the Mauthausen concentration camp was already a byword for savagery and death in early 1941.

Much is made in Kersten's account, and that of his French biographer, of his run-ins with Reinhard Heydrich, the most sinister of Himmler's murderous technocrats. Kersten even claims to have been arrested at one point. Perhaps he was. In the snake pit of Himmler's court, where everyone suspected everyone of skullduggery, it is quite possible that Heydrich was suspicious of Kersten's proximity to Himmler, and thus of having too much influence over his boss. But Kersten's idea that Heydrich suspected him of saving the Dutch population from deportation is certainly an invention. There had been no such plan. Maybe, as Kersten claims, Heydrich did think Kersten had a hand in Rudolf Hess's bizarre solo flight to Scotland. That Heydrich tried to enlist Kersten to spy on his rivals in the SS is also easy to imagine.

Still, in Kersten's telling, despite Heydrich's unwelcome attentions, his resolve to rescue as many individuals as possible from the maw of Hitler's executioners remained as firm as ever. His first chance to do so concerned his own adopted country, Finland.

Although Finland had managed to remain officially neutral until it was attacked by Soviet bombers on June 25, 1941, three days after Germany invaded the Soviet Union, the Finns had cooperated closely with the Germans. They were given arms, and a Finnish Waffen SS battalion was formed. This wasn't so much because the Finns were Nazis—their president, Risto Ryti, was an Anglophile and a Freemason—but they needed German help to avenge their losses in the Russo-Finnish War of 1939–40. After the German invasion, the Finns were military allies against the Soviets. This alliance of convenience lasted until September 1944, when it was clear that Germany was losing the war, and the fraying partnership, much to the chagrin of the Germans, was ended by the Finns in a separate peace with Stalin.

Kersten often liked to boast of his splendid Finnish credentials. He supposedly persuaded Himmler to supply Finland with much-needed supplies of grain, for which he was awarded the Order of the White Rose in 1942 from the Finnish government. Some skepticism might be in order here too. In a letter to the Netherlands Ministry of Foreign Affairs in 1948, the Dutch representative in Helsinki reports that Kersten was not much trusted by the Finns. His claim to have "saved the Finnish people" in the Russo-Finnish War by persuading the Germans to intervene on Finland's behalf in Moscow in 1940 was not believed.

This much is true: In July 1942, Kersten was looking after Himmler at his field headquarters in Ukraine, just as the organized killing of Jews was reaching an atrocious climax. Himmler decided that a visit to Finland might be in order, ostensibly to inspect the Finnish Waffen SS battalion, but also for some rest and recreation after months of overexertion. According to Kersten, Himmler was sent to Helsinki by Hitler on a mission to get the Finns to hand over roughly two thousand highly assimilated Jewish citizens, who would be sent straight to the Majdanek death camp in Poland. Germany promised to send more grain to Finland, if the Finnish government would agree to this request.

Kersten arrived in Helsinki with Himmler and his chief of personal staff, Karl Wolff, a man Kersten describes as "helpful and always friendly." Wolff would be convicted after the war as a war criminal. He was with Himmler when they witnessed the shooting of Jews in Minsk. One of his murderous tasks, among many, was to supervise, along with the dreadful Bach-Zelewski, the extermination of Jews in the Warsaw ghetto.

As soon as they settled in their hotel, Himmler had an attack of cramps. Kersten used the opportunity to dissuade Himmler from pressing the Finns to deliver their Jews. Himmler, in great pain, agreed to discuss the matter further with the Finnish leaders. Since he was still feeling unwell, Himmler declined to attend President Ryti's dinner in his honor. Kersten slipped away to discuss the Jewish question with the Finnish foreign minister, Rolf Witting. They concluded that the best tactic was to stall. Witting would tell Himmler that a transfer of Jews had to be decided by parliament, and parliament was not presently in session. Kersten convinced Himmler the next day that it would be unwise to ignore Finnish wishes. Himmler telephoned Hitler, and the Führer agreed to leave the Jewish problem in Finland until later.

The more conventional account of Himmler's attempted transaction in Finland is that he brought up the matter with Prime Minister Johan Wilhelm Rangell. They met at Petäys, a lakeside resort that Kersten had recommended to Himmler for its sunbathing facilities. The "magnetic healing" of the northern sun would do him good. Rangell replied that there was no "Jewish question" in Finland. And that was the end of it. How much Kersten had to do with this isn't clear. But at least the two thousand Finnish Jews were safe. Himmler repaired to Lapland to inspect the troops. This was the famous occasion described with such verve by the Italian writer Curzio Malaparte in his book *Kaputt*, when Himmler was flogged with twigs by his adjutants in a sauna. It was on this same trip that Kersten asked the Finnish foreign minister whether he would lose his Finnish passport if he were to join the SS.

And so, the legend was set: not only had Kersten saved the Dutch population from being deported to Poland, but he had saved the Finnish Jews from certain death in Majdanek. And all this after he saved the Finnish people from being swallowed up by the Soviet Union in 1940.

He did more than that, however. One more act in his legend took place in 1943. First, he supposedly repaid the Dutch royal family for their patronage before the war by rescuing his former patient Duke Adolf Friedrich of Mecklenburg, brother of the Dutch queen's husband, from Nazi retribution. The story goes that Joseph Goebbels was so angry about Wilhelmina's flight to London that he sought to punish her husband's relatives in Germany. When Duke Adolf Friedrich was supposedly in danger, Kersten wrote a letter to Himmler full of guileful flattery. "As the great Germanic leader," he wrote, Himmler had always "treated his enemies with respect." He would surely not wish to smear them with calumnies "as some people have done who do not share your views."

This letter is fishy for several reasons. It was hardly likely for a masseur, even one as trusted by his patient as Kersten, to openly criticize a powerful member of the Nazi elite, such as Goebbels. But the main reason for doubt is that Duke Adolf Friedrich, the man who made trips to Africa and South Africa on behalf of the German regime, and who corresponded with Hitler, was on perfectly good terms with the Nazi leadership. His nephew, Georg Alexander, who was born in Russia and had a Russian mother, was indeed arrested by the Gestapo in 1944 on suspicion of hiding enemies of the Reich in his home, but this had nothing to do with the Dutch monarch's brother-in-law. Another close relative, Friedrich Franz, was an active member of the Waffen SS. Some historians believe that Kersten forged his letter to Himmler after the war to ingratiate himself with his royal patrons.

Kersten's intervention on behalf of a well-connected aristocrat was trivial compared with something else he supposedly did. He saved the French, Belgian, and Dutch people from being murdered by deliberate starvation. Oddly, the story of this remarkable act is recounted by Joseph Kessel, but not by Kersten himself, either in the English or in the Dutch edition of his memoirs. All Kersten mentions is a Nazi plan to abolish the French state and establish a new Nazi state called the Burgundian Free State, to be administered by Belgian Nazi leader Leon Degrelle.

Kessel's account is quite remarkable. In August 1942, Himmler's secretary, Rudolf Brandt, told Kersten of a plan to loot most of the food from France, Belgium, and Holland, and buy up everything that was left on the black markets. The people in those countries would starve of course, but that didn't bother Himmler, who told his masseur that he would be happy to see them all die of hunger. But that's diabolical, cried Kersten. What about French culture, its great artists and writers, and its glorious history? "My dear Kersten," Himmler replied, "you are too much of a humanist. Anything is allowed in a war to the death. Why did those people fight us? All they needed to do was come to our side."

At the beginning of 1943, Kersten saw his chance to do something about it. Not only was Himmler in crippling pain, but he was depressed. The incessant railway travel had frayed his nerves. He was feeling lonely. Heydrich had been assassinated, the Germans had been beaten back at Stalingrad, and the Allies had landed in Sicily. This was the moment of weakness that Kersten used to save millions. If Himmler would only give up his plan to starve the people of three European nations, "the great Germanic leader's act of generosity" would be "celebrated for a thousand years." Somehow, Kersten had managed to appeal to his client's sentimental streak and his vanity. Himmler was deeply touched. His eyes brimmed with tears. "My dear Kersten," he said, "my magic Buddha, you are quite right. I will talk to the Führer immediately and do everything to persuade him."

Kessel seems to have conflated two Nazi plans. There had indeed been a so-called Hunger Plan, but the idea was to starve citizens of the Soviet Union and Poland to feed German soldiers and the people back home. Consequently, millions of Soviet POWs, Jews, and others died of hunger. There was also systematic looting of food and other products from France, Belgium, and Holland, but there was no plan to starve their populations to death.

By the end of 1943, Kersten could see that the Third Reich certainly was not going to last for a thousand years, or indeed for much longer than another year or two. He knew that German relations with Finland were deteriorating fast. Himmler and Ribbentrop had been ranting about Finnish treachery. And so, in Kersten's words: "It seemed to me that, in light of the developing situation between Finland and Germany, it would be sensible for me to begin slowly and unobtrusively distancing myself from Germany."

By then most Jewish victims of the Nazi genocide had already been killed. More than one million people were murdered in the fall of 1942, just one year after Ribbentrop's shooting party.

2: Tianjin

World War II officially began in Europe with the German invasion of Poland on September 1, 1939. The Germans concocted a casus belli out of a fake event: the staged attack on a German radio station in Gleiwitz at the Polish border on the night of August 31. The attackers were Germans dressed in Polish uniforms. The corpse of a freshly murdered victim of the Gestapo was left on the spot. The dead man played the role of a Polish saboteur. Reinhard Heydrich was the man who made up this fatal charade, quaintly named "Grandmother Died," but better known as the Gleiwitz Incident.

But for many western Europeans, the war began only in May 1940, when the German blitzkrieg overwhelmed France, Belgium, and the Netherlands, or a month earlier, when Denmark and Norway were invaded.

The start of the war in Asia is harder to pin down. The Mukden Incident in 1931? The Shanghai Incident in 1932? Claims have been made for both dates. But July 7, 1937, was the first day of an all-out war that would eventually cause the death of more than twenty-five million people in Asia alone, most of them civilians. The immediate trigger was a misunderstanding rather than a deception. Just ten miles from the center of Beijing lies the arched Lugou Bridge. The bridge was noted by Marco Polo on his travels, hence its name in the West, Marco Polo Bridge. On July 7, a Japanese private was sent out to patrol the area. (An alternative story is that he simply drifted off for a toilet break.) When he failed to return at the agreed time, the Japanese commander got jumpy and demanded access to the nearest town. The Chinese refused. The Japanese soldier soon returned to his base. But negotiations broke down, fighting began, and soon Beijing and Tianjin were in Japanese hands.

Yoshiko wrote her memoir, *In the Shadow of Chaos* (*Doran no kage ni*), in the same year. She blamed the Chinese Nationalist Generalissimo Chiang Kai-shek for the outbreak of war. He had "incited anti-Japanese feeling among the Chinese people," she wrote. Her book was aimed at the Japanese market. This was the official line in 1937. She was giving interviews to the Japanese press in the summer of that year, while recuperating from an old wound that gave her terrible back aches. Her romantic explanation was that she was still suffering from the bullet wound she sustained while fighting off "bandits" in the Mongolian desert.

The fighting in Shanghai that broke out in August was far bloodier than at the Marco Polo Bridge, or indeed the Shanghai Incident in 1932. A Japanese officer tried to barge into a local airport. He was shot by a Chinese guard. The Japanese demanded a withdrawal of Chinese troops from the city. The Chinese saw no reason to comply. Whereupon Shanghai was shelled, bombed, and strafed. Whole neighborhoods went up in flames. Refugees came pouring into the foreign concessions, which were not safe from bomb attacks either. The Japanese had heavier weapons, formidable battleships, and more bombers. The Chinese had more men, but often little to fight with apart from machine guns, hand grenades, and some howitzers. Chiang Kai-shek decided he had to make a stand in Shanghai, nonetheless, hoping in vain that Western powers would rush to his aid. He refused to negotiate and promised "a war of resistance to the end." Chiang's patriotism was admirable, but it proved to be a reckless move. Chinese troops were ordered to fight to the death, often in suicidal attacks. Street fighting in Shanghai and nearby towns was so ferocious that there was not enough time to bury all the bodies. By the time the Battle of Shanghai was over, around three hundred thousand people, including many of Chiang's officers, were dead.

On the common assumption that the Chinese were a cowardly race, the Japanese were shocked by the intensity of Chinese resistance to their Imperial Army. Frustration, lack of discipline, too many unscrupulous officers, and the brutal nature of their army training made the Japanese increasingly vicious. Once the Japanese high command decided in November to march on the Nationalist capital of Nanjing, the stage was set for one of the worst war crimes of World War II. Whether the killing, looting, and raping in towns large and small on the road to Nanjing was a deliberate policy of "shock and awe," as it were, an attempt to terrorize the Chinese into submission, or a way to allow ill-fed, tired, and brutalized soldiers to let off steam is still disputed. Japanese troops also behaved in the way foreign soldiers in unfamiliar places, surrounded by hostile enemies, in or out of uniform, often do. They killed anyone who might conceivably pose a threat. When in doubt, shoot.

The bloodbath that ensued once the thick walls of Nanjing were blasted through, and the city had been abandoned by Chiang Kai-shek's officer corps, leaving only common soldiers who hastily changed into civilian clothes, haunts Sino-Japanese relations to this day. Anyone suspected of being a Chinese soldier was rounded up and killed. Some were machine-gunned, others hacked to death with swords, and some were used for bayonet practice in a gruesome parody of military drills. Many thousands of women were gang-raped, in most cases as a prelude to being murdered. Buildings were set on fire; homes, museums, and stores were looted, with officers often taking the pick of the antiques and other precious goods. This orgy of violence went on for six weeks beginning on December 13. The exact number of deaths and rape victims will never be known. The official count in Chinese history books is three hundred thousand, which is a symbolic approximation. Some Japanese estimates arrive at a much lower number. But crimes on this scale are not just a matter of statistics. Comparisons with Auschwitz were made at the Tokyo War Crimes Tribunal after the war. This was inexact, but it showed how much the crimes had shocked public opinion.

What Yoshiko thought of the Nanjing Massacre isn't known. There is no mention of it in her book, or in any of the articles she published. After her well-publicized adventures as Commander Jin in Manchukuo, she had moved back to Japan in 1933, where she became a celebrity and behaved like one, often making a thorough nuisance of herself. This was to remain a pattern in her life, flitting between China and Japan, staying until her welcome in either place ran out. She got easily bored. Her

private army was disbanded, supposedly because she didn't wish to follow the example of Chinese warlords whose opposition to Japanese en-
croachments had made the situation in China so much worse in her view.
In this respect, she was consistent. No matter how badly the Japanese
behaved on the continent, Chiang Kai-shek and his Nationalists were
still her main enemies. Since she happened to be in Tokyo at the time of
the Nanjing Massacre, she wouldn't have been aware of the scale of Japanese brutality, let alone the gory details. The fall of the Chinese capital
was described in the Japanese press as a great victory. What happened
afterward was heavily censored. Yoshiko still boasted of her untiring efforts to "build a paradise in Manchukuo," but she clearly sensed that
something was going badly wrong in China and was sometimes critical
of Japanese policies in public. Moral outrage could have been part of
this, but there was also a strong element of pique in her remark that
while Japanese soldiers who died in China were worshipped as heroes at
Japanese military shrines, her own Manchurian men were buried in un-
marked graves in the desert. More and more, a feeling of hurt pride, even
indignation, crept into her professions of willingness to collaborate in
the Japanese cause, creating a tension she was never able to resolve. This
could have contributed to her increasing dependence on opiates.

Three months before the savage Sino-Japanese War was triggered at
Marco Polo Bridge, Yoshiko gave one of her most remarkable speeches.
She had been invited to her high school reunion in Matsumoto. The talk
took place in the evening, at the town hall. It was a cold night. The winds
from the surrounding mountains made it seem even colder. Such was
Yoshiko's fame that a huge crowd gathered outside just to get a glimpse
of her. Inside, there was barely room to stand. Yoshiko looked gaunt and
exhausted. She was giving herself regular injections of morphine, often
startling people when she lifted her robe in a public place to stick a needle in her thigh. An assistant had to help her onto the podium, where she
was introduced to the audience by the mayor of Matsumoto. Yoshiko was
barely thirty, but she looked many years older.

She began by stating how grateful her compatriots in China and Manchukuo would be if only they were to receive a fraction of the good-will that she was getting from her Japanese audience that night. Alas, she continued, China and Manchuria were overrun by greedy Japanese ruffians who "terrorized the Chinese people." It was no good for Japanese diplomats or military officers to talk about Sino-Japanese friendship; reconciliation had to come from the bottom up. Japanese foreign policy in China was a disaster. She said: "Every time there is war, I risk my life to rush around for the sake of peace. . . . I didn't become a commander to make war, I continued to use all my power as a commander to stop the fighting."

Even though Japan was not a totalitarian society quite yet (things tightened considerably after the war in China began), this was a very bold speech to make in 1937. Her criticism, though couched in her usual dreamy air of self-aggrandizement, still stung. Whatever the reasons for the Japanese military in China to get her out of their way, the last thing they wanted was for Yoshiko to start bad-mouthing Japanese policies, or to draw attention to Chinese suffering. That she wasn't arrested might have been due to her great fame in Japan, and her on-and-off performances as a spokesperson for Japanese propaganda. She was a nuisance, but still sometimes a useful nuisance.

Yoshiko's celebrity had been greatly boosted by Muramatsu Shofu's fictionalized story of her life, published in 1933, and quickly dramatized (something repeated many times since; most recently in a television drama in 2008). She gave interviews, wrote popular songs, and never turned down a chance to speak on the radio. There is a rather sad photograph of her, looking haggard in front of a microphone, dressed in a man's white jacket and a dark bow tie. Her slicked-back hair is cut short and her melancholy eyes, lined with mascara, peep out from a heavily made-up chalk-white face.

Yoshiko had the confusing habit of alternating comments about Japanese louts and failed policies with propaganda about heroic Japanese

efforts to build a new Asia, and wicked Chinese warlords standing in the way of this grand ideal. This is the story she tells in her memoir. The performance of her own life, preaching the virtues of racial harmony in Manchukuo, while dressed in silk Chinese male gowns or, occasionally, in a Japanese female kimono, was a gaudy advertisement for the belligerent strategies that went under the name of Sino-Japanese friendship. When called upon, she could still perform her role to perfection.

Her first abode in Tokyo, after she moved back from Manchukuo, well before the invasion of China proper, was the Manchukuo embassy. Yoshiko's latest male companion was a writer, public speaker, fraudster, stock market speculator, and man-about-town named Ito Hanni. They would flit around Tokyo in his Buick limousine frequenting nightclubs, which still thrived in Japan until the China war and especially the attack on Pearl Harbor put a stop to such "frivolous entertainments," along with Hollywood movies, jazz music, and other forms of "enemy culture." (That great paean to American democracy, *Mr. Smith Goes to Washington*, was playing in Tokyo cinemas until the eve of Pearl Harbor.)

Ito, who had the slim figure and brilliantined hair of a fashionable crooner, had made a fortune by buying shares cheaply after the Wall Street crash. His financial moves were inspired by his personal astrologer, or so he claimed. He met a variety of literary and political oddballs through a friendly group of astrologers. A flair for self-promotion and lavish donations to the Japanese Imperial Army, among other worthy causes, made him into a public figure, much written about in the gossip columns of popular magazines.

As well as writing several unsuccessful novels, Ito dabbled in politics, first as a promotor of what he called popular sovereignty. He founded a journal called *The Japanese People* (*Nihon kokumin*). But it was a peculiar concept of sovereignty that he was touting, based on ideals of friendship, labor, and love inspired by Rudolf Steiner, the Austrian spiritual guru and founder of anthroposophy. This, too, was apparently prompted by his astrologer. Ito added to his fame by traveling around Japan as an inspirational speaker. One of his gushing followers was inspired to write a novel comparing him with the Count of Monte Cristo for rather mysterious reasons.

Sadly, the magazine venture ended badly. The money ran out. And Ito decided to seek new adventures in China, which is where he first met Yoshiko at a dance hall. The China trip took Ito to new flights of political fancy, even more flowery than his ideals of popular sovereignty. He called it "New Asianism." Japan would take over Asia after kicking out the Western powers. The following thoughts were expressed in one of his collected speeches: "The day will come when Japan will fly over the Pacific like a swallow to unite the world. . . . The Japanese people must never forget that the world will be united, inspired by thousands of years of the rising sun, as well as our mountains, forests, birds, the bottomless ocean filled with beautiful fish, Japanese rice, paddies, silent snow, our traditional warrior spirit, and the nobility running through our veins."

The spirit of Ito's New Asianism was more succinctly expressed in the lyrics he wrote for a popular tune that he first played on a phonograph for a group of Japanese military staff officers at a geisha party. He and Yoshiko gave a demonstration of a new dance, in which the partners rubbed up against each other while improvising the steps. It was called the "walking dance." The words are as obscure as in his political speeches, but the expansionist nature of Ito's nationalism shines through:

Pointing to the new Orient, we will die in the palace of Peking
Ah, the purple sun, ah, the Pacific, ah, the Continent!

Ito and Yoshiko were a well-matched couple. A possible marriage was speculated upon in the press. Both were largely self-invented characters. Ito was not even his real name. He was born Matsuo Masanao. Both were addicted to the nightlife. And both operated in a fantasy world that over-lapped dangerously with that of military and political figures, whose aims were more hardheaded and openly bellicose but often no less outlandish. As usual with her amorous liaisons, there was money to spend lavishly. She moved in with Ito after leaving the Manchukuo embassy sometime in 1934. The couple lived in a large apartment in Tokyo. A sign on Yoshiko's bedroom door indicated that this was the "commander's room."

Yoshiko's social life in Japan reflected her confused politics. She at-tended the sumo championship in Tokyo with Toyama Mitsuru, the ideological gangster who had founded the ultranationalist Black Dragon Society. Toyama's views on Japan's role in Asia were the most extreme version of policies that were now beginning to enter the mainstream. An-other old friend was the radical right-wing terrorist Iwata Ainosuke, the man who once offered Yoshiko his gun when she threatened to commit suicide. Sometimes, on these public occasions, she would dress up like a geisha, with her hair arranged in the traditional Japanese manner. Mem-bers of Yoshiko's disbanded private army would also make their appear-ance at some of her parties, adding an exotic element to the proceedings when they kowtowed to her on the tatami floor, as though they were courtiers in the Forbidden City in Beijing.

Yoshiko never stuck to one man for long. Her relationship with Ito came to an end in 1935, when he was arrested for stock market fraud. Beaten up in prison, he was released on bail after confinement had sup-posedly driven him mad. In bad health, financially strapped, and seeing her dreams of a continental comeback drifting ever further out of reach, Yoshiko appeared to be more and more bewildered. Perhaps her critical speech in Matsumoto was a result of her confusion. She was trying to express incompatible sides of her public persona, which was a splintered concoction anyway, assembled from her aristocratic Manchu roots, the extreme right-wing circles around her adoptive father, her assortment of Japanese lovers in positions of power, the increasingly jingoistic Japanese press avid for sensational gossip and patriotic *bidan*, and her own rich imagination.

Yoshiko was not arrested in 1937, but her presence had once again become annoying to the Japanese authorities, and so she returned to China, where she set up house in Beijing, still in the company of her faithful Japanese companion, Chizuko, various members of her old private army, and a number of guards whom she dressed up in fancy uniforms. But she spent most her time in the fall of that year, when Japanese troops were fighting their way toward Nanjing, managing a Chinese restaurant in Tianjin, specializing in Mongolian lamb hot pot. The restaurant was named Tokoro.

Tokoro, located in the Japanese concession, was in a large villa with many rooms and a pretty Chinese garden. Guests were served tea and rice cakes, as well as more elaborate Chinese meals. Hot baths were also provided. And those who couldn't afford the more lavish facilities could enjoy simple snacks in the courtyard. The financial backing behind this establishment was opaque. But many people believed that Yoshiko's former lover in Manchukuo, General Tada Hayao, had a hand in it. Setting her up as a restaurateur was the latest Japanese effort to keep her out of trouble. Tokoro's staff consisted of about fifty young men, all members of Yoshiko's former private army. As she explains in her memoir, a growing hostility toward the Japanese among the local population had made their presence at home in Manchukuo untenable.

Most of the guests at Tokoro were members of the Japanese armed forces. This was by design. Yoshiko wanted to thank the brave Japanese soldiers by "offering solace to the officers on their way to the battle fronts and to the men coming back from the interior of China." Her restaurant would help "to bring the Chinese and Japanese peoples together."

Banquets at Tokoro were attended not only by Japanese soldiers, however, but also by figures from Chinese high society. One was Pan Yugui, the collaborationist mayor of Tianjin's foreign concessions. He brought along a seventeen-year-old student from Beijing, dressed in a simple Chinese student uniform. Her name was Pan Shuhua, in honor of the mayor who was her godfather. But she had a stage name too, Li Xianglan, or Ri Koran in Japanese, ever since she made a name for herself singing Chinese, Russian, and Japanese songs on the radio in Manchukuo, where she was born. Her real name was in fact Yamaguchi Yoshiko. She was the daughter of Japanese parents. Her father, Fumio, was a shiftless Sinophile who taught Chinese to Japanese employees of the South Manchurian Railway Company and gambled away much of what he earned—hence his daughter's temporary adoption by Fumio's Chinese friend Pan Yugui.

Pan/Li/Ri/Yamaguchi remembers her first glimpse of Kawashima Yoshiko at the restaurant. Dressed in a black silk Chinese robe, Yoshiko looked to the younger woman like a beautiful man in drag. Her face and arms were "deathly pale," her lips and eyebrows lightly made up with mascara and lipstick. She was entertaining a group of admirers with risqué jokes. Introduced by the mayor to his young goddaughter, the elder Yoshiko slowly examined her from top to toe. "Ah," she murmured in Chinese, "so you're Japanese. . . . Isn't that curious. And we have the same name too." She told the other Yoshiko to call her "big brother." And for the duration of her stay in Tianjin, Yamaguchi, lapping up the heady atmosphere of adult life in the foreign concessions, became Yoshiko's constant companion on her rounds of the nightspots. The two Yoshikos continued to meet back in Beijing, despite the Chinese godfather's disapproval. Kawashima Yoshiko would turn up late at night with several uniformed guards in tow, ready to go dancing.

They made a most peculiar Sino-Japanese pair, soon made even stranger when Amakasu Masahiko, the Japanese army propaganda chief, opened a movie studio in Manchukuo to produce films promoting the Japanese cause. This, too, was in that same fateful year, 1937. Unable to find Chinese movie actresses with good enough Japanese to star in these celluloid visions of the New Asia, Amakasu decided that Yamaguchi

Yoshiko would be ideal to play the roles of young Chinese women who fell in love with heroic Japanese soldiers. Henceforth, she would be known only as Li Xianglan, or Ri Koran, and her identity as Yamaguchi Yoshiko would have to remain a well-protected secret. Even as Japanese troops were going on a brutal rampage through China, leaving hundreds of thousands of dead in their wake, a Ri Koran boom of pseudo-Chinese exoticism was sweeping across the home front. Young women in Tokyo cafés wanted to look like Ri Koran. Her story, too, was a fiction wrapped in a fiction inside a fiction.

The two Yoshikos, the young exotic actress and her "elder brother," one a Japanese woman pretending to be a Chinese collaborator, and one a Manchu, educated in Japan, donning a Japanese uniform to fight the Chinese Nationalists, were both embodiments of sentimental propaganda designed to endorse a brutal form of imperialism. They embodied something else, too, something more perverse. As objects of an erotic fetish, they offered female impersonations of the exotic East dominated by masculine Japanese conquerors. The exact nature of their many affairs with Japanese soldiers, policemen, politicians, studio bosses, and movie stars cannot not be known with any certainty, but they aroused a great deal of fantasy of power and submission, fantasies to which they themselves were hardly immune.

Relations between the two women soured after a while. Ri Koran claims that she couldn't keep up with Yoshiko's pace, rising in the late afternoon and carousing all night. She was warned by her Chinese godfather, as well as her various Japanese minders, to stay away from this unsuitable companion. Despite her carefully cultivated air of youthful naïveté, Ri Koran could be quite calculating. "I came to realize," she writes in her memoir about her older friend, "that her life as Commander Jin was all washed up." Gone were the glory days of being the Oriental Mata Hari, or Asia's Joan of Arc: "She had been rejected by the Japanese military and the Manchukuo army. Even the right-wing continental *ronin* wanted nothing more to do with her." Perhaps inevitably, there was also a man involved.

One of Ri Koran's Japanese minders was Lieutenant Yamaga Toru, who first appeared in this story as Yoshiko's suitor in Matsumoto in the 1920s. It was their aborted affair that prompted her to say that she wished she were a man. Yamaga was yet another Japanese China enthusiast who fetched up in Manchukuo in search of adventure. As a frequent guest at the Yamaguchi family home, he had known Ri Koran since she was a girl. A genial, womanizing bon vivant, he "went native," speaking fluent Chinese, having affairs with Chinese actresses, getting addicted to Chinese opium, and on occasion deploring the way Chinese were treated by their Japanese masters. When he wasn't dressed in white sharkskin suits, he wore silk Chinese robes. He went by the Chinese name of Wang Jiaheng.

Yamaga/Wang was not just a Sinophile but an insider in the Manchukuo military establishment, at least for some time, until his Chinese affectations raised suspicions of disloyalty. His job was to spy on Chinese cultural figures as an undercover agent for the Japanese secret service, a job for which he was perfectly suited. It was he who suggested Ri Koran to Amakasu as the ideal vehicle for Japanese movie propaganda. Ri always swore that her relations with Yamaga were entirely chaste.

There is no proof that Yamaga was in fact one of Ri's many lovers, but Yoshiko, who had resumed a stormy affair with him in Beijing, certainly thought he was. In a fit of jealousy, she denounced him as a double agent to the Kempeitai, the Japanese military police, widely feared as ferocious torturers. The Kempeitai didn't believe her at first. But after being sent back to Japan in 1943, Yamaga was arrested as a traitor. Perhaps Yoshiko spread more malicious rumors, or perhaps one of his jealous Chinese mistresses did. Ri Koran saw him once more after the war, when he suddenly appeared at her apartment in Tokyo asking her for money. She could barely recognize the old dandy. He now looked haggard, unshaven, dressed in rags. Not long after that, he tied himself to a pine tree, together with his new young wife. They took a heavy dose of sleeping pills. Their bodies were found some days later, ravaged by mountain dogs. One of the last things he said to Ri Koran in Tokyo was: "The vengeance of Chinese women is a terrible thing."

While fighting for the affections of Lieutenant Yamaga, Yoshiko almost came to a sticky end herself. Her own account is soaked in melodrama. She was friendly with a Madame Wang, sister of the Manchu warlord Su Bingwen, the man Yoshiko was supposed to negotiate with after parachuting into his Inner Mongolian redoubt. Madame Wang had just ended her relationship with a member of the anti-Japanese resistance. Tianjin was a dangerous place in those days, with "terrorists" and Japanese agents lurking on every street corner. Wang was savagely attacked by members of her former lover's resistance group. She knew too much and had to be silenced.

When Yoshiko heard that her friend was dying in a hospital in Tianjin, she rushed to her side. As she was stroking the dying woman's hand in her hospital room, three masked "Chinese bandits" suddenly burst in wielding axes. Yoshiko tried to fight them off. Since there were three of them, and she was unarmed, there was not much she could do. The ring finger on her left hand was almost severed, and she received a hard blow to the back of her head. Wang's skull, meanwhile, was crushed and her pillow was soaked in blood.

Japanese newspapers, always keen to report on the latest Kawashima Yoshiko scandal, announced her tragic end in a fight to the death with Chinese bandits. In fact, as she writes in her memoir, she miraculously survived the ordeal and vowed to dedicate the rest of her precious life with renewed energy to "the building of a greater Asia." Fiction or truth? Who knows? Yoshiko's story was getting stranger and stranger, but not quite so strange as the Japanese newspaper reports from Nanjing just a few months earlier, when the massacre was in full flow. The *Asahi Shimbun* reported on December 21, 1937, "At first the [Chinese] would hide themselves in the shadows every time they saw a Japanese. But soon they became friendly with Japanese soldiers and even offered their services with smiles on their faces."

And here, the advertising copy for a magazine attached to the same newspaper two days earlier: "All is bright and cheerful in northern China. And soon after Shanghai, Nanjing fell into our hands! Our relations with China will get deeper all the while. We Japanese must realize the need to better understand China and the Chinese people from now on."

Eight

THE ENDGAME

̄o͞o̅o̅

1: Westerbork

The Nazi police had a word for their civilian helpers: V-Mann, short for *Vertrauensmann*, "trusted person." Friedrich Weinreb gives a succinct description of a V-mann in his memoir. To be a V-mann, he writes, "is to be a provocateur, a police spy, a snitch." He knew a person like that who had infiltrated a resistance group to betray its members to the Gestapo. The odd thing, according to Weinreb, was that this V-mann "managed to continue his game for so long, and that no one had warned about him sooner."

Fritz Koch, the SD agent who arrested Weinreb twice, called him "an excellent V-mann." He "betrayed many families, I can't remember how many. . . . He told us everything, and really did his best. He did all this to protect his own family and himself."

Koch said this after the war. Depending on the words of a former Nazi officer would be foolish. But there are other reports of Weinreb's behavior in 1943—not only from Nazis, but also from their victims—that confirm Koch's statement. The question is when exactly Weinreb became a V-mann. Claims that he was already in touch with the SD office in Villa Windekind before he was arrested the first time have never been proven. Accounts of what happened after his second arrest on January 19, 1943, when he was held at the Orange Hotel prison in Scheveningen, could not be more conflicting.

Weinreb himself goes on at great length and in considerable detail about how he was tortured. He tried to convince Koch of the truth, that he, Weinreb, had made everything up, that his list had been a fantasy to give his fellow Jews hope, and that there was no General von Schumann, or indeed any other German officer who supported his bogus plan. Koch wouldn't believe him. He was convinced there had to be a conspiracy rooted somewhere in the German army, and the truth would have to be thrashed out of Weinreb. Koch discreetly left the interrogation room when the rough stuff started. He was squeamish about that sort of thing. Weinreb was kicked, stomped on, and punched in the face, until he could barely walk or sit up straight. One of his torturers was a German brute with a glass eye named Lemcke. But the Dutch SD men were even more vicious than the Germans. This went on for days, perhaps even weeks.

Weinreb's insistence that he was simply a brilliant fantasizer still failed to convince his interrogators. Perhaps the notion that he had been duped was too hurtful to Koch's professional pride. And so, the thrashing and stomping continued. Weinreb consoled himself with the thought that "they wouldn't be allowed to kick me to death, because then they would lose their conspiracy. Koch first needs to get to the source of the supposed plot."

As usual in Weinreb's stories, he can't refrain from commenting on how much he was admired, even as a torture victim. "Koch hissed: That man is unbreakable. He must have been trained well. He is much more dangerous than we thought. I wonder whether he really is a Jew. That could be another disguise."

Who knows if Koch ever said such a thing? If Weinreb really was tortured, anything he might have said should not be judged harshly.

None of us can know how long we would stand extreme physical pain. But Weinreb claims to have prevailed. The question is whether he was ever put to the test.

A Dutch collaborator named Krijna Peeren, who worked for the SD, filling in as Koch's secretary, claimed after the war to have been present during Weinreb's interrogations. He had seemed nervous and fidgety, but Peeren maintained that Weinreb was never physically harmed. He spoke nonstop, she said, regaling the SD men with stories. She noticed how he mentioned the names of Jews and certain addresses, as though inadvertently, so as not to leave the impression that he was a snitch.

Again, maybe not the most reliable witness. About certain events, however, while Weinreb was in prison, there is no doubt. Several people who had been in touch with him to distribute funds and ration coupons to Jews in hiding were swiftly arrested, as were the men who introduced him to the petty criminal who pretended to be his imaginary associate, the aristocratic Six.

Then there was the notorious Reinkenstraat raid in The Hague, where twenty-four Jews were picked up while Weinreb was in prison. Some of them had paid money to be on Weinreb's list. They were concealed in an apartment by a Eurasian nurse named Sarah Wahlbeem, a woman of great courage who never turned down a request for help. Soon, there were too many people cooped up in the apartment to be safe. Some slept on the floor, some in the bathtub. They had to keep quiet at all times, tiptoeing around in their socks. Even flushing the toilet might draw unwelcome attention from the neighbors. Then, one night in March, the SD, led by Fritz Koch, came banging on the door and arrested them all. Wahlbeem survived her ordeal in prison, but she was so badly tortured that her health never recovered. All the people she had hidden were gassed at the Polish death camp Sobibór. The youngest was a six-month-old baby. Weinreb always denied that he had anything to do with the raid. Koch insisted that it was Weinreb who told him where the Jews were hidden. He added, by way of explanation, that Weinreb's assistance in this and other matters ensured that Weinreb and his family would be spared from being sent to Poland themselves.

We know that Weinreb's memoir cannot be trusted. But it contains detailed descriptions that are of interest—too detailed, in fact, for his self-serving stories go on and on, until his voice begins to grate. But some of the stories might be true and reveal more about Weinreb than he may have intended, especially when it comes to his complicated feelings about being Jewish. There is the bizarre story of a cellmate named Schellevis, an anxious young Jew who trembled all the time, as though constantly anticipating a beating. Schellevis had been arrested at random in Amsterdam by a German who took him home and treated him as his pet dog. The young man was ordered to bark, walk on all fours, and lick up leftovers from his bowl. When there were guests, large men in SS or Dutch police uniforms, he would crawl under the table, so people could use him as a footstool. What astonished Schellevis was the fact that everyone behaved as though having a human dog was perfectly normal.

Another cellmate was a working-class Amsterdam Jew named Blik. He knew all about Weinreb, and said he never trusted his so-called lists. How could the Germans possibly have believed such an unlikely tale? And now the great Weinreb himself was in prison, well, well. . . . No, this business was clearly fishy from the start.

Weinreb was deeply offended. There, he thought, was "the true voice of the people." They were nice to his face, when there was money to be made, but now they were only too happy to see his downfall: "So that's who I was doing it all for, risking the lives of my own family, my own grandfather. For these merchants, these sly creatures. And now they're pleased they were right, laughing at my fate."

Both stories are believable.

In May, Koch decided he'd had enough of Weinreb. His usefulness to the SD had been exhausted. Or in Weinreb's own telling, his tormentors had failed to get him to change his story, and they simply gave up.

In any case, he was sent to Westerbork with an S attached to his name, S for *Strafe*, or punishment, meaning that he would be treated as the lowest of the low, and his swift transit to Auschwitz or Sobibór was assured.

Westerbork was constructed in 1939 as a camp for German Jewish refugees—up to fifty thousand Jews had already crossed the border since 1933. It is in one of the bleakest parts of the Netherlands, cold and damp and always exposed to strong winds, which covered the camp in dirt from the soggy moors. Rain turned the primitive tracks between the flimsy wooden huts into seas of mud. The main strip was dubbed the Boulevard of Misery by the inmates. In summer, swarms of flies got into everything: food, eyes, noses, beds, water supplies, open sores.

Built to contain less than one thousand refugees, the camp was overwhelmed by tens of thousands of Dutch Jews in the summer of 1942. There wasn't nearly enough room to house them all. Jews rounded up in Amsterdam, The Hague, and elsewhere arrived in packed trains that ran in and out of the camp, announcing arrivals and departures with a shrill steam whistle. Hungry, bewildered, and filthy, the prisoners, some of them picked up at night and still in their pajamas, would be shoved around by Dutch military policemen, German "Green Police" (green because of the color of their uniforms), and Jewish camp police selected to keep a rough order among their fellow inmates.

Westerbork was a desolate, squalid place, and yet the people sent there for days, weeks, months, and sometimes years prayed for a chance to stay just a little bit longer. Even though they may not have known precisely what awaited them in Poland, they knew enough to be in a constant state of terror. Transports to the east, in ordinary third-class carriages at first, then in cattle cars, would leave like clockwork on Tuesday mornings, after the lists of deportees, commonly known as "transport material," had been announced the night before. Every transport had to contain up to a thousand people of all ages, including the sick and the infirm.

Always there were lists, and more lists, to queue up for, sign off on, pay to be exempted from, and pay to be included on—that is, if one still had any cash after men from the Nazi bank had robbed the prisoners of all their assets. There was the so-called Palestina List, for Zionist Jews who might be allowed to go to Palestine in exchange for German prisoners. None made it to Palestine. Most ended up in Poland, or Bergen-Belsen, the camp where Anne Frank, who passed through Westerbork, would die of typhoid. There was the Calmeyer List, named after the German lawyer Hans Georg Calmeyer, who determined whether someone was wholly, half, or only a quarter Jewish. And then there were the Weinreb lists, which reached into the confines of Westerbork. While they lasted, some people still had a chance that their deportations would at least be delayed. Most people on the lists ended up being murdered anyway.

Presiding over Westerbork as the absolute ruler of his little fiefdom was the camp commandant, Albert Konrad Gemmeker. Always impeccably turned out, Gemmeker, a minor Gestapo officer before the war, liked to think of himself as a gentleman, who knew how to take care of "my Jews." Handsome, in the affected way of a matinee idol in German operettas, he rarely raised his voice, smiled often, and took pleasure in attending entertainments by his Jews, some of whom had been major stars in prewar German and Dutch theaters and concert halls. Some of Berlin's finest comedians and revue artistes passed through the camp, as did leading musicians of the Amsterdam Concertgebouw Orchestra. A special gala night was organized, with music and stage performances, to celebrate the forty-thousandth Jew dispatched to Poland.

Gemmeker prided himself on running a tight ship. Maximum efficiency and a minimum of fuss were his aims, as he stuffed up to one hundred thousand Jews onto the eastbound trains. In a more lethal way, Westerbork was as phony and fantastical an enterprise as the perfect multiracial puppet state of Manchukuo. For a quasi-normality marked this last stop before mass death, which was of course not called mass death, but *Arbeitseinsatz*, literally labor assignment. Jews were supposed to be put to work in Poland. There were football matches in Westerbork, concerts, excellent dental care, factory workshops, a post office, schools, a yeshiva, and even a synagogue. Etty Hillesum, whose diary of Westerbork would become famous, and who met Weinreb in the camp and rather liked him, wrote in her letters that quite a few teenage girls were secretly in love with Gemmeker, the smiling "gentleman-criminal." Hillesum left on a transport in September 1943. Children were singing as they boarded the train, while waving goodbye to family and friends, almost all of whom would soon follow. Hillesum was murdered in Auschwitz two months later.

Like most people with unlimited power over other human beings, Gemmeker could be capricious. But his capriciousness was typical of the peculiar make-believe that was so much a part of Nazi mass murder. He vaunted his love of small children. One newborn baby, named Machiel, was barely alive when his mother was pushed onto a cattle train and forced to leave her child behind. Gemmeker asked a famous Jewish pediatrician named Simon van Creveld to do everything he could to revive him. An incubator was especially ordered from Groningen. Gemmeker visited the boy every day, to make sure he was all right. He offered his own best Hennessy brandy for a medical prescription Dr. Van Creveld had devised. Finally, to everyone's relief, the infant began to gain strength. When he weighed six pounds, Gemmeker decided that little Machiel was now ready for the labor assignment. He was sent to Auschwitz on the next transport. Reading about Machiel's case, I thought Dr. Van Creveld's name sounded familiar. Then I realized he had been a close friend of my grandfather, a fellow pediatrician, giving this grotesque little story a chilling sense of proximity.

Weinreb was lucky after he arrived at Westerbork as an S prisoner. That he was greeted as a hero by other prisoners, as he claims, is doubtful.

Many distrusted him after the first list was abolished by the Germans—
geplatzt was the term for this, meaning something that "bursts," like a
bubble. Children in the camp sang a song that went:

Who is Weinreb, Weinreb is a Schweinrebb
Weinreb is a friend of the rulers in The Hague
Who is Weinreb, Weinreb is a Schweinrebb
Weinreb helps the Jews from Portugal to Prague

Luckily, Weinreb's wife, Esther, had secured a job in the camp. Having a job, even a fake job with a title, was vital, for it meant a temporary
reprieve from deportation. Everyone who was physically able would give
anything for a job, providing opportunities for corruption of all kinds.
Esther had good contacts among the power brokers at Westerbork and
managed to get her husband transferred from the punishment hut to the
hospital, allowing him to drop his S status. Medical care at Westerbork
was apparently superb, for some of the best Dutch and German doctors
were prisoners there, including a Dr. Spanier, who also treated Gemmeker. (They were both from Düsseldorf. Dr. Spanier survived the war and
continued to treat Gemmeker in their hometown after the former commandant was released from prison.) Providing medical care to people
destined for murder was yet another aspect of Nazi make-believe at
Westerbork. Weinreb declared that the food in the hospital barrack was
delicious.

Once he was able to move out of the hospital, Weinreb became quite
a shrewd observer of his fellow inmates. That he and his wife and children were not yet sent to Poland might have been due to Esther's contacts; drawing up the lists of deportees, like all other distasteful jobs, had
to be done by prisoners themselves. This created hostile hierarchies in the
camp that Weinreb, with his touchy social antennae, was well placed to
describe. At the top of the pecking order was the German Jewish elite,
most of whom had been in the camp since 1939. They were, in Weinreb's

eyes, rather like the Jewish Council, haughty and drunk on their limited power. In turn, the German Jews looked down on the eastern European and Dutch working-class Jews, who had no *Kultur*. But at least some of the poorer ones had a knowledge of Jewish religion. Educated Dutch Jews had neither a sense of tradition, nor the sophistication, in German eyes, of their brethren across the border. In some ways, a man like Dr. Spanier probably felt closer to the camp commandant than to a Yiddish-speaking Amsterdam Jew who had made a living selling pickles at the Sunday market.

Weinreb's Jewish social status was hard to classify. He was an *Ostjude*, but his sympathies probably lay more with the German than with the Dutch Jews. After all, he thought of himself as a man of high culture. His assessment of the camp elite does not seem unfair: "The Germans felt comfortable with people they could understand, who knew every side of the camp, who had built the administration and managed it. As people, the Germans were no better or worse than the Dutch. They just expressed themselves differently." This didn't stop the Dutch Jews from regarding the German Jews as arrogant and typically German disciplinarians.

Weinreb wouldn't be Weinreb if he didn't soon establish cordial relations with the commandant himself, at least in his own recollection. He might indeed have seen him once or twice. Gemmeker declared after the war that he had heard the name, but he had no memory of ever having had an extensive conversation with Weinreb. That Weinreb met Gemmeker in June 1943 is possible. For that is when one of Koch's henchmen, a Dutch collaborator named Bolland, accompanied by Lemcke, the German brute with a glass eye, appeared at the camp to take Weinreb back to The Hague. According to Weinreb, the transaction took place in Gemmeker's office. The commandant introduced himself with great courtesy, shook hands with his prisoner, and said: "So you are Weinreb, the famous Weinreb."

This might conceivably have happened, even though Gemmeker was not in the habit of speaking directly to any Jews, except to his doctor or possibly some famous German actors or musicians. Still, Weinreb was soon back at the Orange Hotel in Scheveningen, leaving his wife and three children behind in Westerbork as hostages (one son, David, had died of pneumonia despite the doctors' best efforts). Back in his old cell, Weinreb expected the worst. He thought he might be executed in the dunes outside the prison walls. Why else call him back from Westerbork?

Soon, however, he would be writing a letter to his wife about how well he was being treated in prison. He was given special meals, entirely to his liking. "Eating may not be the most important thing in life," he wrote, "but having a good solid meal is not to be despised. Especially in these days. I do miss sweet things. But that will have to wait."

A few months later, in November, Esther and the children were released from Westerbork, and the family moved into a new house, well furnished, luxurious even, in the center of The Hague. They could come and go as they pleased; they didn't even have to wear the dreaded yellow star. What could possibly explain this miraculous transformation, unheard of in an occupied country where more than 70 percent of the Jewish population never returned from the camps? Again, the stories diverge widely. What happened is not just a matter of interpretation, but a question of whom one chooses to believe: Weinreb, or pretty much everyone else.

Weinreb's version is long, detailed, and bizarre. This does not necessarily make it unbelievable. Much of what occurred at the time was bizarre. He begins with a description of his train ride from Westerbork to The Hague with Bolland and Lemcke. Bolland was one of those corrupt Dutch goons who would have been a common criminal if he hadn't been employed by the Germans. Weinreb was struck by a novel note of politesse, even friendliness in his SD minders. Gone was the barking arrogance. They even bought their own train tickets, instead of ordering some hapless railway clerk to hand them over. Weinreb put this down to the worsening prospects of Germany winning the war. "Stalingrad lay between January and now," he wrote, and "there was fighting in Sicily. The Russians were gaining ground, and the bombings in Germany had become more frequent and destructive." Bolland hinted at new schemes that would enable Weinreb to make up for having led the SD up the garden path. What menace lurked under the surface of affability?

Koch's proposal was this: Weinreb was obviously a trusted figure in a vast Jewish network of underground resistance. He had the knowledge, and the superior intelligence, to infiltrate this network, deliver the ring-leaders to the SD, and soon there would be no more Jews left to round up. In exchange, Weinreb and his family would be exempted from trans-ports to Poland. They would be allowed to survive in the relative safety of Theresienstadt, the camp in Czechoslovakia where privileged Jews were sent (many of them to be killed in Auschwitz anyway). Now, of course, if Weinreb failed to come up with the goods, he and his family would go straight to Poland. "Don't forget," Koch said, "that you are all Jews!"

Weinreb knew perfectly well that there was no such Jewish resistance network, and the scheme was absurd, but he decided to play for time until he could devise an alternative scheme. After Stalingrad, Germans appeared to be more willing to make deals. There was talk of prisoner exchanges, mostly bogus. One proposal was to allow Jews to go to South America, in exchange for Germans held in prisons there. This gave Wein-reb the idea for an intricate scheme to dupe the Germans, as well as Jews, but all for a good cause. He conjured up the idea, which Nazis wouldn't find at all hard to believe, of vast riches of money and diamonds that re-mained hidden in Jewish hands. A second list would be drawn up that promised rich Jews who were still in hiding an escape to South America. They would surely be glad to hand over all their wealth to the SD in exchange for their lives. The sponsor of this ruse would not be an imag-inary German general this time, but a Wehrmacht general who actually existed, named von Kleist. This would reassure the rich Jews of the plan's bona fides, even though the general himself would be kept in the dark. Since there was no way that the SD could organize safe passage to South America, the rich Jews would in fact be sent to Theresienstadt. Weinreb was very insistent on this last point. He wanted to do the right thing.

Koch was deeply impressed. "What brilliance!" he thought. "How clever you are. What a pity you're a Jew. Man, are you really Jewish?" The SD was greedy, however. They demanded ten thousand Jews.

To facilitate his second list and show potential takers that he had the trust of the German authorities, Weinreb was given an office in Westerbork. He could enter and leave the camp whenever he felt like it. Even though many Jews now preferred to dodge Weinreb as a fraud, other prisoners were so desperate to avoid being deported that they still wanted to sign up. This did nothing to help them in end, since the killing machine ground on relentlessly, list or no list. But it didn't hurt them either. And Weinreb was convinced that Jews still in hiding would not be foolish enough to emerge in the open just to be on his list.

One of Weinreb's claims after the war was that he managed to manipulate Gemmeker into stopping transports to Auschwitz in December. Since he was supposedly on amicable terms with the commandant, he kept him informed on the progress of his list. Gemmeker needed a thousand people to make up enough "transport material" for one load. But Weinreb kept stalling him. Before he could complete his list of exemptions, he needed confirmation from the SD in The Hague. And this confirmation kept being delayed. Gemmeker had to send the trains back empty.

That trains to Auschwitz stopped running for a few weeks in December is true, but not for the reason given by Weinreb. There had been an outbreak of polio among the children at Westerbork. The camp was quarantined for a time, until the death trains could resume their journeys east with lethal and monotonous regularity.

What may have transpired in The Hague and Westerbork in the summer of 1943 was less heroic than Weinreb's account, and much more sordid. Again, we must not forget that Weinreb and his family were always in mortal danger. And little can be proven beyond any doubt. But the following story was pieced together in the careful analysis of Weinreb's war record by the National Institute for War Documentation (RIOD). He was never brought back to The Hague to infiltrate a nonexisting Jewish resistance network. It was more prosaic than that. Bolland, the Dutch SD helper, had just returned from a stint with the SS in Italy, where he injured himself by falling off a tank. His new assignment was to find the last Jews still in hiding. Since Weinreb had proven his use as a V-mann before, the SD thought he might be good for one more job. There was indeed a second list, but the aim was not so much to steal diamonds and cash as to flush out any remaining Jews from their hiding places.

But first Weinreb had to prove his worth in another way. Bolland, Lemcke, and Koch all made statements after the war about the nature of Weinreb's assistance. Jewish prisoners were put in his cell, where he would gain their confidence by posing as a resistance man. He would pass on whatever he found out to the SD agents, who used the information when they interrogated the prisoners. The RIOD report concludes that at least twenty-two people lost their lives because of Weinreb's spying. One case might serve as a grim illustration. A medical doctor named Joseph Kalker was arrested in July with other Jews in hiding. His wife, who survived the war, testified that he was tortured horribly but somehow managed to hang on without revealing any names or addresses. Dr. Kalker then spent two or three days in Weinreb's cell. Immediately after that, several people who had hidden Kalker and provided Jews with food and money were arrested. Weinreb later claimed that Kalker seemed a little confused, perhaps even drunk, when he arrived in his cell. The doctor even threatened to kill Weinreb. But in a letter from prison to his wife, Esther, Weinreb mentions Kalker without saying anything about him appearing to be drunk or confused. In fact, the threat to kill Weinreb came only after the arrests of Kalker's former benefactors, which suggests that he knew precisely who had betrayed them. Kalker himself could no longer testify because he died in Auschwitz that same year.

Bolland declared after the war that he had "no doubt Weinreb had been used by the SD to pump fellow prisoners for information. I can state with absolute certainty that this produced results for the SD. I am also sure that Weinreb betrayed many Jews who were in hiding." Again, Bolland was a thug. But the writers of the RIOD report were convinced that he was telling the truth.

Weinreb had another task to perform for the SD. Through his wife, who was born in Antwerp, Weinreb knew people in the Belgian Jewish community. Koch sent him on several trips to Antwerp with another Dutch SD collaborator, a man named Krom. The idea was to test whether a second Weinreb list would work in Belgium. Since Weinreb was unknown in that country, there would be less reason for suspicion, and Jews might be easier to dislodge from their hiding places. In fact, there were few Jews left in Antwerp. Most of them had already been caught. But Weinreb promised the SD diamonds and money (in his version of the story), so he had to find a way of getting some cash to convince the Germans he was on the case. Then follows a tale so implausible that it's hard to see how it could have convinced anyone.

While the SD men waited outside, Weinreb went off to look for Mendel Landau, a wealthy relative of his wife who lived in one of Antwerp's grand mansions. The place still looked the same, richly decorated and furnished with superb Persian carpets. But Landau had long gone. The house was now an office for the German navy. Weinreb was ushered inside by a polite German officer. When Weinreb asked about Landau's whereabouts, the officer understood the situation instantly and said how sorry he was for the way his country had been treating the Jews. Germany was bound to lose the war anyway. Might there be some way he could be of help? Weinreb asked him for some money. Of course, no problem, said the noble officer, and he handed Weinreb a wad of ten thousand Belgian francs. "It was like a fairy tale," Weinreb writes in his memoir. The SD men were enormously impressed by the way Weinreb had managed to get money off rich Jews so easily.

Other adventures on that trip are fondly recalled: Weinreb was able to persuade the Brussels SD to release a distinguished Jewish doctor, and there were pleasant encounters with the Flemish police, who had such fine manners, unlike their coarser Dutch colleagues. About two hundred Belgian Jews had paid five hundred francs each to be on Weinreb's second list. But apart from supposedly receiving the ten thousand francs from a friendly naval officer, nothing much else had been achieved. Weinreb was clearly still playing for time.

There was more, however. Several people claimed they saw Weinreb take part in a German raid on a Jewish hiding place in Belgium. If true, this was one of the worst examples of Weinreb's treachery. The raid occurred on October 16. It had been well prepared by Krom, the Dutch SD agent. He had convinced a Dutch resistance group that he was a sympathetic policeman wholly on their side. They revealed their smuggling operation of Jewish fugitives into Belgium. Krom knew about a Jewish woman, Nanny Marie Vieyra, and her two small children, who were hiding in a suburb of Antwerp. Her husband was already in Westerbork. Krom was a frequent visitor to Nanny Vieyra's hideout, to find out where other Jews were concealed, and to extort money from her. He was absent when the Vieyras were arrested. The party consisted of Bolland, Lemcke, and Koch, dressed in a green loden winter coat, and Weinreb, who was told to guard the family while the other three ransacked the house for valuables. Mrs. Vieyra's fur coat was all they could find. There were several eyewitnesses, including the son of the owner of the house, and a doctor who was looking after one of the Vieyra children. Both remembered seeing Weinreb, swaggering about as though he were a Gestapo officer himself. The son even recalled seeing him brandishing a gun. Bolland confirmed this. The doctor was not sure about the gun. But if ever there was an example of the hunted man identifying with the hunters, this was it.

This trip was a "success" for another reason. While the Vieyra family was sent to Westerbork, where they were reunited with Anthony Vieyra, the father, and quickly deported to Auschwitz, Weinreb traveled to Brussels. He had managed to secure a meeting with the wife of Franz Fischer, an SS officer in Holland whose zeal as a Jew-baiter earned him the nickname *Judenfischer*. Why she should have felt any sympathy for Weinreb is not explained, but she apparently prevailed upon her husband to release Weinreb's family from Westerbork. A possible reason for this unusual act of "generosity" is that Weinreb deserved a favor in exchange for his services to the SD.

However, if he wanted his family to survive, Weinreb still had to prove to the Germans that his second list would bear the desired fruit. This was a problem. Since Weinreb was no longer trusted, Jews in hiding refused to come out into the open to sign on to his list. The only place where people still lined up for this dubious privilege was Westerbork, but even as many were clinging to Weinreb's list as their last hope, his reputation in the camp was going from bad to worse. Seeing his family leaving the camp with him was the last straw. This confirmed that he had to be a traitor.

Weinreb acknowledges this ill feeling in his memoir, but he puts it down to jealousy, or to Dutch Jewish prejudice against a Jew born in Poland. He quotes a man in the camp who told him: "There are Dutch Jews who can't stand German Jews, but they hate the Polish Jews even more. And they see you as a Polish Jew. They think all Polish Jews are swindlers and cheats. They would be quite prepared to beat you to death."

Again, whether or not this story is true, Weinreb put his finger on a sore spot. Like any successful fraudster, he had a sharp eye for human weakness. And he consoled himself with delusion and self-congratulation. Managing to get Gemmeker to stop the trains to Auschwitz was terrific. Keeping the SD at bay with promises of vast riches to be plundered was brilliant. Even Koch himself had called Weinreb's operations in Belgium "a masterpiece." And he still had true friends at Westerbork too, who thanked him "with tears in their eyes and called me a magician." He had to keep going, even if his list was to save just a few lives. "I am convinced that I *have* to resist," he wrote. "That is my work of art. Only someone who lives in the world of our enemy, in the enemy's reality, would call my work of art a lie or a fraud. For such a person feels that I am an enemy of his world."

This is the clearest key to understanding Weinreb. He was proud of having created an alternative reality, like an artist. But even an artist should be able to distinguish his own fictions from the world in which he lives. A work of art can reflect the real world, comment on it, and find an expression for it, but to believe that it *is* the real world is a categorical error with often dangerous consequences.

Weinreb may have sensed this himself on occasion. For all his lies, Weinreb can be an astute reporter on his own states of mind, and a certain kind of truth is revealed. He knew his second list was going to burst at any moment. His SD masters in The Hague were getting impatient. Then, one day in December, just when he supposedly stopped the train from going to Auschwitz by convincing Gemmeker that his list still needed to be approved by higher authorities, Weinreb was wandering along the Boulevard of Misery in Westerbork: "I feel dizzy. I can't believe all this is true. The fraud has reached such a scale that I don't dare to think about it. I will just have to get used to living as though everything about my deception is real. But that is impossible too. I am shivering. I feel as if I have a fever."

2: Stockholm

Weinreb was not the only one to notice a change of mood after the German disaster at Stalingrad in the summer of 1943. The expectation that

Germany might lose the war had an effect everywhere, not least in neutral Sweden. Staying out of the war, while aiding Nazi Germany, came at a price, which began to make some Swedish officials distinctly nervous.

The Swedish coalition government of liberals, leftists, and conservatives, led by a Social Democrat prime minister, was not exactly pro-Nazi. But many Swedish politicians and businessmen were more afraid of the Soviet Union than of Hitler's Germany. So a deal had been struck early on: Sweden would remain neutral while agreeing to export iron ore to Germany and allow unarmed German troops to travel through Sweden to and from occupied Norway. In 1941, Sweden broke the rules of neutrality by extending this privilege to armed German soldiers. And Swedish borders were closed to Jews who tried to escape from Germany and neighboring Scandinavian countries until the end of 1942, which was precisely when things were no longer going Germany's way.

Not everyone in Sweden was happy with their country's tilt toward the Third Reich. Carefully guarding its formal neutrality, the government tried to make sure that public opinion would not turn against Germany. Articles about Nazi crimes—"atrocity propaganda"—were suppressed. Left-wing newspapers that printed stories about torture and murder by the Germans in Norway were confiscated. A book published in the fall of 1942, *Poland's Martyrdom* (*Polens martyrium*), describing in detail the horrors inflicted on that country, was also impounded.

The ghastly facts about Poland were reported by some brave Swedish businessmen based in Warsaw. Appalled by what they saw, they cooperated with the Polish resistance, smuggling money in and information out. The Germans arrested seven of them as spies in the summer of 1942. Four were sentenced to death.

Felix Kersten enters the scene once more. He claims to have been asked for help by a Berlin lawyer named Carl Langbehn, who had volunteered to defend the "Warsaw Swedes" in court. Langbehn was one of Kersten's patients. Extremely wealthy, conservative, and a Nazi party member since 1933, Langbehn became Himmler's friend in the mid-1930s; their daughters were classmates in Berlin. Despite his friendship with the SS chief, Langbehn was disturbed by the brutality of the Nazi regime. Oscillating between Himmler's court and dissident figures in the Nazi bureaucracy and the armed forces, Langbehn made several attempts in the last years of the war to see whether the British or the Americans might be persuaded to negotiate a favorable peace. Himmler knew about these efforts but never committed himself. Langbehn would pay for this later.

After having approached Kersten about the Warsaw Swedes, Langbehn withdrew from the case. The other person interested in the Swedes was Walter Schellenberg, Himmler's crafty chief of intelligence. He was anxious to keep the Swedish government happy, partly to safeguard the smooth flow of iron ore, and partly because he, too, like Langbehn, was already thinking of ways to arrange a peace deal with the Allies that would be to Germany's, Himmler's, and his own advantage. Kersten's claim that Schellenberg, a committed SS officer since 1933, was "sincerely opposed to the Nazi system," seems fanciful, but he was a survivor, not a fanatic.

Kersten took part in some of these efforts, as a major player in his own account, as a mere go-between in the view of others like Schellenberg. Kersten had his own reasons for getting involved. He needed to establish a base in Sweden, to ensure his own and his family's safety in the event of a German defeat. So began a new phase in his collaboration. The Swedes needed to distance themselves from the Germans. Kersten needed the Swedes for protection. Schellenberg needed Kersten to furnish introductions. And both men needed Himmler to keep them out of the clutches of other Nazi bosses, such as Ernst Kaltenbrunner, who had succeeded Reinhard Heydrich as the head of the Gestapo. Kaltenbrunner, a brutal Austrian with dueling scars running up his horselike face, was deeply suspicious of smooth international operators like Schellenberg and Kersten, whose influence on Himmler he deplored. Any attempt to make peace with the Allies smacked of "defeatism." Many men were hanged for lesser offenses.

In fact, Kaltenbrunner, too, would gingerly put out feelers for a possible peace deal, in his case with the Soviet Union, hoping to drive a wedge between the Soviets and their Western allies. Himmler, however, loathed Russians almost as much as Jews. If any deal was to be made, it would have to be with the "Anglo-Saxon races," whose bloodlines he could respect. Indeed, he is supposed to have told Kersten that an even greater Aryan race could arise from the mixing of German and Anglo-Saxon blood. But Hitler was adamant to fight to the end, and Himmler was not about to defy him, not yet at any rate.

Kersten played a part in persuading Himmler to save the four Warsaw Swedes from execution. Whether Himmler was persuaded because Kersten's magic hands made his life more tolerable or because he didn't want an unnecessary row with the Swedes is unclear. Either way, the Swedish government was grateful for Kersten's intervention. And Kersten was well rewarded by the employer of the Warsaw Swedes, who paid him 55,000 Swedish kronor for his services. This big boss, Jacob Wallenberg, was another one of those powerful figures in Kersten's life. Head of the biggest bank and various companies in Sweden, Wallenberg was close to some of the Nazi leaders, including Hermann Göring. His bank did business in gold bullion looted by the Nazis. He was pro-German, but like Carl Langbehn he had some contacts with conservative anti-Nazi dissidents in Germany.

When Kersten landed in Stockholm in September 1943, he was received by Christian Günther, the conservative minister of foreign affairs. The minister proposed to Kersten that it was time to make a serious effort to get the Germans to release Scandinavian prisoners from prisons and concentration camps. Kersten in his memoir ascribes this to "Sweden's humanitarian and neutral traditions." Possibly, but if so, why did Sweden close its borders to desperate Jewish refugees before 1942? For once, the more elaborate account of Kersten's gullible French biographer, Joseph Kessel, seems closer to the truth. In Kessel's version of the story, Günther complained about pressure from the Allies to enter the war on their side. He thought this would be a catastrophe for Sweden. What if Stockholm were bombed like Rotterdam or Warsaw? Perhaps a human-itarian gesture would keep the Allies happy. Sweden would try to pry as many people as possible out of the camps, first fellow Scandinavians, and later possibly others too. Then the Swedish Red Cross could bring them to Sweden. Their vice president was Count Folke Bernadotte, a nephew of the Swedish king. He thought Kersten's influence on Himmler might be of some use in this enterprise.

Kersten was more than happy to be an agent for the Swedish govern-ment, in exchange for the right to live and work in Stockholm, but he still had a serious problem. To assure Himmler that he would return to Germany to attend to his stomach pains, Kersten was compelled to leave his wife and children, as well as the ever-faithful Elisabeth Lüben, at Hartzwalde, his country estate in Brandenburg. But he found a way to fix this problem. He needed a safe way to communicate by telephone with his Swedish contacts without the Gestapo listening in. Kersten claimed after the war that a story was concocted with the help of the Finnish embassy. He would be called up for duty in the Finnish army, in effect terminating his massage therapy. But the Finns would let him off if he agreed to treat wounded Finnish soldiers in Sweden. That way he could continue his ministrations to Himmler, while basing his family in Stockholm. Himmler conceded. Astonishingly, Himmler also agreed to a safe private telephone line from Hartzwalde to Stockholm.

Joseph Kessel mentions an even more extraordinary concession: Ker-sten's estate was granted extraterritorial rights. The story of how Kersten managed this is extremely far-fetched, but too entertaining to leave un-mentioned. Since food was strictly rationed in Germany, slaughtering animals for private consumption was absolutely forbidden. Kersten was terrified that Kaltenbrunner's Gestapo would find out that the sausages and pork he consumed in large quantities came from his own pigs. One day in early 1944, Kersten visited Himmler at his office in Berlin carry-ing a large ham. Although not normally a meat eater, because of his care for living creatures, Himmler was happy to accept a slice of the finest German ham. Quite delicious, he exclaimed, but how the hell did Kersten get his hands on so much meat? Kersten told him the truth. Himmler went pale. The Reichsführer SS had broken one of Nazi Germany's tightest regulations. Kersten said Himmler now had a choice: to be arrested for his transgression or keep quiet and grant extraterritorial rights to the Hartzwalde estate. Himmler dropped his head in shame and granted Kersten's wish. A good story, but . . . Himmler may have been a stickler for the rules, but the notion of the head of the SS being arrested for eating illicit ham is ridiculous. This, by the way, is supposed to have occurred around the same time that Himmler proudly announced to an audience of German generals that the "Jewish question" had been "solved uncompromisingly, as was appropriate in view of the struggle in which we are engaged for the life of our nation, for the survival of our blood."

Less absurd, but still quite unrealistic, were Kersten's further maneuvers in Stockholm, as a middleman, or negotiator, depending on whom one believes. Jacob Wallenberg introduced him to a new patient with back problems. His name was Abram Stevens Hewitt, ostensibly an American businessman, described by Kersten as "Roosevelt's special representative in Stockholm." Since Kersten spoke no English, and Hewitt's grasp of German was rudimentary, there may have been a misunderstanding. Hewitt knew a lot of important people in politics and business, but he was in Sweden to gather intelligence for the OSS, the intelligence agency that later became the CIA, and not as the U.S. president's representative. Kersten's familiarity with Himmler and his circle must, however, have been of great interest to Hewitt. Kersten sensed his chance to play the role of an important diplomat.

Hewitt and Kersten discussed possible ways of bringing the terrible war to an end. When the American told his masseur that the Allies were unlikely to make peace with Hitler, Kersten replied that he might be able to arrange an alternative solution. He would talk to Himmler.

Since Himmler feared that Germany and Europe would fall into the hands of the barbaric Russians, he might well be ready to come to an arrangement with the Anglo-Saxons. Maybe Hewitt would like to visit Germany himself? Hewitt declined this offer but supposedly drew up certain conditions for making peace. Hitler's regime had to relinquish power. Occupied countries needed to be liberated. And the Nazi leaders would be tried as war criminals. Kersten took the view that Himmler might be receptive to this, if an exception were made in his case. He diligently wrote the conditions down and, in his version of the story, sent them to Himmler.

There is something preposterous about these "negotiations" between an American spy and a Finnish masseur, neither of whom had any authority to negotiate, let alone decide on any official policy. If Kersten is to be believed, he flew back to Germany and met Himmler at Hochwald, his headquarters near the Russian front. In his journal entry of December 4, 1943 (re-created after the war; the original was supposedly lost), Kersten writes: "This morning I tried to make Himmler realize that it was time for him to come to a decision about my negotiations in Stockholm. . . . I told him: 'No country in Europe is getting anything out of this war; it's time it was stopped.' . . . Himmler replied: 'Ach, don't torment me, give me time. I can't get rid of the Führer, to whom I owe everything.'"

About Himmler's awestruck fear of the Führer there can be no doubt. But Himmler's own diary reveals that he wasn't in Hochwald on that day, but in Berlin, and there is no mention of a meeting with Kersten. In fact, when Schellenberg, who had sounded out Hewitt himself on several occasions, after being introduced by Kersten, tried to get Himmler to consider coming to terms with the Americans, Himmler showed little interest but said he didn't want his masseur to be meddling in any diplomatic overtures.

All this seems quite detached from reality. The Allies had no intention of dealing with Hitler or Himmler. They stuck to their demand for unconditional surrender. And if there were to be war crime trials, Himmler would be the first to be summoned. But it is true that attempts were made, with or without Himmler's knowledge, to see what could be saved from the coming wreckage of the Third Reich. Some of these maneuvers were simply weird. In Operation Modellhut, for example, Schellenberg tried to contact Winston Churchill through the French couturier Coco Chanel, who was living in Paris with her lover, a German military intelligence officer. (She knew Churchill because of her long affair with the Duke of Westminster.) Then there was Himmler's friend, Carl Langbehn, who had been talking to Allen Dulles, an OSS operative in Switzerland, about finding a way to avoid unconditional surrender. Langbehn introduced a man named Johannes Popitz to Himmler, and this former Prussian finance minister suggested that Himmler might stage a coup against the Führer. Schellenberg had made a similar proposition to Himmler before. And Langbehn himself had been on trips to Stockholm to see what kind of peace might be brokered on Himmler's behalf.

Popitz and Langbehn, like Schellenberg, had links with the growing resistance among members of the military elite. These men genuinely sought a way out of Hitler's madhouse and Germany's impending doom. So did Kersten, in his way. After the war, Kersten made it seem as if they were all motivated by a shared hatred of the Third Reich. In most cases, the reasons for resistance were far more complicated. And they help to explain actions that might now strike us as fantastic. When Schellenberg was interrogated after the war, he stated that Hewitt, his interlocutor in Stockholm, "emphasized especially the great danger to Germany that bolshevizing the masses would mean, and considered it essential that the SS should be strengthened as a stabilizing factor inside the country and on the Eastern Front." Until the very end of the war, some Nazis, including Himmler, kept hoping that the Western allies would wake up and realize that their armies were pointed in the wrong direction. They should be fighting shoulder to shoulder with the Germans against the Asiatic hordes.

John H. Waller, a former CIA officer and author of a book about Kersten, writes that it "is likely that the sentiments expressed [purportedly by Hewitt] are essentially those of Schellenberg, not Hewitt." Quite possibly. Even though such sentiments were not absent among the Allies (General George Patton expressed similar ideas after the war), they were not widely shared in Washington or London, which is why efforts to broker a compromised peace in Stockholm, Paris, or Switzerland didn't go anywhere. By the time Himmler expressed an interest in hearing more from Hewitt, the American had already left for the United States. That Himmler still hoped to play a leading role in a post-Hitler Germany is certain. This hope was perhaps encouraged by Swedish conservatives such as Jacob Wallenberg.

What about Kersten himself? He wanted a good life, a grand life, attending to the comforts of people of wealth and power. He probably wasn't all that interested in politics. But he had sympathies and antipathies. His loathing of the Russians was a constant theme. His fear of Bolshevism was real, to do with his background in Estonia and Finland. And his fears were shared by many of his patients, including top Nazis, whom he continued to defend as basically decent men long after the war.

Many dissidents who wanted Hitler gone were indeed decent and brave people: Carl Goerdeler, Ludwig Beck, Hans von Dohnanyi, among others. Most were upper-class conservatives who had served in Hitler's regime as bureaucrats or military officers. They feared for the fate of their country, and in some cases of their class. Kersten mentions Himmler's hatred of monarchs, aristocrats, and upper-class elites. During a short visit to Holland in early 1944, Himmler went on about the Dutch elite's disloyalty to the great Germanic cause and wanted to send several wealthy businessmen to the Dachau concentration camp. Kersten claims that since Himmler was in dire need of another massage, the masseur was able to save them from this terrible fate. His memoir mentions the names of some of the biggest art collectors in Holland. They were not exactly heroes of the resistance; one of them sold pictures to Hermann Göring for a considerable profit. They were certainly of great help to Kersten once the war was over.

On July 20, 1944, when the attempt by German army officers to assassinate Hitler with a bomb failed, the resistance movement quickly fell apart. Himmler regarded the Führer's survival as an act of divine providence, and he vowed to round up the entire "reactionary gang" and kill all of them. The leaders were indeed arrested, tortured, humiliated in a show trial, and suspended from meat hooks. And not just the leaders. Himmler decided the families of some of the leaders should be locked up as well. Among the people killed on Himmler's orders were Johannes Popitz and Himmler's old friend Carl Langbehn. It was as though the Reichsführer SS was ferociously compensating for his failure to stop the attempt on his leader's life. Maybe he was compensating for something a little more than that.

The problem for Himmler was that he was a bit too close to the plot, if only indirectly. A figure like Langbehn knew too much. Himmler had listened to suggestions by Schellenberg and others that Hitler's demise might be helpful. Kersten says he told Himmler that it would have been better if the plot had succeeded (an unlikely story). Kessel writes that Himmler was panicking and told Kersten to destroy all their correspondence from Stockholm (unlikely too). Wilhelm Wulff, who had been introduced to Himmler by Kersten to read his astrology charts, says that Kersten called him in great agitation. He wanted the astrologer to consult the stars to see whether Himmler, and Kersten himself, would now be in danger.

None of these reports are reliable. And yet they throw an interesting light on the crazy house of mirrors that Himmler's court, and the Nazi regime in general, had become. We now know that the Third Reich was never the efficient, well-oiled, bureaucratic machine that many people once thought it was. But the stories from peripheral figures like Kersten and Wulff offer an extraordinary glimpse at what a pit of paranoia and vicious rivalries the regime really was. And these were fought out between men whose grasp on reality had become increasingly slack. Accounts by the astrologer and the masseur may be partly fictional, but the deranged atmosphere they describe rings true.

According to his biographer Peter Longerich, Himmler emerged from the events of July 1944 with more power than before. Hitler sacked generals of the Wehrmacht, from whose ranks many of the plotters came, and put Himmler, a man of very limited military experience (in the sense of fighting armies rather than killing helpless civilians), in charge of the Reserve Army. But this didn't make Himmler feel more secure. The fact that he would ask an astrologer to use his arcane powers to advise him on military strategies is a sign of how unhinged his court had become. Whether he always took Wulff's advice is another matter. The astrologer, like the masseur, was also used to spy on and influence the behavior of others in the top Nazi ranks.

Wulff's remarks after the war need to be taken with as much salt as Kersten's, but he was clearly a sharp observer. Schellenberg, in Wulff's view, knew more about the politics and military strategies of foreign powers than Himmler did. This was no doubt the case. According to Wulff, Schellenberg tried to "prevent or mitigate some of the enormities" perpetrated by the Nazi leaders. Wulff adds: "To what extent he was motivated by humanitarian feelings and to what extent by the desire to furnish himself with an alibi for future use, it is difficult to say." The latter seems more likely. That Kersten "exploited [my] astrological knowledge to make himself more interesting in the eyes of Himmler and Walter Schellenberg" is catty but might also well be true.

The fact is that the Nazi bosses, as they began to sense the end coming, either pushed the thought away in wishful thinking about special weapons, last-minute victories, and superior German fighting spirit or lashed out in more and more murderous policies, trying to bring down as many people as possible with them, while becoming increasingly dependent on quacks, astrologers, doctors, and masseurs who could offer temporary relief with magic charts, magic potions, or magic hands. To keep operating amid this madness was never safe. That Kersten managed to use Himmler's insecurities to persuade him to release some people from the gallows is to his credit. Among them was Karl Seitz, the former socialist mayor of Vienna.

If Kaltenbrunner was already suspicious of Kersten, the July events and Kersten's pleading for the lives of men like Seitz would have made his paranoia worse. In his memoir, Kersten reproduces a letter he received on August 2, 1944, from Schellenberg. In this "secret and confidential" letter, Schellenberg warns Kersten that Kaltenbrunner is gunning for him because of "the Langbehn case." The files in this case, concerning Langbehn's alleged complicity in the July plot, were supposed to prove that Kersten was working with the British secret service. Ever since Kersten left for Sweden and moved his family to Stockholm, Schellenberg claims, the Gestapo had wanted to kill him. He should speak to Himmler, carry a gun, and please destroy this letter immediately. The letter bears no official letterhead. Either Kersten didn't destroy it, or he wrote it himself after the war.

Both Kersten and his biographer Kessel mention another letter from Schellenberg, also dated August 2, which warns him of a specific plan to assassinate him on his route from Hartzwalde to Berlin. This note is not reprinted in Kersten's memoir. But Kersten claims that he took an alternative road to Berlin. He then informed Himmler of his narrow escape. The Reichsführer SS was furious. Kaltenbrunner was immediately summoned to Himmler's private train. Kersten and Gottlob Berger, the man Kersten described as a decent fellow, were present too; Berger was engaged at that time in consolidating the power of the Waffen SS on the eastern front. Kaltenbrunner politely asked Kersten how he was doing. Not so well, replied Kersten, for he had just lost his job. After years of working for the British secret service, he said, he still hadn't succeeded in killing Himmler. Kaltenbrunner was too stunned to speak. Himmler thought it was a terrific joke and said that if anything were to happen to his masseur, Kaltenbrunner would pay with his life.

As so often with Kersten's stories: perhaps, maybe, but then maybe not. At the very least, it shows his lively imagination. He survived, but the war was not yet over. Himmler still had power over the life and death of millions. On August 9, SS and police units started liquidating the ghetto in Łódź and deported sixty thousand Jews to Auschwitz. Between August and October, Gottlob Berger's SS crushed a rebellion in Slovakia, and more than twelve thousand Slovakian Jews were deported to Auschwitz. On October 30, the last transport from Theresienstadt left for Auschwitz and eighteen thousand Jews were gassed, most on arrival. On November 25, Himmler, hoping to destroy all traces of his systematic mass murder, ordered the destruction of the gas chambers and crematoria at Auschwitz. The last transport from Westerbork had left with 279 people on September 13; Anne Frank was on the train the week before that.

3: Beijing

Kawashima Yoshiko's active collaboration in the Japanese war had effectively ended before the attack on Pearl Harbor. By the time Japan's defeat became inevitable, Yoshiko's eagerness to play her part, however fictitiously, as a booster of the Japanese war effort had curdled into a feeling of abandonment. Having betrayed her native country, she now felt betrayed by the men who had used her, for their own pleasure and for presenting the invasion of China as a heroic enterprise. She was not shy about expressing these feelings, which put her in great danger.

Holed up in a hot spring hotel on the Japanese island of Kyūshū in 1940, feeling sorry for herself, Yoshiko bumped into Ri Koran, the movie actress, in the lobby one day. Ri was on her way back to Shanghai after shooting *China Nights*, in which she plays a young Chinese woman who improves Sino-Japanese relations by falling in love with a brave Japanese sea captain. As soon as she spotted Ri, Yoshiko hitched up the hem of her kimono, showed her a livid scar on her thigh, as well as needle marks, and said: "This is how I've suffered. For all I've done for the Japanese army, this scar is proof of my terrible fate."

Yoshiko had already outstayed her welcome in Kyūshū after falsely accusing a hotel owner of cheating her on her bill and the director of a hospital of sexual abuse, and sending the police hither and yon with a false complaint about a stolen diamond watch. Her loyal secretary ascribed these antics to her loneliness. But one of the policemen in her escort gave a different explanation. He believed that Yoshiko enjoyed making a fool of Japanese officials because she "bore a grudge toward Japan."

She expressed her state of mind most clearly in a letter that she slipped under the door of Ri's hotel room. Addressing Ri by her real name, she wrote:

> *My dear little Yoshiko,*
>
> *It was so good to see you. I don't know what will happen to me. We may never meet again. . . . Looking back over my life, I don't know what it was all for. It fills me with great sadness. Life is wonderful when the world celebrates you, but things will soon turn bad when people come to exploit you. Stay away from such people, whatever you do. Stick to your own beliefs. Do what you want to do. I'm a good example of what happens when you are used and then discarded. Take a good look at me. I'm giving you a warning from bitter experience. I feel like I'm watching the sun go down in a vast desert. I'm all alone. Where can I go now?*

There is a little too much self-pity, but her words, written in masculine Japanese, sound genuine. Kawashima Yoshiko was trapped in her own myth. There was no more place for her to go. And so, she retreated more and more deeply into her fantasies, which were as conflicted as her political loyalties and her affairs with the men who exploited her. One of them was the closest figure there was to a true Japanese fascist.

Sasakawa Ryoichi, the son of a sake brewer, was a shady businessman and political operator who grew rich in the 1930s by speculating on the rice market and then branching out to a variety of rackets. He was one of those fixers on the extreme right who linked the criminal underworld with politics and the armed forces. His private militia with a fleet of airplanes was put at the disposal of the Japanese Imperial Army. In Shanghai and Manchukuo, he made a fortune shaking down Chinese merchants and supplying the Japanese military with minerals and diamonds, as well as providing other services, including, it is alleged, a highly profitable trade in opium. His goons were employed in certain violent tasks that the Japanese Imperial Army preferred to delegate—political assassinations and the like. Sometimes, Sasakawa's methods went too far even for the Japanese to officially condone. He was arrested for extortion in 1935, but later released for lack of evidence. A great admirer of Mussolini, whom he visited in Rome in 1939, Sasakawa dressed members of his Patriotic People's Party in Italian-style black uniforms.

Although he was imprisoned by the Americans in 1945 as a class A war criminal, Sasakawa was never indicted. Like some other right-wing figures of his type, with close connections to gangsters as well as conservative politicians, he prospered during the Cold War, when he made himself useful as a staunch anti-Communist. A betting operation on motorboat racing made him immensely wealthy. Sasakawa called himself the "world's richest fascist," perhaps only a little bit in jest. His outfit, named the Nippon Foundation, was a major donor to the United Nations, as well as several charities. His dream was to win the Nobel Peace Prize, an honor that still eluded him by the time he died in 1995.

In June 1940, Sasakawa was involved in a plan to murder Yoshiko. He had flown to Manchukuo on his private aircraft, named *The Patriot*, and then to Beijing, where he was met at his hotel by Brigadier General Yuri of the military police, the Kempeitai. Yuri wished to speak about a problem that was giving him a "headache." General Tada Hayao had ordered Yuri to "dispose of" Yoshiko. This same Tada had of course been her lover, patron, and source of cash. Yuri felt sorry for Yoshiko since she had done much to help the Japanese cause. But now she was such a serious nuisance that Tada wanted her out of the way. Still, Yuri couldn't bring himself to kill her. The Kempeitai was not a softhearted organization, but this went against his moral principles.

What Sasakawa did next comes from his biographer, Yamaoka Sohachi, whose book is so fawning that he can hardly be a dependable source. Kawashima's biographer Phyllis Birnbaum quotes him at length anyway. Although his book is a hagiography, Birnbaum believes that Yamaoka got Yoshiko basically right. Sasakawa told Yuri he would handle this awkward affair himself and rushed to Yoshiko's home in Beijing, where she was kept under close guard by several Kempeitai officers. She looked pale and run-down and was in a mood of profound melancholy. "Papa," meaning Tada, had done this to her, she said. After all her services to the Japanese, this is how they were treating her, like a common criminal. She denounced Tada and Tanaka Ryukichi, her former lover in Shanghai, as "two-bit generals" and "ungrateful thugs" who had only wanted her for her body and then threw her away like "some old rag."

Yoshiko may well have said something like that. Several people have claimed that she was in the habit of writing letters to the minister of war and the foreign minister, as well as other Japanese leaders, denouncing General Tada and the Japanese military for their behavior in China. Yoshiko had become more than a nuisance; she posed a direct threat to Tada, who had plenty of enemies in the military establishment already, including Tojo Hideki, the war minister. Her provocative criticisms of Japan, in radio broadcasts and speeches, lend plausibility to the story of her inflammatory letters.

Brigadier General Yuri may not have been the first candidate to assassinate Yoshiko. At least one other person might have been landed with the same task. He was Lieutenant Yamaga Toru, Yoshiko's former lover and Ri Koran's mentor. This alleged assignment is mentioned in Ri's memoir. Being ordered to murder one's ex-lover would have been extraordinarily perverse. But that is no reason to dismiss the possibility. Perhaps Tada wanted to test Yamaga's loyalty to Japan. Perhaps he felt an amorous rivalry. Or perhaps it never happened at all.

In any event, Yamaga did not kill Yoshiko. It's safe to assume that Yoshiko was indeed, as they say in Japanese, "a lump on the eye" of the Japanese military authorities. For whatever reason—personal pique over the behavior of her lovers, remorse over her own betrayals, a residual sense of patriotism, or a combination of all three—she was becoming more and more openly disparaging of the Japanese war in China. Why then did she seek solace and protection in the arms of a lawless ultra-right-wing Japanese nationalist like Sasakawa? Perhaps the question is naive. For a dominant theme kept running through her life, like a leitmotif in an increasingly lurid opera. Even as she resented Japanese domination, she sought it out, craving the humiliation of its punishing love.

The precise nature of her relationship with Sasakawa is difficult to fathom. She called him "big brother." In Sasakawa's version of their first encounter at her house in Beijing, she broke down in tears, begging for his help. He bundled her off to her family house in Dalian, before flying her to Fukuoka, the largest city in Kyūshū, to keep her out of trouble in China. Although in the latter stages of his life, Sasakawa liked to present himself in paid television commercials as a cuddly figure who carried his old mother on his back as a token of his filial devotion, he was proud of having been a bit of a lothario as a younger man, keeping many mistresses. Yoshiko appears to have been deeply attached to him, following him around everywhere he went, from Fukuoka to Tokyo, from Tokyo to Osaka. She never let go. Every time he wanted to go off somewhere on his own, she kept him up all night in floods of tears. "Hold me," she is supposed to have cried one night, "I want to be held by a real

Japanese." Sasakawa recalls that he was impressed by the way she dutifully folded away his kimono trousers, or *hakama*, at night: "Not many women knew how to fold a *hakama* properly any longer."

As was the case in most of her erotic entanglements, Yoshiko's relationship with Sasakawa was colored by her political fantasies. One of them was a fanciful idea that Ri Koran would star in a film about Yoshiko's life. She also imagined herself as a peace envoy to Chiang Kai-shek, whom she would meet in Chongqing, Chiang's wartime capital. Sasakawa received a letter from her stating this intention. In her stilted Japanese, she advised Sasakawa to connect his patriotic party to the fate of China: "I, your little Yoshi, am planning to go and see Chiang Kai-shek. Time is running out. Please come, so we can discuss this. After speaking to Matsuoka [the foreign minister], we should travel to Chongqing."

Apart from his erotic interest, Sasakawa probably had reasons to indulge Yoshiko for a while. She was still a celebrated public figure in Japan, someone who could boost the fortunes of his fascist party. Having the support of a Manchu princess would add glamour to his shady enterprises in China and Japan. And she, once again, was a pleasing object for another powerful man to be toyed with. But Yoshiko was too unreliable to bolster his public relations. Asked to give a public speech, she would fail to turn up, or break off in the middle, or veer into unscripted and unhelpful remarks. She would spend much of the day in bed. Her drug problem was getting out of hand. There were threats of suicide. She was always in need of more money.

As usual in Yoshiko's life, it was not clear which side was the greater exploiter: the master or the slave. Sasakawa's biographer believes that his hero supported her for as long as he did because his "heart had been greatly moved by Yoshiko's pure passion for her unfinished dream of an imperial state, which she had staked her life on." The question is which imperial state: the Qing Dynasty or the Japanese empire? In any case, Yoshiko didn't fit into Sasakawa's plans for long. He dropped her.

Yoshiko did finally manage to get out of Kyūshū. Apparently, Matsuoka Yōsuke, the foreign minister, had something to do with this. She met him at Fukuoka airport, when he was on his way back from Berlin to Tokyo, pleased with himself for signing a pact with Nazi Germany and fascist Italy, something he later deeply regretted. They hugged each other, which is a distinctly odd thing to do in public in China or Japan. But Matsuoka's goodwill was sufficient for her to receive permission to move to Tokyo, where she bought three monkeys and moved with them into the Sanno Hotel, the place where in 1936 young military extremists had launched a doomed coup d'état to establish a fascist state with the emperor as a divine dictator.

It was there, listening to the radio with her monkeys perched on her shoulders, that she heard the announcement of Japan's aerial attack on Pearl Harbor. The news was received by many Japanese, including some liberals, with immense relief. At least now Japan was fighting an honorable war against its true enemies: the Western imperialist powers. The war in China was a sordid embarrassment. Manchukuo had become a dumping ground for impoverished Japanese farmers. Now that this had become a sideshow in the true war against the "Anglo-American brutes," Yoshiko's role in Japan's Asian ambitions had become irrelevant as well.

In the room next door to hers at the Sanno Hotel lived a tall, mustachioed figure named Charles Cousens. He was a major in the Australian army, captured by the Japanese in Singapore. As an experienced broadcaster, he was brought to Japan, apparently against his will, to produce a propaganda radio show aimed at Allied soldiers. The star of his show was the Californian daughter of Japanese immigrants named Iva Toguri. She became known, and reviled, as Tokyo Rose, and sometimes as the Tokyo Mata Hari.

This story, too, is filled with make-believe. There was no Tokyo Rose. It was a myth, a generic name for several female broadcasters with seductive voices meant to undermine the morale of enemy troops. Toguri was a pure victim of circumstances, stuck between two nations at war.

Toguri happened to be visiting relatives in Japan when the attack on Pearl Harbor turned her into an enemy overnight. She spoke no Japanese. She could barely eat with chopsticks. As an American, she was not allowed to stay with her Japanese family, and her parents were in an internment camp in the United States. With no money and nowhere to go, Toguri, adopting the radio name of Orphan Annie, survived by broadcasting in English on Japanese radio. She never spread any political messages, and she and Cousens maintained that they deliberately injected subversive jokes into their shows, which featured mostly music and comic sketches.

But the myth of Tokyo Rose was potent. Americans wanted a scapegoat after the war. Even though neither the U.S. Department of Justice nor the U.S. military thought she had done any harm, Toguri was tried in America as a traitor. The trial was held under highly dubious circumstances; jurors claimed they were put under pressure to convict. Toguri was sentenced to ten years in prison, and she lost her American citizenship. Here was a person who truly had no home. In 1977, following reports that she should never have been convicted in the first place, President Gerald Ford finally granted a full and unconditional pardon. At the age of sixty, Toguri was an American once more.

Yoshiko, meanwhile, moved from Japan to China yet again and sat out the rest of the war in Beijing, bored, idle, in an increasing state of physical decrepitude, with her three monkeys as company. Unlike the Tokyo Mata Hari, however, she would not survive after her own trials as a traitor once the war was over.

Nine

FINALE

∞

1: The Hague

It was 1944, shortly after the new year, and Friedrich Weinreb knew his game could not last for much longer. His services as an informant had helped the Germans round up some Jews, soon to be murdered in the east. But this wasn't enough. It was never going to be enough to still the bloodlust of the SS. And Weinreb's dithering over his phantomlike second list of rich Jews was beginning to seriously annoy officials at the SD in The Hague. Weinreb was right. No one was so foolish as to leave their hiding place just to sign up. The ones who did enlist at the Westerbork camp were no good to the Germans, for they were ready to be dispatched as "transport material" anyway.

Weinreb writes in his memoir that Albert Konrad Gemmeker, the suave camp commandant, was still courteous, but there was a new tone in his voice that had begun to sound a little forced, a trifle suspicious even. Weinreb thought he could tell; the German mind was an open book to him. Germans, in his view, were bad actors.

Weinreb considered going into hiding, an event for which he was well prepared. The only reason he didn't, he said, was his care not to let down the people on his list. He was still playing for time. Surely, the liberating Allied armies would come soon; then everyone could go home. He said he worried about the fate of his signatories if the list should "burst" before that happy day. Lest no revenge be taken on them, Weinreb decided to destroy any documents containing their names—documents that in fact mostly existed in his own head. Inevitably, the list did burst in February. It was finally time for Weinreb and his family to make their "dive" underground.

Before this dramatic change of fortune, however, Weinreb was given one more task, which sounds preposterous but makes sense as another imaginary episode in his personal odyssey. In one of his regular meetings with the SD agents in The Hague, Weinreb expressed an interest in how the Germans ferreted out their hidden victims. How did they know where the Jews were concealed? Fritz Koch and his Dutch helpers assured him that informants, or V-men, played only a minor part. Most of their information came from denunciations mailed in by ordinary Dutch citizens from all walks of life—doctors, schoolteachers, housewives, businessmen, and so on. Perhaps, the SD men suggested, Weinreb should make a proper study of this interesting phenomenon. He was such a brilliant scholar, after all. A meticulous research paper on catching Jews with all the facts and figures would be the perfect thing for him, and much welcomed by the German authorities.

Weinreb accepted the assignment and was given access to the Gestapo files. He found exactly what the SD men had said: letters, some of them written in impeccable German, from highly educated burghers who needed some favor, and were prepared to reveal Jewish hideouts in exchange. Others wished to be rid of irksome fugitives who made too much noise living under the floorboards or squeezed into a closet over the bathroom. There were businessmen who wanted former associates to disappear, so they wouldn't owe them anything after the war. Weinreb was particularly struck by one letter from a pious Christian who claimed that God had told him to denounce the murderers of Christ.

The point Weinreb was trying to make is that the Dutch were really no better than the Germans. That, and the unimportance of V-men, letting Weinreb himself off the hook. The Jewish catastrophe was made possible by petit bourgeois bigotry, a fetish for order, greed, and obedience to authority. He wrote about this in the late 1960s, when antiauthoritarian student protesters and left-wing intellectuals, inspired by Chairman Mao, the French philosopher Jean-Paul Sartre, and the sociologist Herbert Marcuse, were attacking "the establishment" in all its class-ridden manifestations. New historians were busily "demythologizing" conventional narratives about heroic wartime resistance by uncovering, or even exaggerating, the extent of Dutch collaboration. Subverting the institutions of power was the order of the day. Weinreb's story perfectly fitted the times.

Even if his "research project" was never real and his examples of treachery were made up, Weinreb's point would still hit home. The Nazi occupiers *had* successfully exploited the obedience of a largely docile population, as well as the basest instincts of some people. There is no doubt that the Gestapo was much helped in its murderous enterprise by denunciations from ordinary citizens who acted out of avarice, cowardice, or malice. In the Netherlands, like in France and other countries under Nazi occupation, the Gestapo received so many anonymous letters that they didn't know what to do with them. Even in his self-interested fictions, Weinreb knew how to press his thumb into sore places.

For a man who prided himself on his intelligence and know-how, Weinreb could also be, or pretend to be, remarkably obtuse. He insists that it wasn't until 1944 that he became aware that Jews were being systematically murdered in gas chambers. Anne Frank had already learned about this from the BBC radio in 1942. But not Weinreb. He claims to have been given the terrible news in The Hague by a German bureaucrat who was married to a Jewish woman. The worst thing, in this man's view, was that people who knew the awful truth, people like Gemmeker, or the agents of the SD, just carried on with their work, as though everything were perfectly normal. No one felt responsible.

The second Weinreb list ceased to exist after February 3, 1944. German patience had run out. The list had burst at last. Weinreb and his wife and children quickly left their home in The Hague and found a place to hide in a rural part of the country. They were helped by old friends, a German Jewish family named Birnbaum. Uriël Birnbaum was a painter of mystical scenes inspired by his religious faith (he also did some fine illustrations of Lewis Carroll's *Through the Looking-Glass*). His sister Miriam met the Weinreb family at the local railway station. Even in hiding, a terrible ordeal for most fugitives, Weinreb was special. "We are received with such warmth," he recalls in his memoir, "that we felt at home straight away. Here it is light. . . . We smile at one another in the light. It is good to be together. But outside it is still night."

The Weinrebs were also helped by another remarkable Jewish family named Durlacher, all of whose members worked for the resistance. Jetty Durlacher is identified in Weinreb's memoirs as "the little peasant," because of her unassuming appearance. She had been active in finding places for Jews to hide. One of her sons, named Evan, supplied false identity papers. Immediately after the war, this Jewish resistance man, along with quite a few other former members of the anti-Nazi underground, was sent to the Dutch East Indies as a soldier. In a macabre reversal of roles, their task was to crush Indonesian resistance to Dutch colonial rule.

Evan's brother Leo was the reason for the family's connection with Weinreb. Leo was arrested and sent to Westerbork in 1942 after being caught riding his bicycle without a proper back light. (Such petty infringements could have dire consequences in a system where power was routinely exercised on a whim.) It could have been worse. The police could have found out that Leo had been helping a British airman escape back to England. His mother, "the little peasant," asked Weinreb to include Leo on his list. Weinreb did so. Leo and his mother were convinced that Weinreb's list had saved him from deportation, and certain death. Leo then developed an alarmingly high fever, caused by pills smuggled into the camp by his brother Evan. After being transferred to an outside hospital, he managed to escape. In hiding together, Leo and Weinreb spent their days and half the nights discussing theology. Weinreb could count on the Durlachers as his most loyal defenders after the war was over.

The whole country was liberated in May 1945, mostly by Canadians. British, American, and Polish troops had already freed the southeastern parts of the Netherlands in the summer of 1944. The Weinreb family was holed up on a farm. Before returning to The Hague, Weinreb decided it might be prudent to find out how he might be received there. His former contacts with the SD, whatever his intentions might have been, were bound to cause him trouble. The first person he consulted in The Hague was a Jewish lawyer named Hes, who gave a sympathetic hearing to Weinreb's tales of General von Schumann and other wartime escapades. Curiously, Weinreb refrained from telling Hes that the general was an imaginary character. What Weinreb really wanted to know was whether his own name was on any wanted list. Hes was unable to reassure him.

In a short book written in 1988, just before his death in Switzerland, Weinreb described his arrest as a Nazi collaborator. The book, like his memoirs written two decades before, was self-serving, with a lot of fiction and a great deal of exaggeration. But the picture he paints of the newly liberated country, where idle young men suddenly became resistance heroes and the thirst for vengeance was raw and not always discriminating, is not entirely inaccurate. Here, too, he managed to hit the Dutch where it hurt.

The Hague, in his memory, was the "Wild West." Suspected Nazi collaborators were being gunned down in the streets. Sadistic Dutch thugs went around bullying and humiliating their victims just as the Nazis had done. The first Dutch policeman Weinreb asked for directions to the Canadian headquarters was a rabid antisemite who told him to go back to Poland. Why wasn't he gassed along with the others of his kind?

It is not inconceivable that Weinreb really did meet a policeman like that. But the anecdote fits a little too neatly into his caricature of a country full of cowards and antisemites. It is true that Jewish survivors were not always warmly welcomed back, especially when they tried to reclaim lost property. Postwar bureaucracy could be extremely callous: people who had been deported and barely survived the horrors of Auschwitz or Bergen-Belsen were sometimes asked to pay backdated taxes or rents on properties that no longer existed. Empty homes where they had once lived in Amsterdam were gutted and plundered for firewood during the freezing winter of 1945. Families like the Birnbaums and Durlachers, who had fled Germany or Austria in the 1930s and never managed to get Dutch passports, were treated as enemy aliens. One of the most poisonous effects of Nazi occupation was that antisemitism stuck like a filthy stain. Perhaps uneasy feelings of guilt, for having looked the other way, or worse, had something to do with this. A more likely explanation is that the noxious fumes of propaganda have a way of lingering.

Still, The Hague in the summer of 1945 was not the Wild West. It was a milder version of other parts of formerly occupied Europe. Women who had slept with German soldiers were dragged through the streets, with their hair cut off, and spat on by jeering mobs. Suspected collaborators were locked up in prisons and camps just recently vacated by the German SS. They were often treated badly. But compared with France and Belgium, let alone Poland or Czechoslovakia, with their large German-speaking populations, Dutch vengeance was quickly brought under control. There was nothing like the French "wild purges" of late 1944, when thousands of men and women were murdered, often by members of the Communist Party, who used the chaos of liberation as an opportunity to purge political opponents. Dutch antisemitism, odious in any case, never resulted in violence, which is not saying much. One of the problems in the war's aftermath was the government's decision that Jews should not be singled out for special consideration; they were Dutch citizens to be treated like everyone else. Before the Nazi occupation this was the only sensible attitude; after what happened during the previous five years, it was thoughtless at the very least.

Weinreb first went to see the Canadian military authorities, but they expressed little interest in his stories of lists and German generals. His next stop was a former girl's school, where the BS, or Internal Armed Forces, the Dutch equivalent of the Free French, had set up their headquarters. Weinreb's account of what happened there is quite different from the stories told by others. His own version is far more dramatic. The commandant of the BS, a shifty-looking fellow in horn-rimmed glasses named Van Maaswijk, wanted to know what Weinreb had been doing at the Gestapo office in Brussels at the end of 1943. Wondering how this man could possibly have known about his visit to the Belgian capital, Weinreb suddenly realized he had seen him before—at the Gestapo office in Brussels, clearly up to something sinister.

Van Maaswijk asked if Weinreb had said anything to the Canadians about Brussels. Weinreb said no and made to leave, whereupon the commandant started shrieking: "This man had his family murdered at Auschwitz! He robbed people of all their money! People, come quickly. He deserves to be punished right now. We have no time for a trial. The biggest scoundrel in history!" Here was the Wild West in action. "Nazi methods," thought Weinreb. "Evil is contagious." It was, he felt, "as though these people had always envied [the Nazis], and now they could be just like them." Weinreb was spun around against the wall, with guns pointed at his back. He protested that his family was alive and well. "Liar!" yelled the commandant. "We are in charge now. We have the power to decide what's true."

This last sentence is especially chilling. Whether the commandant really said it or Weinreb made it up is in a way irrelevant. Weinreb understood the nature of authoritarianism. His form of rebellion against tyranny, real enough during the war, and imagined after it, was to adopt this attitude to the truth himself.

A discussion ensued on what to do with the prisoner. Should he be executed on the spot? It was obvious to Weinreb that Van Maaswijk wanted to destroy a witness to his own shady dealings with the Nazis. If he were shot, no one would say a word. Those "simple obedient citizens" would look the other way, just as they had done before, when Jews were dragged from their homes. Things hadn't changed at all. Daylight does not follow darkness in an instant. Weinreb was reminded of the German idea of the *Gotterdämmerung*, the twilight of the Gods. Someone must be sacrificed in the twilight. And he thought of himself as the sacrificial lamb, the *korban*. The word is Hebrew, the concept is perhaps more Christian, more Jesus Christ than Isaac.

The report of the National Institute for War Documentation on the Weinreb affair tells a very different story. Weinreb was indeed arrested at the BS headquarters in the girl's school in The Hague. The name of the commandant who arrested him was not Van Maaswijk, but J. C. van Heukelom, a lawyer who had never been at the Gestapo office in Brussels. Weinreb was not arrested on a whim, but because several people had filed complaints against him. A former associate in Weinreb's prewar economic consultancy, H. L. Swart, accused him of "treachery on a large scale." Weinreb had told the Gestapo that the money from Jews on his list had gone to Swart, which was untrue. As a result of Weinreb's betrayal, Swart spent a year in one of the worst concentration camps. The other accuser was D. Kelder, a former member of the resistance; he was a baker, still famous for his delicious hazelnut tarts when I grew up in The Hague. While sharing a cell at the Orange Hotel, he trusted Weinreb and mentioned several Jewish hideouts. The SD quickly followed up with raids. None of the inhabitants would survive.

In the summer of 1945, Weinreb found himself back in the familiar surroundings of the Orange Hotel, this time as a defendant in a so-called Special Court. These courts were established after the war to deal specifically with cases of betrayal and collaboration. Defense lawyers were mostly recruited from the junior members of the bar. Established lawyers had little taste for such cases; they were beneath their dignity. My father, fresh out of law school, was one of the defense lawyers who cut his professional teeth in Special Courts. His experience left him with a lifelong distrust of hasty moral judgments. He had seen too much ambiguity to believe that light and dark, good and evil, could always be easily determined. What to make of the young Dutch citizen (one of his clients) born from a German mother and Dutch father, who was drafted into the German army? Was he really a traitor? Most people, from factory owners to urban planners and traffic cops, cooperated in one way or another with the German occupation. Establishing criminal culpability was not always straightforward. Not all prosecutors were immune to the pleasures of vengeance either. At one point in 1945, there were about 150,000 suspected collaborators in jail, a high number for such a small country.

That Weinreb was a Jew muddled things even further. Even though antisemitic reflexes were hardly absent from public life, nothing points to a concerted desire to take the humiliations of Nazi occupation out on the few Jewish survivors. But trying a Jew, one who had barely escaped with his life, added an extra layer of complexity. Guilt in this situation was a dangerously loaded concept. Another notorious case of a Jewish collaborator was that of Ans van Dijk, a lesbian milliner in Amsterdam. She was the only woman to be tried by a Special Court. Refusing to wear the yellow star, Van Dijk spent the first few years of the war helping people find places to hide. Arrested by the SD in 1943, she was given the choice: work for the German police or be sent to the east. She agreed to assist the German police. Pretending to be her old self, she offered Jews a place of refuge and then betrayed 145 people to the SD. One of these unfortunates was her own brother. Van Dijk confessed her crimes to a Special Court. After converting at the last minute to the Catholic faith, she was executed by a firing squad on the dawn of January 14, 1948. One wonders why a Jewish lesbian would be the only woman to receive this harsh punishment. Just a handful of collaborators were executed, even as the lives of some of the top Nazis, responsible for mass murder, were spared.

Weinreb's first prosecutor, F. Hollander, was himself Jewish. He was also known as a liberal-minded man who tended to go easy on minor collaborators. Vengeance was not his style. One of his cases concerned a relatively well-known painter, who had been a member of the Nazi party and joined the Nazi Culture Chamber, but no one's blood had stuck to his hands. He was acquitted. Hollander was more interested in prosecuting more powerful figures, people who had enriched themselves in business with the occupiers. Still, Weinreb objected so vehemently to Hollander that a different prosecutor was appointed. Hollander knew Weinreb and had said that, as a Jew, he had had unpleasant experiences with him during the war.

At first, Weinreb's trial in the Special Court attracted little public attention. It was also slow going. Changing prosecutors had delayed the proceedings. The new prosecutor took a long time to prepare his brief, and Weinreb's lawyer, C. Smit, only managed to read his files in 1946. Smit asked Weinreb to put his side of the story on paper, twice in fact. His client was more than willing to do so. As would be true of his later memoirs, Weinreb put great emphasis on what he believed to be the antisemitic prejudice of his accusers. He was a victim of the Dutch establishment, which had collaborated with the Germans, and so on. He even compared the Special Court with *Der Stürmer*, the vile antisemitic Nazi paper.

Moral pressure was applied in his defense in other ways too. Weinreb threatened to reveal the names of prominent Dutch figures who had secretly worked for the Germans. This so-called Mauretania file (why Mauretania isn't entirely clear; perhaps it referred to the Berber kings of Mauretania who became vassals of the Romans in 25 BC) was supposedly the fruit of Weinreb's research in the Gestapo archives. The dossier was never published. Most likely it never existed.

Weinreb made his case so convincingly, however, that Smit based his entire defense on his client's fiery and eloquent account. Smit believed in Weinreb's story: that he had been a heroic savior of thousands of Jewish lives, that he had taken enormous risks selflessly, and that the money he received had been spent to help fugitives survive in hiding. The allegations of sexual abuse in Weinreb's "medical examinations" did not come up. Nor did Weinreb's alleged betrayal of twenty-four Jews hidden in a single apartment in The Hague. The accusations of having spied on fellow prisoners for the SD were mentioned but were quickly dismissed by Smit as vengeful fantasies. And the prosecutor, P. S. de Gruyter, was faced with a problem.

The most damaging testimonies about Weinreb's collaboration with the SD came from the former SD agents themselves. Alas for the prosecutor, one of them, Bolland, was declared insane and committed to a mental institution. Fritz Koch, the German official at the SD in The Hague, was vague and said he had left much of the work to his Dutch subordinates. This left Krom, the menacing figure who had accompanied Weinreb on his trips to Belgium. But Krom withdrew his damning testimony in 1946 in exchange for a positive statement from Weinreb on Krom's behalf.

In the initial trial, then, the prosecution chose to concentrate mostly on Weinreb's efforts to defraud his fellow Jews by taking money in exchange for false promises. This was *faute de mieux*, but several Jewish witnesses convinced De Gruyter that Weinreb's fraud was more serious than a simple scheme to enrich himself. The swindle, in the prosecutor's view, cost lives because people's trust in him prevented them from finding other means of escape. For this, and for Weinreb's spying and betrayals, De Gruyter asked that he be sentenced to ten years in prison.

The judges were not as unequivocal in their views as the prosecutor. Their verdict in 1947 was judicious to the point of indulgence. Weinreb would be sentenced only for crimes that could be proven beyond any doubt. That is, two cases of spying on a fellow prisoner, one betrayal, four cases of giving information to the SD under pressure, and the crime of cheating Jews out of money for Weinreb's own profit. But the judges were prepared to consider the possibility that the defendant might have believed he was offering his victims a real prospect of delaying their deportations. They also assumed that some people could have benefited from a respite to find other ways of saving their lives. Weinreb was sentenced to three and a half years in prison and a lifetime loss of his voting rights.

Not quite the Wild West, then. But the way Weinreb and his loyal supporters chose to present his trial is telling, especially after the prosecutor, disappointed by the court's leniency, appealed for a trial in the higher court. Weinreb's most fervent defenders were his companions in hiding, Jetty Durlacher and Uriël Birnbaum, the painter. Birnbaum was convinced, like Weinreb himself, that his friend was the victim of a conspiracy. A Jewish hero was being smeared as a traitor to distract public attention from the pusillanimity and even abject collaboration of Dutch officials during the war. Durlacher started a Weinreb Committee to raise money and mobilize opinion behind her friend's defense. A letter was published in the main Jewish newspaper that presented Weinreb as perhaps "a little too impulsive measured by sedate Dutch standards," but certainly not a fraudster.

Uriël Birnbaum went further than that. He did his best to turn a local case into an international cause célèbre, or more specifically a worldwide Jewish cause. In 1946, Birnbaum wrote an impassioned plea, in German, entitled "The Weinreb Case: A Dutch Dreyfus Trial." Weinreb, he wrote, was clearly a victim of antisemites. To call him a traitor was to continue Nazi propaganda about Jewish treachery: "A conviction of Weinreb will brand all Jews in the world as treasonous, criminal and inferior." Birnbaum was convinced that Weinreb was innocent; "he will be judged by the world *because* he is innocent. Because what he really did would make him a Jewish hero, which is even more reason to depict him as a Jewish traitor and mass murderer."

Friends in New York were mobilized by Birnbaum to send letters to the World Jewish Congress, which then contacted the Dutch embassy in Washington to intervene in the case. The International League for Human Rights, based in New York, promised to send someone to monitor the trial. *PM*, a liberal New York daily paper, reported on the "Dutch Dreyfus."

While preparing for his trial, Weinreb shared a prison cell for a time with a journalist named W. H. M. van den Hout, who would later become a successful writer of adventure stories for children. Before the war, he had written a satire about Hollywood. During the war, he was a propagandist for the Nazi press. He, too, was evidently convinced by his cellmate's story and offered his services as an experienced journalistic PR man. He wrote an article aimed at American readers under the headline "Famous Gestapo-Foe Who Saved Hundreds of Jews from Deportation, Still Kept in Jail by Dutch Nazi-Collaborators—Secret Anti-Semitism in Holland."

Despite the efforts of Birnbaum and Weinreb's defense lawyer, Smit, the article was never published. But the story of the Dutch Dreyfus wouldn't go away. Everything Weinreb wrote in later years must be read in this light. It didn't save him from punishment, but it would one day have a dramatic second life.

After the prosecutor appealed the first verdict, the Weinreb case was tried again, this time in the Special Court of Cassation. His legal team echoed the sentiments fanned by Weinreb and his supporters. Weinreb, Smit declared, was being hunted by Dutch authorities in ways "that the SD could hardly have improved on during the war." The judge told Smit to control himself: the analogy didn't fit. "Surely it does," Smit replied. "It's high time for this trial to be ended. Considering actions taken in the U.S., it has become a matter of prestige."

Smit was clearly referring to Dutch prestige. The charge of official antisemitism was taking its toll. Smit reminded the court that "almost every Jew in Holland—and many outside too—is up in arms. And not just the orthodox . . . but orthodox and liberal Jews. All feel the same: TUA RES AGITUR [a matter that concerns you]."

There was a risk in widening the case to encompass all Jews, and to make Weinreb into a scapegoat or sacrificial lamb. The new prosecutor, W. P. Bakhoven, remarked that what was being forgotten by those who cried antisemitism in the courtroom, and elsewhere, was that most people testifying against Weinreb were Jewish themselves. Weinreb was being tried, not for deceiving the Germans or for being a fantasizer but for cheating other Jews in deadly circumstances. H. Drion, a law professor and Supreme Court judge, later made an even sharper argument against projecting Weinreb as the victim of antisemitism. He questioned the suggestion of collective guilt. If all Jews should regard Weinreb's case as an attack on all Jews, Orthodox and liberal, the implication would be that all Gentiles who find him guilty must be antisemites. Drion feared that this kind of collective thinking could backfire and actually become the source of more antisemitism: "If collective guilt is pitted against collective guilt, the minority will end up being victimized. This danger is not unimaginable even if that minority is as tragically small as the Jewish minority in the postwar Netherlands."

Even though the second trial dealt only with accusations judged in the first one, new witnesses and information, damaging to Weinreb, were introduced by the prosecution. The prosecutors have been criticized for being overzealous in this respect. But Weinreb's behavior was distinctly odd as well. To elicit favorable witness accounts, he wrote the statements himself and asked people to sign them. Some did so, and some didn't. Mention of the raid on the twenty-four Jews hidden in the apartment in the Reinkenstraat, although not part of the original indictment, could affect Weinreb's case badly. Sarah Wahlbeem, the woman who had hidden the Jews in her apartment, received a visit from Weinreb's wife and one of his friends. For more than six hours, they pressed her to sign a statement that none of the people in her safe house had had anything to do with Weinreb or his lists. They threatened, they begged, they cried. She refused.

Neither the international campaign nor the pressure on witnesses helped Weinreb much in the end. The verdict was harsher than after the first trial. The judges argued that Weinreb was blinded by his "highhanded confidence in his own intelligence" and the presumption of pushing his "grand scheme." This had "resulted in the sacrifice of individual people to save himself, his family, as well as more people whose fate he had taken and thought he could continue to take into his own hands, despite the tremendous risks in so doing."

Whatever the merits of specific allegations against him, it appears from everything we know about Weinreb that the prosecutor Bakhoven got him about right. He saw Weinreb

> as a combination of an operator and what Germans call a *Hochstapler,* a man who wants to be in the center of things. He set up and played a game with the SD using his almost pathological imagination and took as much pleasure in the thrills and dangers of this game as he did from the adoration of his "wards," some of whom worshipped him as a Messiah. He certainly didn't aim to betray Jews to the Germans. He helped many Jews to go into hiding. But he used Jews as the stakes in a game, even though he knew from the beginning that he didn't have the cards to win it. . . . This game with the SD had no solid basis and was bound to have a horrible end.

Some people might have reached a more severe conclusion. The court sentenced Weinreb to six years in prison. But luck was with him once more. To celebrate fifty years of her reign, Queen Wilhelmina granted a certain number of pardons. Weinreb's lawyers asked for her clemency. It was granted. Weinreb was a free man. A request from the lawyer of Ans van Dijk, the other Jewish traitor, to spare her from execution, was turned down.

So, all in all, Weinreb had spent about three years in jail. Albert Konrad Gemmeker, commandant of Westerbork, who had sent up to one hundred thousand Jews to the death camps, was sentenced to ten years, just four more than Weinreb. He got off lightly because he maintained that he had no idea what would happen to "my Jews" once he had done his duty and they had been loaded into the trains at Westerbork. The court was unable to prove beyond reasonable doubt that he did know. Some people continue to believe that Weinreb's sentence was too tough. Many more think that the verdict on Gemmeker was not nearly tough enough.

2: Beijing

Kawashima Yoshiko was still dozing in bed at 3:00 p.m., as was her habit, when a policeman from the Chinese Nationalist government came for her. This was on October 11, 1945, two months after the Japanese emperor announced his country's surrender in stilted court language that most of his subjects found incomprehensible. The policeman ordered Jin Bihui (her Chinese name) to get up. On her bare feet and still in her blue pajamas, she was handcuffed, blindfolded, and pushed into a waiting car. All her belongings, including jewels that once belonged to her mother, were confiscated. They included a diamond watch, a jade necklace, a gold hairpin, and some precious bibelots on platinum stands.

Yoshiko vented her outrage over this treatment in her diary. Her prose is sometimes hard to follow, but the aristocratic contempt for her jailers is clearly expressed. She spoke to them in the haughty manner she once adopted toward her Japanese primary school teachers. The police-man "looked like a coolie," she wrote. At the police station, she de-manded a cigarette and ordered a guard to light it for her. Casting her eye on the torture instruments available for the more severe interroga-tions, she sighed, "Ah, China," and deplored how old-fashioned they looked.

It wasn't as though she hadn't been warned. When the end of the war was near, a friendly Japanese fortune-teller suggested an escape to Mon-golia. But Yoshiko was stubborn. She was a Sino-Japanese woman with-out a home, she said, but her heart was with the Chinese people. And so, she stayed at home in Beijing, with her three beloved monkeys, spending much of her time listening to a blind musician play melancholy Japanese tunes on his lute.

Before Yoshiko was arrested, the Manchukuo emperor Puyi had already been intercepted by Soviet soldiers on his escape route to Japan. Vengeance after the humiliations of conquest and occupation was harsh and often arbitrary everywhere. But some places were worse than others. In the former Manchukuo, once again a northeastern part of China, revenge was particularly brutal. After the senior officers of the Japanese Kwantung Army had gotten away with their loot in the comfort of the last trains heading for the coast, hundreds of thousands of Japanese civilians, cajoled by years of imperial government propaganda to settle in Manchukuo, and made destitute overnight, now bore the brunt of popular rage from people who had been promised "harmony of the five races" and never received it. Many Japanese were robbed or killed by furious Chinese. But the Chinese were relatively restrained compared with the invading Soviet Red Army troops, who behaved as they had earlier in Germany and eastern Europe. Looting was the least of it. A person could be hacked to death just for his watch. The most vulnerable people, again as in Europe, were the women, many of whom were raped by gangs of marauding soldiers. Parents were so desperate to save their children from the carnage that babies and small children were left behind to be taken care of by Chinese peasants, if they were taken care of at all. Up to eighty thousand Japanese never made it home.

One of the worst Japanese war criminals was General Okamura Yasuji. In 1942, he oversaw a savage effort to wipe out Communist guerrillas in northern China. His strategy, called *Sanko Sakusen*, usually translated as the Three Alls—that is "Kill all, burn all, and loot all"—was devised by Major General Tanaka Ryukichi, Yoshiko's former lover in Shanghai. The broad goal was to crush the guerrillas by killing all males "suspected of being enemies." Peasants were forced into chain gangs. Villages were burned to the ground. Grain and other vital foodstuffs were confiscated, and cattle were slaughtered until there was nothing left for the guerrillas to live on. Some historians have claimed that the Three Alls cost the lives of 2.7 million Chinese civilians.

Even as Yoshiko was arrested as a suspected traitor and spy, General Okamura was declared innocent by a hasty war crimes tribunal and taken on as a military adviser by Chiang Kai-shek. This was not just an arbitrary move, or even a sentimental one, just because Chiang himself and some of his generals had studied at Japanese military academies and knew Okamura personally. As soon as Japan was defeated, the civil war between Chiang's Nationalists and Mao Zedong's Communists, always simmering behind the facade of an anti-Japanese alliance, broke out in furious fighting. Because Chiang wanted Japan to be on his side, relatively few Japanese were tried for war crimes in China, unlike in other parts of Asia, such as Singapore or the Dutch East Indies. The official line was that Japanese people, even Japanese soldiers, were not China's enemies, just a few militarists at the very top.

And yet the Chinese had suffered more than any other people in Asia. Up to twenty million Chinese died because of the Japanese invasion. So, even as the military war criminals were let off easy, something had to be done to settle scores in public. In Europe after the collapse of the Third Reich, women were often used as the prime symbols of national humiliation, hence the ferocious treatment in France and other countries of women who had slept with German occupiers. Something comparable happened in China. Posters appeared all over the country denouncing three especially egregious traitors who collaborated with the Japanese: Li Xianglan, "Tokyo Rose," and Kawashima Yoshiko. Li Xianglan (or Ri Koran, or Yamaguchi Yoshiko) was accused of being a spy and a collaborator. Kawashima Yoshiko was charged with not only spying but also aiding the Japanese invasion of China, selling out her country, and having had many sexual affairs with leading Japanese war criminals. In a letter to her Japanese secretary, Yoshiko wrote that she was being "made into a public spectacle" by the Chinese newspapers "as a way of offering a bit of relief to the poor."

Unfortunately, Yoshiko did everything to make her case worse. In police interrogations, she was either supercilious or full of braggadocio, boasting of the astonishing feats that had made her a legend in Japan, even if half of them weren't true. The old story about parachuting into Qiqihar to get an anti-Japanese warlord to surrender was recounted, despite her having admitted in her own book that this never happened. Tall tales from wartime Japanese magazines were regurgitated. Her military exploits, never much more than a zany costume show, were exaggerated. It is possible that she confessed to all this under duress, as she soon claimed. She may indeed have been bullied and humiliated in jail. Her nicknames among her fellow prisoners were "crazy sister" or "mad brother." But she was above all a victim of her own myth.

Meanwhile, Ri Koran, the other purveyor of Japanese wartime myths, was under house arrest in Shanghai, together with a well-known Japanese movie producer who was her lover at the time. One day, a Chinese general appeared at her door, asking her to sing at a party for Allied military officers. The Americans were keen to hear "China's number one singer" perform Chinese songs. She protested that she was no longer a Chinese movie star, but an ordinary Japanese citizen named Yamaguchi Yoshiko.

In 1945 it had become a matter of life and death for both Yoshikos to prove they were not Chinese. As Japanese, after all, they couldn't be accused of being traitors. They needed papers to prove their citizenship. Every Japanese citizen must be entered into the family register. Yamaguchi was fortunate. A Russian friend retrieved a copy of her family register from her parents, who were living in Beijing.

The other Yoshiko had no such luck. Pretending not to understand Chinese, she asked for a Japanese translator in jail. But her adoptive father, Kawashima Naniwa, had neglected to enter her into the Kawashima family register. Officially, she had always remained a citizen of China. No matter how many letters she sent to Kawashima Naniwa from jail, begging him to send documents proving her Japanese nationality, even if they had to be forged, this sealed her fate. She would be tried as Jin Bihui, a Chinese traitor, with maximum public exposure.

The trial of "the female spy" opened in October 1947, with great and often juicy publicity. She was the "beauty in men's clothes worshipped by young women under a militarist regime." She was a "poisonous thistle dancing on the waves of an aggressive war." The Japanese newspaper *Asahi* reported that the small court where she would be tried was swamped by so many people who wanted to get a glimpse of "the Mata Hari of the Orient" that the windows and furniture were in danger of being smashed.

Finally, on October 15, Yoshiko faced her judges in the court garden, with five thousand people craning their necks to get a glimpse of her. The list of her alleged crimes was long: she had formed her own army to  conquer Chinese territories in Manchuria; she helped put Emperor Puyi on the throne of the puppet state; she plotted the invasion of China; she helped to start the Battle of Shanghai; she passed along Chinese military secrets; she spread Japanese propaganda; she sought to revive the Qing Dynasty; she betrayed the motherland by supporting Chinese collaborators; she postured as a male war hero and was corrupted by the "samurai spirit" through her intimate relations with Japanese militarists. Yoshiko sat through it all, smiling serenely.

The accusations were not surprising. But the nature of the evidence was. The prosecutors claimed that her crimes were all vividly described in the book *The Beauty in Men's Clothes*, Muramatsu Shofu's fictional account of Yoshiko's adventures in Shanghai. Evidence of her treachery was also found in the propaganda movie *Dawn in Manchuria*, supposedly based on this book, starring Ri Koran and directed by the great filmmaker Mizoguchi Kenji. There was indeed such a film, but it did not star

Ri Koran, nor was it based on *The Beauty in Men's Clothes,* or indeed on anything to do with Yoshiko's life. It was a piece of hackwork produced to celebrate the founding of Manchukuo. But these errors aside, it was of course highly irregular to allow fictions as evidence. Yoshiko's entanglement in her own myths now proved to be her undoing.

One myth she had indisputably promoted was the aim of building paradise in Manchukuo. The crash of this much-cherished Japanese enterprise was symbolized by the end of Amakasu Masahiko, the Kwantung Army officer in charge of propaganda, the killer with the bland face, the man who made Ri Koran the star of the Manchukuo movie studio. Two days after Japan's surrender in August 1945, he had watched the sun go down over the film studios in Shinkyo. He spoke to an associate about his efforts "to put a smile on the peaceful people of this great land." He said: "The Manchuria we Japanese have built will go under, but their smiling faces will never disappear." The next day, dressed in his uniform of the Racial Harmony Society, Amakasu withdrew into his office and took a cyanide pill.

Yoshiko's end was more sordid. She awaited her fate alone in a tiny prison cell. A photograph of Ri Koran was pinned to the wall. Spencer Moosa, a reporter for the Associated Press, was granted a last interview. He wrote: "She no longer looks the part of the Oriental siren, who used her charms to help Japan in the war. At the age of 33, her upper teeth are gone, her hair is cut in a mannish bob, and she wears padded gray jacket and slacks that make her small figure look bigger than it is." She didn't like men, she told Moosa. "They only make trouble for women." I'm sure she meant it. But even at the very end of her life, she couldn't help indulging in a few more fictions. She was born in Tokyo when her parents were in exile, she said. She also told Moosa she had never been married, forgetting to mention her Mongolian husband. Like Weinreb, she refused to renounce the reality she had created for herself.

Yoshiko asked to be executed away from the public view and to be dressed in a white Japanese kimono. The first request was granted, the second was not. The *Yomiuri* newspaper reported that on March 25, 1948, she was ordered to kneel and asked to confirm that her name was Jin Bihui. She received one bullet in the back of her head. "According to the Chinese guard, she died without flinching, like a true lady."

3: Stockholm

By the time American, British, and Soviet leaders gathered at Yalta, in February 1945, to decide on the fate of the world after Germany's imminent defeat, Heinrich Himmler, Reichsführer SS, Reichsminister of the Interior, commander of the Reserve Army, and commander in chief of Army Group Upper-Rhine, was so desperate that he was consulting his masseur and his astrologer about staging a coup against Hitler. France, Belgium, and parts of the Netherlands were already liberated. Soviet troops were launching rocket artillery from "Stalin's pipe organs" less than forty miles from Berlin. One after the other, former allies, including Finland, Felix Kersten's country of citizenship, had turned against the Third Reich. Most major German cities lay in ruins after being bombed at night by the British and in daylight by the Americans. Wilhelm Wulff, Himmler's astrologer, urged his boss to get rid of the Führer. At the end of his tether, according to Wulff, Himmler, "a man feared by millions, said softly and almost plaintively, 'I will make this confession to you, gentlemen—I simply cannot do it.'"

Himmler may not have said such a thing. Perhaps this bizarre conversation never even took place. Wulff, as prone as Kersten was to fables and exaggerations, was not a witness to be trusted. But it could have happened. Himmler may have said it. We know that since the autumn of 1944 he swung wildly between utter despair and moods of delusional confidence in a miraculous German victory, because of Hitler's genius, or a devastating "secret weapon." We also know that he had been looking for ways to save himself, using proxies to probe for a peace deal with the Western allies, who would surely come to realize that they should join Himmler in a war against the Russians. To survive as a German leader, the rightful incarnation of Henry the Fowler, Himmler was quite prepared to barter a few Jewish lives. Prominent Jews had been held at the Theresienstadt camp for that very purpose, and Bergen-Belsen, too, was meant to be a clearing place for "exchange Jews" dispatched there from various other camps, including Westerbork. But even the head of the SS had to tread carefully, since he knew that Hitler would never countenance such cynical maneuvers. The Führer's war against the Jews was total.

For the Swedish government, saving at least some lives by negotiating with Himmler was its best chance to side with the victorious nations and end up on the right side of history. The same thing applied to Kersten. Opportunities presented themselves in the winter and early spring of 1945. Even if Kersten overstated his role in the rescue of thousands of people—Scandinavian, Dutch, French, Polish, many of them Jews—who had barely survived the camps under Himmler's whip, he did more than most people, at some risk to himself. Wulff said that Kersten did it all for money. He claimed that Kersten used him, as well as Himmler, to promote "his selfish plans for business deals in Sweden." Perhaps so. But it is more likely that Kersten was preparing for a world in which his job as Himmler's private masseur was not the ideal credential for starting a new life. He always enjoyed being a man of importance. And we should not discount the possibility that the bon vivant was also moved by a sliver of human decency.

Kersten's involvement in Himmler's trafficking in Jewish lives began in August 1944. He had been asked by a former patient to support a plan to rescue twenty thousand Jews, who would be transported to safety by the Swiss Red Cross. Might he put in a word to see whether Himmler could be persuaded? In his memoirs, Kersten is a little vague on the details of the scheme, but he soon realized that Himmler—or, more specifically, his intelligence chief Walter Schellenberg—was already negotiating with other Swiss figures about a similar plan. We know who they were: a married couple, Orthodox Jews named Recha and Yitzchak Sternbuch. Recha was a courageous woman who had done everything she could since the 1930s to save Jewish lives. Like Weinreb, she was a member of the Orthodox Agudath Yisrael, but that is where their resemblance ended. She used her religious contacts to give aid to all persecuted Jews, believers and nonbelievers alike. Even during her pregnancy, she would hide out in the woods on the Swiss border to help people escape from Austria and Germany. She and her husband had turned a hotel in St. Gallen into a home for refugees, some smuggled into the country, some exchanged for cash. The religious habits of the Orthodox Jews astonished the local people, who came to stare at these exotic creatures in their prayer shawls and their black hats.

In the summer of 1944, the Sternbuchs asked Jean-Marie Musy, the former president of the Swiss confederation, to go see Himmler, whom he knew slightly. Himmler and Schellenberg hoped that Musy might open the door to secret talks with the Western allies. Musy and his son, Benoît, traveled to Germany, where they spent many hours with Himmler on his private train, and made a deal with him. Himmler agreed to release prisoners from Theresienstadt in exchange for money. For each monthly transport of 1,200 people, five million Swiss francs would be deposited in a Swiss bank account. The money would be used to procure tractors and trucks for the German army.

This peculiar trade of Jews for trucks was not unprecedented. In May 1944, Adolf Eichmann, Himmler's main organizer of the Jewish genocide, offered a similar deal to a Jewish representative in Hungary: a million Jewish lives for trucks, cocoa, coffee, tea, and soap. "Blood for goods" (*Blut gegen waren*), Eichmann called the arrangement.

Kersten claims in his memoir that he condemned Himmler to his face for his sordid financial transaction. How could he exchange human lives for money? His name, Kersten supposedly told Himmler, "would be tarnished in the history books forever." Gottlob Berger, then busily organizing Waffen SS units on the eastern front and cracking down on a Slovakian uprising with great brutality, was staunchly on his side, according to Kersten. If so, humanitarianism or fastidiousness about trading in lives cannot have been the reason. As soon as Slovak resistance to more Jewish deportations was crushed, trains filled with Jews resumed their service to Auschwitz. Still, in Kersten's story, he and Berger prevailed. Himmler backed down.

In fact, he did not. The money was indeed paid, and 1,210 Jews—not 2,700, as Kersten mistakenly records in his book—crossed into Switzerland through the Czech and Bavarian countryside. But the deal collapsed because publicity about Jews being exchanged for German military matériel alarmed American Jews and outraged Hitler, who not only put a stop to such transactions but threatened to kill all Jews remaining in Germany and any German who helped them escape. The Eichmann trade in Budapest came to a similar halt; the British saw it as a ruse to seek a secret deal with the Western allies and drive a wedge between them and the Soviets.

The British, by the way, stayed away from any secret dealings with Himmler and left all such undertakings to Swedish and Jewish agencies. They also had great misgivings about Kersten himself. Sir Victor Mallet, the British ambassador in Sweden, reported to the Foreign Office that he considered Kersten to be "a Nazi and a thoroughly bad man."

But it was not the end of human barter. Kersten maintains that "from that moment on I received the means and the contacts to really lend help to the Jews." This part is true. In February 1945, Kersten met another one of those shady operators that regularly turn up in his professional and social life: Ottokar von Knieriem the head of the Dresdner Bank in Stockholm. Von Knieriem a patient of Kersten, was suspected after the war of having been a Nazi who engaged in all manner of squalid dealings to the benefit of wealthy Swedish industrialists as well as the German military. Since he was involved in German attempts to come to a beneficial agreement with the Allies, both on the western and eastern fronts, it was not surprising that it was he who introduced Kersten to Hillel Storch, the representative in Stockholm of the World Jewish Congress.

Storch was a Lithuanian Jew who fled to Sweden in 1940. Besides representing the World Jewish Congress, Storch also worked for the Zionist Jewish Agency. He contrived to save some Polish and Norwegian Jews, who then found refuge in Sweden. Such efforts were not universally popular in Sweden; some prominent Swedish Jews worried that it might provoke antisemitism in their country. But the Swedish government was keen to do more.

The main Swedish organizer of last-minute rescue operations was Count Folke Bernadotte. He was something of an aristocratic boy scout, a man who liked uniforms and drilling young men for action—indeed he was the president of the Swedish Scouts, as well as vice president of the Swedish Red Cross. When Himmler tried to contact Winston Churchill to see if he could make peace behind Hitler's back, he went through Bernadotte—without success. In any case, Bernadotte had informed Storch of Himmler's release of Jews from Theresienstadt in 1944, and he suggested that Himmler might be open to further concessions. But, pressed by the Norwegian and Danish representatives in Sweden, Bernadotte made it his first mission to secure the release of Scandinavians.

Since the respective roles of Bernadotte and Kersten in negotiating with Himmler are murky, and their rivalry would have dramatic consequences, it is important to note that the Swedish nobleman first met Himmler in February 1945. Himmler had agreed to allow thousands of Scandinavian prisoners to be placed in a camp under Red Cross supervision. Bernadotte found Himmler surprisingly pleasant to deal with, indeed he appeared "obliging . . . and liked to make a joke to lighten the tone a little."

This appearance of the obliging Himmler, ready to lighten the tone, was probably accurate. Unlike his raging Führer, who would rather go down in flames than compromise, especially on Jewish lives, Himmler was ready to cooperate, if it would help him. However, Kersten's speculation, noted in his diary of March 21, 1945, that Himmler, knowing the Nazi cause was lost, might no longer have felt "obliged to carry out his fearful task of annihilating the Jews and [feels] that he can now revert to his original ideas" of solving the "Jewish problem" in gentler ways, sounds highly implausible. This is like Kersten's notion that Brandt and Schellenberg were helping his rescue efforts because of their "devotion to the good cause." Considering the cause they had served for the last decade or so, this is unlikely.

Since Hillel Storch was aware of Kersten's direct access to Himmler, he was keen to meet him. Hitler had just announced that concentration camps would be blown up and all the prisoners killed as soon as Allied troops came near, and because it would be Himmler's job to carry out the grisly order, it was essential to try anything to talk him out of it. Kersten promised to do his best and flew from Stockholm to his country estate in Germany.

That some kind of negotiation took place in March between Himmler and Kersten is probable. Exactly what was said and promised is not clear. Kersten's diary was reconstructed after the war. Joseph Kessel, his French biographer, has the most dramatic account, laying heavy stress on Kersten's magic hands that did all the persuasive work when Himmler was once again in agony. Himmler, he writes, "lay slumped on his metal bed, red in the face, hollow-cheeked, covered in sweat." Once Kersten had dulled the sharpest pain, he asked whether it was true that the camps would be blown up once the Allies came near. Himmler confirmed it. If Germany was to go down, her enemies would go down too, he said with great conviction.

Kersten then resorted to his usual approach: oily flattery. Surely, he said, the great German rulers in the past would never have done such a terrible thing. Himmler was the greatest German leader of his time, more powerful, even, than Hitler himself. If only he could show some compassion, Himmler would be remembered forever as the glorious savior of eight hundred thousand people.

Days went by of dithering, toing-and-froing, and professions of Himmler's impotence in the face of Hitler's terrifying will. Then, finally, in the presence of Brandt, Himmler drew up a document, promising not to blow up the camps, or to evacuate them at terrible human cost, but to hand them over in an orderly fashion to the Allies, and to stop killing Jews and allow delivery of food parcels. Kersten wrote that he felt as though he were "the representative of an invisible power, above all the powers of the earth." He signed the document "in the name of humanity." Brandt, he noted, was "thunderstruck."

Kersten didn't stop there. He persuaded Himmler to release French prisoners from Ravensbrück, the female camp, since France was liberated anyway, to allow Jewish inmates to leave Bergen-Belsen for Sweden, and eventually to assemble all Jews in a camp under control of the Red Cross. He presented lists drawn up by the Swedish government of different categories of Jews to be sent to Sweden or Switzerland. He even talked Himmler out of a plan to blow up The Hague in retaliation against the treacherous Dutch people. Hitler himself had ordered it, said Himmler. But could Himmler not defy the order in name of humanity? Did he really want to be guilty of destroying a great Germanic town? Well, all right, said Himmler, he would spare the Germanic town of The Hague, even though the Dutch really didn't deserve it. Kersten thanked him "in the name of history for this benevolent act by which so many lives will be spared."

If such a plan ever existed, there is no record of it. Since The Hague was where the Germans had based their V-2 rocket launchers, designed to do maximum damage to London, it seems doubtful.

Still, the attempt to get Himmler to release Jewish and other prisoners was real and not without hazard. Kersten had played his role with aplomb. One thing that makes his story a little confusing, however, is that Count Bernadotte claimed in his memoir to have arrived at similar arrangements with Himmler roughly at the same time. At the very least, Bernadotte got Himmler to agree to allow Scandinavian prisoners to leave several camps under the auspices of the Red Cross. And Himmler later promised the release of prisoners, including Jews, from Ravensbrück.

The rescue mission started in March, when Bernadotte led a fleet of buses, painted white with red crosses and Swedish flags, to a few concentration camps, including Dachau, Mauthausen, and Ravensbrück. Despite their markings, the convoy was sometimes strafed by Allied fighter planes who mistook the buses for German transports. Bernadotte had to dive into a ditch a few times himself. The buses, some of them driven by Canadian POWs, were not allowed to enter the camps, to prevent foreign eyes from seeing what the Germans had done, but after several weeks more than twenty thousand people had been pushed out of the camp gates. Many of them were so weak that they could barely walk. Often, the prisoners were forced to drag themselves to the buses for several miles. But many eventually made it to Denmark and Sweden. About eight thousand of the evacuees were Norwegians and Danes. The rest came from various countries, including several thousand Jewish prisoners. All this took place in secrecy. Any publicity would have infuriated Hitler and endangered the mission.

How much of this operation was due to Kersten's negotiations, and how much to Bernadotte's, is hard to tell. Wilhelm Wulff writes that he heard from Schellenberg that Kersten had introduced Bernadotte to Himmler. It also seems that initially Bernadotte concentrated on getting only Scandinavians released. There is barely any mention of Jews in his memoir. But then, he was negotiating on behalf of the Swedish Red Cross. Kersten had been asked to speak to Himmler by the World Jewish Congress.

Himmler wrote Kersten a letter on March 21, the hypocrisy of which is so extreme that one might think it was meant as macabre mockery. Or perhaps not. Himmler's delusions might have been alarmingly sincere.

He was happy to announce to Kersten that 2,700 Jewish men, women, and children had been freed. This, he continued, was what he had always intended until "the war and the unreason unleashed by it" made it impossible to carry out. He was sure that once "demagoguery and superficialities" were excluded, "wisdom and reason would prevail, despite the bloodiest wounds on all sides, as will human sentiments and the willingness to help."

Before returning to Stockholm, Kersten managed to extract one more concession from Himmler. He suggested that it would be a good idea for the SS chief to meet in person with the representative of the World Jewish Congress. Himmler couldn't believe this at first. What would the Führer say if he found out? Kersten replied that no one needed to know apart from Himmler, Schellenberg, and Brandt. And so, Himmler, still hoping to strike a deal with Churchill or Eisenhower, agreed to meet Hillel Storch at Kersten's country estate.

Back in Sweden, Kersten, in his own account, basked in effusive praise. Christian Günther, the Swedish foreign minister, called Kersten's efforts "a political event of global importance," and Storch told him that "Jews all over the world will be eternally grateful to you." Joseph Kessel gives the story an extra flourish. In his book, Günther, hearing about Himmler's agreement to meet the representative of a Jewish organization, exclaims: "My goodness! It is extraordinary, it is absurd! I know you are the Miracle Doctor, but this, even for you, sounds impossible."

There was indeed something surreal about this last-minute negotiation between a Jewish representative and the man who tried to wipe out the Jewish people. Since Himmler could never be trusted, it was also dangerous. There is some doubt whether the document Himmler supposedly signed with Kersten, laying out his promises to stop killing Jews and hand over the camps in an orderly way to the Allies, really existed. Only a carbon copy without their signatures survives. But even if Himmler did make these promises, verbally or in writing, he failed to keep them. Bergen-Belsen was indeed handed over to the British on April 15, but only because a typhus epidemic had made moving the inmates too risky. Weeks before that, Himmler ordered tens of thousands of prisoners from Buchenwald and the Dora-Mittelbau camp to leave on forced marches without food or drink and dressed in rags. The exhausted survivors who couldn't keep up were shot. Himmler also told the commandants of Dachau and the Flossenburg camp that no prisoners should fall into enemy hands. Bernadotte mentioned the charred corpses piled up at Buchenwald when the Americans arrived. Himmler told him that was because American tanks had caused a fire in the camp.

Storch, a stateless person without a Swedish passport to give him some protection, quite sensibly decided it would be unsafe to put himself at the mercy of Himmler's SS. Another World Jewish Congress representative, Norbert Masur, would accompany Kersten instead to the meeting at Hartzwalde. Masur was a German Jew who had moved to Sweden before the war. He recalled how he felt before boarding the plane to Berlin on April 19: "For me, as a Jew, it was a deeply moving thought that in a few hours, I would be face to face with the man who was primarily responsible for the destruction of several million people."

Kersten slept soundly on the flight. Masur apparently did not. His description of the trip to see Himmler is one of the most extraordinary documents of World War II. They were met by police officers at Tempelhof, the modernist airport in the middle of Berlin, with cries of "*Heil Hitler!*" Masur raised his hat and politely wished them good evening.

The city looked deserted. In fact, there was barely any city left. Their SS car traveled in the dark with dimmed headlights through miles of rubble with checkpoints and tank barriers to make the trip more arduous. They drove through the outskirts of Berlin, past Sachsenhausen, one of the first concentration camps in Nazi Germany. The name jolted Masur. Some of his relatives had had the terrible experience of being incarcerated there. Once they were clear of the city limits, they stopped the car and watched in awe as searchlights fingered the sky for enemy bombers. The destruction of Berlin "was a fascinating spectacle in all its horror. We could hear the hum of airplanes coming in from all directions. The chauffeur said they were Russians. Colorful flash bombs slowly descended and spread like a carpet over the city. We saw planes caught in the searchlights, but there was no sound of anti-aircraft guns. The chauffeur explained that the flak batteries had all been sent away to the eastern battle fronts."

They reached Hartzwalde just before midnight. Schellenberg arrived two hours later. His "somewhat feminine appearance" made him look quite different from the "hard Nazi type" Masur had expected. Schellenberg was depressed about the future of Germany and told Masur that Hitler was still very much opposed to treating Jews more humanely. Masur slept badly again, not because of the incessant noise of bombers overhead, but because of anxiety about his forthcoming meeting with the mass murderer.

The next day, April 20, was Hitler's birthday. Himmler would be attending a celebration dinner that night in Berlin. He promised to come to Hartzwalde straight from the Führer's bunker. Masur remained on tenterhooks. What if Himmler suddenly changed his mind? What if there were no safe way back to Sweden? After breakfast, he strolled around the grounds, listening to atrocity stories from the Jehovah's Witnesses who worked Kersten's estate. There were also some German refugees from Prussia and other areas now in the hands of Soviet troops.

Himmler finally arrived in the early hours of the morning. Masur found him surprisingly relaxed, neatly dressed in his SS uniform, polite. This is when Himmler is supposed to have uttered the famous words "I want to bury the hatchet between us and the Jews. If I had had my own way, many things would have been done differently." Kersten wrote in his reconstructed diary that these words were spoken to him, not Masur. This is possible, and only slightly less grotesque than if Himmler had said this directly to the representative of the Jewish people.

Himmler, Schellenberg, Brandt, Kersten, and Masur sat down for coffee and cakes. Then, Himmler began to hold forth, as was his habit, about the historical necessity for Germany to solve its Jewish problem once and for all. He mentioned problems the Germans had had with eastern European Jews, who were all infected with dangerous diseases. This, he explained to Masur, who kept his cool despite a building rage, accounted for the crematoria in the camps, to burn the bodies of Jews who had succumbed to typhoid fever. Himmler became agitated. For this, he exclaimed, the Germans were to be hanged! It was all so unfair! The camps, by the way, should not be called concentration camps but training camps. The Nazis had been very successful at reducing crime through reeducation. And, by the way, the Jews had made everything worse by shooting at German soldiers from their ghettos. But still, Himmler wished to impress his Jewish interlocutor with his magnanimity: he had "left 450,000 Jews behind" in Budapest. What had already happened to the other 430,000 Hungarian Jews who disappeared (to Auschwitz) in the summer of 1944 was discreetly left unmentioned.

At some point in Himmler's monologue, Masur managed to interrupt. There was little point dwelling on what happened in the past, he said; "we now have to make sure that all Jews in Germany and countries occupied by Germany remain alive." The conversation could have ended there, as Himmler made it clear that the Führer would never allow the liberation of any more Jews. Whereupon Kersten suggested that Himmler look at the lists of prisoners compiled by the Swedish government. Himmler agreed but not in the presence of Masur, who was asked to leave the room. When Masur was allowed to come back and resume talks, Himmler declared that he was prepared to release Scandinavian, Dutch, and French prisoners on the Swedish list, as well as one thousand Jewish women from Ravensbrück. This, Himmler thought, would surely please Masur. But only on one condition: they had to be identified as Poles, and never as Jews.

By the time Himmler left at five o'clock in the morning, the conversation had lasted for two and a half hours. The Reichsführer's words to Kersten, as he got into his car, were: "With us, the best of the German people will perish. As for the rest, we don't care about them." He also thanked Kersten with tears in his eyes: "Whatever happens, don't think badly of me. Please help my poor family if you can."

On the way back to Berlin, where they tried to locate Count Berna-dotte without success, Masur saw something he would never forget: the German *Herrenvolk* on the road. He was shocked by the view of this "heap of human misery, piled into an endless succession of carts filled with hastily rescued household items. It kept moving away from the front in wind and rain, from town to town, without ever being able to stay long. . . . These were the images of desolation that we saw in photo-graphs or in our imagination, of French, Poles, Russians, and Jews forced to flee from German soldiers, images that were cheered on by the Ger-man people. Now, finally, the Germans are suffering what they had done to others."

Kersten, too, was moved by his farewell to Germany and his beloved Hartzwalde. It made him reflect on his past, back to the time he first discovered the healing power of his hands in a Finnish field hospital. "It has been my fate ever since," he thought to himself, "to heal people and to help them, wherever they are threatened in a system of violence. I was grateful to the Eternal One who allowed me to accomplish this." What he thought of his patients who perpetrated the violence, he didn't say.

Ten

AFTERMATH

*The most striking difference between ancient and
modern sophists is that the ancients were satisfied
with a passing victory of the argument at the expense
of truth, whereas the moderns want a more lasting
victory at the expense of reality.*

HANNAH ARENDT

1: Matsumoto

Reinventing history is a constant process. Much of what most people know about the past comes to them through fiction, in novels, movies, musicals, or comic books. Mythology sometimes bypasses history entirely by claims that nothing ever ended, claims that the death of a hero never took place, for instance. The story of Christ's resurrection comes to mind, but his death was never denied. He rose again, just as trees in springtime sprout new leaves after a barren winter. His story is not so much a myth as a parable for the cycle of life and death.

The type of mythology I mean is present in cultures in all parts of the world. The belief, for example, that Elvis Presley never died, and has been "sighted," like a UFO, in Kalamazoo, Michigan, or Carlsbad, California.

In Japan this kind of fantasy is best illustrated by the story of the twelfth-century hero Minamoto no Yoshitsune, a superb swordsman who helped to win an epic war against a rival clan. The legendary warrior was finally defeated by his ambitious half brother Yoritomo, and he was forced to commit suicide by slitting his stomach in samurai fashion. His severed head, pickled in alcohol, was presented at his brother's court. Like Elvis, however, Yoshitsune lived on in the minds of believers, who were convinced that he escaped on a ship to Manchuria and later came back as Genghis Khan.

The Genghis Khan story was written many centuries after Yoshitsune's death. Kawashima Yoshiko's extraordinary survival was already reported shortly after she was executed as a traitor in Beijing. One story goes that a shiftless Chinese family named Liu offered to let one of their daughters be executed instead of Yoshiko. The two women apparently looked alike. For this sacrifice, the Liu family demanded a payment of ten gold bars. When only four bars were received, the elder brother lodged a complaint. Since he failed to leave an address, no further inquiries were made. By then, Yoshiko had already made her way to Manchuria, supposedly in the care of a Chinese Communist general, and nothing more was heard of her since.

Kamisaka Fuyuko, Yoshiko's Japanese biographer, cites an alternative story related by Xianli, Yoshiko's elder brother. In this version, a regional Chinese Nationalist military commander, who was married to a Manchu aristocrat, offered to save her life. One hundred gold bars were demanded for a body switch. Since the Soviet government hoped to use Yoshiko as an informant (presumably on Japanese matters), two Russian planes were waiting to take her to the Russo-Mongolian border. Quite who was going to dispense all that gold is left unexplained in these stories: the Russians? the Chinese Communist general? And what was the general's connection with the Soviets?

In any case, soon after her execution, the Chinese and Japanese press ran stories about the Mata Hari of the Orient still being alive and well.

Yoshiko's adoptive father, Kawashima Naniwa, now a stone-deaf old man, thought there was something fishy about his daughter's death too. In a letter to a friend, he pointed out that a photograph of her corpse, published in Chinese newspapers, showed a long-haired woman, even though Yoshiko always wore her hair cut short. He added that the Japanese Buddhist priest who retrieved her body, in the absence of Yoshiko's relatives (who were afraid of being tainted by her crimes), had told him that her face had been so disfigured by the bullet that passed through the back of her head that she was hard to recognize.

The priest was convinced nonetheless that it could only have been Yoshiko, whose corpse he brought back to Japan, because a letter was found in her pocket with a poem written in her own hand. The original is kept at the U.S. National Archives. The rather poor English translation was done by someone in the American occupation administration in Japan. It goes:

> *I have a home; but where I cannot return,*
> *I have sorrow; which I cannot disclose,*
> *I have a law; which cannot protect me,*
> *I am innocent; but I have no one to appeal to.*

This sounds very much like the real Yoshiko.

In 2003, a Chinese woman appeared in a quiz show on Japanese TV, claiming to have been Yoshiko's daughter. She said her mother had married a Japanese man. Another Chinese woman turned up in 2008. According to her, Yoshiko had been sheltered in the former Japanese police academy in Shinkyo, now Changchun. She then led a quiet life in a small village, playing a recording of Ri Koran singing one of her hits, "Suzhou Nocturne," over and over.

So, if in fact Yoshiko died in 1948, her legend did not. It still lives on in popular culture. A quick glance at Japanese Wikipedia shows that she has been the subject of thirteen nonfiction books, four novels, eleven plays, eight movies, five television dramas, four manga, one musical, and one video game. As recently as 2009, a Japanese television show entitled *The Beauty in Men's Clothes: Kawashima Yoshiko Was Still Alive!* (*Danso no reijin: Kawashima Yoshiko wa ikiteita!*) dramatized the story of the switched bodies. The first postwar movie about Yoshiko, entitled *Shanghai Is Burning* (*Moeru Shanghai*) was made in 1954. The film followed a book of the same title by Muramatsu Shofu, which appeared the year before. Muramatsu, the man who fictionalized Yoshiko's adventures in 1933, was clearly convinced there was more mileage in his story.

The movie is a fiction based on a fiction, with a deep strain of noirish melancholy, inevitable perhaps in the 1950s, when the Japanese war could hardly be shown in a heroic light. Set in Shanghai, the Asian Mata Hari, aiming to revive the Qing Dynasty, embarks on love affairs with Japanese officers to further her goal. After many adventures, featuring a Chinese lover in the anti-Japanese resistance and a Korean terrorist, she realizes that she has been used by the Japanese military all along and returns to Mongolia in a mood of despair. No one emerges well from this moral murk.

A second movie followed three years later: *Clouds of War: The Queen of Asia* (*Sen'un: Ajia no jo-o*) is more like an epic adventure movie, a kitsch forerunner of *Lawrence of Arabia*. Unlike the dark fantasy of dissolute Shanghai, this is a story of heroism and bravado, an even more fanciful version of Yoshiko's wartime myth. Despite being in love with a Japanese officer, Yoshiko marries a Mongolian prince (which of course she did in real life). The wedding ceremony is interrupted by a gang of bandits (which certainly did not happen). The prince is killed, and Yoshiko clips her hair and takes command as the Mongolian queen, looking splendid on her horse dressed in a general's uniform.

The politics are absurd. The plot creaks all over the place. The story has almost no basis in fact. But what is missing is the vague antiwar message of the earlier movie. Yoshiko is no longer a sad victim of history, but the heroic figure she had been in Japanese wartime propaganda. Possibly, the change of mood reflected gradual changes in Japanese society, including ways of viewing the recent past. The early 1950s were a time of serious, often left-wing, national introspection. This did not persist in popular culture.

People who had known Yoshiko protested that the movies got her completely wrong. Shoji Hisako, the former secretary of Yoshiko's adoptive Japanese father, said Yoshiko was never a schemer who used people for her own ends. In fact, quite the opposite was true: powerful figures in the Japanese military and government had used her. What the movies missed, in Shoji's view, was Yoshiko's profound loneliness. The secretary noticed how Yoshiko wept in her room every night in her house in Dalian.

The idea of victimhood, of peace-loving ideals betrayed by evil militarists, fell on fertile ground. Much more than tales of heroism, this became the common story about the past in postwar Japan. The Japanese people, so full of good intentions, with the peace-loving emperor as their prime symbol, had been led astray by warmongers. The production of *Ri Koran: The Musical*, featuring Kawashima Yoshiko as the narrator, in a dashing military uniform, fits the bill perfectly.

Ri Koran: The Musical was first staged in Tokyo in 1991 by a theater company called Shiki, led by Asari Keita, one of Japan's most eminent modern theater producers. Shiki was already well-known for its sumptuous productions of such Broadway musical hits as *Cats*, *West Side Story*, and *Jesus Christ Superstar*. Asari was not a right-wing nationalist who sought to prettify or whitewash Japan's wartime record. But his business was entertainment, so he was not about to ruffle any feathers either, including those of Ri Koran/Yamaguchi Yoshiko herself, who was still very much present. She had switched from being a movie star to hosting a TV show, and then embarked on a long career as a politician for the conservative Liberal Democratic Party. I knew her slightly in the 1990s, when she would repeat the mythical version of her life in a mixture of Chinese and Japanese. She was a small, elegant lady in her seventies, with jet-black hair and not a wrinkle in her carefully tended face.

The musical begins dramatically with a dance number set in Shanghai just after the war. A Chinese crowd is calling for the blood of the traitors. "Kill! Kill!" the chorus sings, "Kill the collaborators who sold out our motherland to the hateful Japanese. Kill! Kill! Kill!" Kawashima Yoshiko, dressed in a brilliant white uniform, then appears onstage to tell the story of Ri Koran, how she got caught in the wheels of history, and by extension how Yoshiko herself got tangled up in the same tragic events.

We see Ri being judged in a Chinese military court. She softly sings: "I loved China. I loved Japan. I just wanted to bring the two countries together in peace and harmony." Whereupon the judge pronounces that hate should not be met with hate and the time has come for reconciliation.

The horrors of war are not ignored. Behind Kawashima Yoshiko, dancing soldiers of the Kwantung Army look menacing as they fire their guns, killing innocent Chinese, tumbling all over the stage. We see Emperor Puyi falling off his phony throne. We see the common Japanese suffering from militaristic policies at home, with their sons forced to die in a hopeless war. But we also see Puyi in a showstopping scene surrounded by people in Chinese clothes, their arms stretched to heaven, with ecstasy in their eyes, waving the colors of the five races living in glorious harmony and belting out "Manchurian Dream."

The point of the show was not to revive Manchukuo propaganda. In fact, right-wing nationalists were annoyed by the negative portrayal of wartime Japan. But there is an unmistakable sense of tragedy in the story, of a beautiful dream gone sour. No one in Japan, even on the far right, would idealize the invasion of China. Some still maintain, with some reason, that the war in Southeast Asia was a bloody conflict with European colonial oppressors, and with less reason that Japanese fought to liberate Asians. Some continue to argue that the United States and other imperial powers forced Japan to go to war. But there is little romance in these events. The Battle of Shanghai, let alone the Nanjing Massacre, would hardly lend itself to a song and dance production, and neither would the attack on Pearl Harbor. But Manchukuo has a lingering romantic appeal.

The myths of Kawashima Yoshiko, who "longed for peace in Asia," and of Ri Koran, who "loved China" and "loved Japan," still play to the imaginations of many Japanese. This has nothing to do with militarism, or even with colonial nostalgia for the acacia trees of Dalian. Something deeper is at stake. The confused identities of the two Yoshikos, one a Japanese raised in China, and the other a Manchu raised in Japan, both acting out roles that promoted a brutal imperial project, and both caught between Japan and the Chinese continent, reflect in different ways the confused identities of Japan itself.

For much of its history, Japan was a peripheral country that looked to China as the center of civilization. When China's weakness was exposed in the humiliating Opium Wars with Britain in the mid-nineteenth century, Japan sought to dodge the abject colonial submission of much of Asia by turning to the West as the center of civilization. "Leave Asia," or *Datsu A*, was the motto coined by the great liberal thinker Fukuzawa Yukichi at the end of that century. Fukuzawa was an admirer of the European Enlightenment. Japan would become a powerful modern enlightened nation by Westernizing as quickly and thoroughly as possible: Western clothes, Western culture, Western architecture, Western military organization, and of course a Western-style colonial empire, in Korea, Taiwan, and the South Pacific.

And yet, Japan never really became a Western country. Leaving Asia did not mean entering the West. When in 1919, Japan, as a proud member of the League of Nations, asked for a racial equality clause (not for everyone, but for members of the League), Australia and the United States refused. This snub was the beginning of a slow reversal in Japanese attitudes toward the West. Nationalists rejected symbols of Westernization, such as Hollywood movies, jazz music, and political liberalism. A revived sense of Japaneseness, often authoritarian and militaristic in tone, was promoted. This Japaneseness would be anchored in Asia once more. But instead of being a peripheral power paying tribute to the Middle Kingdom, Japan, after ridding the continent of noxious Western imperialists, would be the new Asian master.

There was, however, a deeply ambivalent strain running through this militant nationalism. Even as Japan wished to restore Asia to the Asians, its politicians and diplomats still wanted to impress Western powers with Japan's modern prowess and earn their respect as equals. Manchukuo was to be a showcase of Asian modernity, blessed with racial equality and the latest technology. This colonial experiment posing as anticolonialism would draw the Japanese archipelago out of its insularity. The Japanese would be Asian, powerful, culturally advanced, keenly internationalist, and admired, not just by fellow Asians, who were expected to be grateful for Japanese leadership, but by the Western powers too.

But most Asians were no more prepared to accept Japan on its own terms than the Americans and Australians were to regard Japanese as racial equals. Some Asian leaders were happy to cooperate with Japan to free themselves from their colonial oppressors, but not to accept the Japanese as the new colonial masters.

And so, after 1945, the identity of the Japanese nation was as confused as it had been before. Defeated by the West, rejected by other Asians, and especially hated by the Chinese, Japan still had not found its rightful place. Some Japanese saw a renewed attempt to "leave Asia" as the best way to secure the nation's future. Coached by the U.S. occupation authorities, Japan would mimic American ways in politics, education, culture, and social mores. Japan would be the closest thing to being an American state, on the edge of the Asian continent, as it was possible to be for a sovereign nation. Others, on the left as well as the right, tried to reestablish close relations with Asian countries, often in spasms of hostility to the United States and contempt for its culture.

Ri Koran's, or rather Yamaguchi Yoshiko's, role as a politician was precisely that: to repair the links with Asia. She was sent to China, North Korea, and other non-Western countries to build bridges and show contrition for the historical wrongs she herself had helped to promote. This Yoshiko had not only found her place as a symbol of Japan's troubled past, but also as a player in the latest Japanese attempt to adopt a pan-Asian identity, spreading peace, harmony, and liberty.

The other Yoshiko never had the chance to redeem herself, as a bridge between cultures or a symbol of contrition. Speaking of her love for China and asking to be buried in a Japanese kimono, Kawashima Yoshiko was as conflicted in the face of imminent death as she had been during her life. She, too, like Ri Koran, will always be linked in Japanese minds to the lost Manchukuo dream. Whether she is remembered as a glamorous hero, or a tragic victim, she will forever be the exotic continental princess who was on the side of Japan in its quest for an Asian utopia.

For most Japanese under sixty, Manchukuo is now little more than a name in the history books, if that. Japan's relations with Asia are still unsettled, but that particular dream has faded. There is no such thing as Manchuria any longer, just a few northeast provinces of the People's Republic of China. As for a Manchu revival or a new Qing Dynasty, that no longer even exists as a fantasy, in Japan, China, or anywhere else.

And yet, Yoshiko's legend persists, in unexpected ways. Her latest incarnation in popular culture arrived in the form of a manga as recently as 2020. She is depicted on the cover of the comic strip aimed at teenagers as a young woman pointing a gun and half-dressed in a Japanese army uniform, her bare legs and white underwear saucily exposed. It is part of a series by a female manga artist named Tanaka Hosana. The title is *Kawashima Yoshiko Wants to Be a Man* (*Kawashima Yoshiko otoko ni naritai*). The description on the cover goes like this: "A young woman moves to Shanghai with a dream. Her name is Kawashima Yoshiko. Seventeen years old. Her only dream in the city of endless possibilities is—to be a man! . . . In Shanghai the heroine will become a hero. Here is the first edition of her grand adventure of fighting for her country."

The seventeen-year-old Yoshiko was of course not in Shanghai. But the manga is aimed at a young audience, specifically at readers with a taste for androgynous heroes. This has long been a specialized genre in Japanese manga, appealing to the same people who adore the Takarazuka Revue, an all-female theater troupe famous for its productions of *Gone with the Wind* and other musical spectacles. The female actors of male roles are especially admired. Yoshiko never actually said that she wanted to be a man. She did say men caused endless trouble to women. She also said she wanted to "do what boys do." And she said she "was born with what the doctors call a tendency toward the third sex." If not yet a fully transgendered figure in her latest manga incarnation, Kawashima is still the perfect hero for a gender-fluid generation.

Her tombstone in a small Buddhist temple in Matsumoto, near the spot where she once rode her horse to school, is inscribed with her Japanese name, Yoshiko, and with the name of her adoptive father, Naniwa, described simply as "a patriot." Yoshiko always maintained that she was a patriot too. As the manga says, she fought for her country. The question remains: Which one?

2: Stockholm

After the collapse of Hitler's Reich, Felix Kersten badly needed to secure his residence in Sweden, preferably with a Swedish passport. He was still formally a Finnish citizen, but a staunch anti-Communist who had serviced the top Nazis could hardly feel safe on the periphery of the Soviet Union. Nor could he go back to Hartzwalde, his country estate in a part of Germany that was now firmly under Soviet control. Christian Günther, the Swedish foreign minister, was on Kersten's side and supported his application for citizenship, but to no avail. In any case, Günther lost his job at the end of 1945. The Social Democrats who took over were suspicious of Kersten.

Kersten was vulnerable in a way he hadn't experienced before, or at least not for many years: short of cash and without the protection of powerful leaders. Himmler had swallowed cyanide after being caught by British troops, not very far from Bergen-Belsen, dressed in a sergeant's uniform. Gottlob Berger had surrendered to the 101st Airborne Division near Salzburg. Himmler's former secretary, Rudolf Brandt, was a POW in the same camp where his boss killed himself. And other Nazi leaders who had been treated by Kersten, such as Ribbentrop and Hess, were facing war crime trials. Robert Ley, the gauleiter and Labor Front chief, did too, but he hanged himself in his cell with a rope made of toilet paper.

It may be that Kersten's request for Swedish citizenship was turned down because he hadn't spent enough time in Sweden. More likely, it was because he had some potent enemies. Most prominent among them was Count Folke Bernadotte.

Although Kersten was not a war criminal, to get on in the febrile atmosphere of postwar Europe, he needed to rid himself of any taint of Nazi collaboration. Then, so did the Swedes. And the heroic story of Bernadotte's white buses rescuing people from some of the worst Nazi hellholes was perfect for polishing Sweden's reputation. There was not much desire in Stockholm to water down this legendary feat with complicated stories about the interventions of Himmler's Finnish masseur.

Within months after the end of the war, *Slutet*, or *The End*, was published under Bernadotte's name. (The book was published in the United States as *The Curtain Falls*.) This slim volume offers a glowing account of Bernadotte's meetings with Himmler, the way he managed to browbeat the Reichsführer SS into releasing prisoners, the adventures of the white buses, and more. The text is peppered with breathless clichés: "The gloves were off. The fight had begun," and so on. Bernadotte also offers deft little pen portraits of the main Nazi leaders. Ribbentrop was "a man of very small mental stature and, moreover, rather ridiculous," and Kaltenbrunner had "an evil spirit." The hero of the story is of course Bernadotte himself. But his most able helper is Walter Schellenberg, the "good Nazi," as it were. Bernadotte always "felt a certain confidence in Schellenberg," the man who "tried to combat the bestialities of the Gestapo." He would "always be grateful" to him for his "valuable help." Bernadotte's autohagiography even ends with Schellenberg's personal account of the gallant Swedish rescue missions.

None of this should come as a great surprise, since Schellenberg actually wrote the book. Schellenberg, too, needed Swedish protection. He embarked on the management of his own as well as Bernadotte's legend while staying with the count in Stockholm. This worked up to a point. Even though he was soon arrested by the British, Schellenberg avoided a heavy sentence by testifying against the SS at the Nuremberg trials. He was in prison for only two years and wrote a memoir called *The Labyrinth*. A CIA report on the book describes the author deftly: "*The Labyrinth* throws into relief one salient aspect of Schellenberg's personality: his exceptional dexterity in the manipulation of power factions within the leadership of the Nazi party without ever becoming too closely identified with any one of them."

In the immediate aftermath of the war, Schellenberg was happy to use and be used by Bernadotte. One of the oddest things about *The Curtain Falls* is the complete absence of Felix Kersten's name. He might as well not have existed. Kersten was understandably put out by this erasure of his role in the events of 1945. But Bernadotte tried to make sure that Kersten wouldn't make a fuss about it. He is quoted as having said that if Kersten "dared to make a criticism or a comment about [the book], he and his family would be sent back to Finland." This may not have been why Kersten was refused Swedish citizenship, but it certainly didn't help.

Nor did some people sympathetic to Bernadotte who kept insisting that Kersten was a Nazi. This, despite grateful testimonies from the World Jewish Congress on Kersten's behalf.

Before publicly casting himself in a heroic light, Kersten decided to seek his redemption by turning to his Dutch contacts. His main booster in diplomatic circles was Baron J. E. H. van Nagell, who had known Kersten since 1943. He had been happy to meet Kersten during the war, even as the Dutch embassy refused to do so. The baron did everything he could to talk up Kersten's reputation in high Dutch circles, some of whose members had personal reasons to be grateful for the masseur's interventions. One such elite Dutchman was Marius de Beaufort, a prominent figure in shipping and banking. His daughter was one of the prisoners released from the Ravensbrück camp in 1945. De Beaufort spoke to Baron van Boetzelaer van Oosterhout, the Dutch foreign minister, who approached Queen Wilhelmina with the suggestion of making Kersten a Dutch citizen. The queen would have remembered Kersten's solicitous treatment before the war of her late husband, Prince Hendrik. Her son-in-law, Prince Bernhard, was convinced that Kersten had saved his mother and brother, both keen Nazis, from being persecuted by Goebbels. As mentioned earlier, Kersten always maintained that Goebbels wanted to punish Prince Bernhard's German relatives after the Dutch royal family fled to London in 1940, and that Kersten persuaded Himmler to protect them.

Baron Van Nagell has been credited by some as an impeccable source on Kersten's wartime exploits. Whether or not this was true, he was clearly a skillful networker in Dutch high society. But some of his colleagues had misgivings, both about Kersten and the diplomat himself. Van Nagell was yet another conservative in Kersten's circles who had reason to be defensive about his past. He had been removed from his position as ambassador to Sweden in 1941 because his loyalty to the anti-Nazi cause was under suspicion. A speech of his in 1940, praising the Germans as "our great neighbors," had not gone down well. Van Nagell's reputation, too, needed some burnishing.

In a letter from the Dutch embassy in Stockholm, the diplomat in charge of intelligence advised against giving Kersten Dutch citizenship. Kersten, in his view, was not to be trusted. Three years after the war, despite Baron Van Nagell's best efforts, Kersten was still without a safe passport. He also claimed that he was poor. His solution was to come out with a book himself. The first edition in Dutch, *Klerk en beul*, was squarely aimed at making his case to readers in the Netherlands. The text is full of flattering references to the Dutch people, their extraordinary suffering, and plucky resistance. Much is made of Kersten's success in talking Himmler out of deporting the entire Dutch population to Poland in 1941, which was to be expected. Much is also made of Kersten's sensational interventions when Himmler supposedly threatened to blow up The Hague, or when the Germans were apparently planning to rob the Dutch of their artistic treasures.

Loe de Jong, the main historian of the Netherlands in World War II, convincingly debunked the deportation story in 1972. He believed that Kersten's diaries, published in English as *The Kersten Memoirs*, as well as other documents, were largely made up after the war. We know—not least from Baron Van Nagell's account—that much of Kersten's archive was destroyed by the loyal Elizabeth Lüben, when the Soviet Red Army was approaching Hartzwalde. To call Kersten's book the work of a con man may be harsh, but the author had the successful con man's talent for telling his marks what they wished to hear. De Jong concluded that Kersten had been responsible for some fine humanitarian deeds, but that as far as history is concerned, he was an "utterly unreliable witness."

This view was echoed in a letter from A. J. Th. van der Vlugt, the Dutch ambassador in Helsinki, who reported that the Finns distrusted Kersten. "Aside from his special gifts as a masseur," he wrote, "Kersten is seen here as a fantasist and a money-grubber. His book is seen as grandiose propaganda for himself and an important source of income." That Kersten is said to have lobbied for his book to be turned into a movie

would give this view some plausibility. But he probably cared more
about his reputation at this stage
than about making a quick buck.

Still, in 1948, Kersten's claims
were widely believed, first of all
in the Netherlands, where Prince
Bernhard personally pinned a Dutch
Red Cross medal onto his lapel.
There was even talk of proposing
him for a Nobel Prize. But before
that, there was at least one attempt
to make sure everything was above-
board. A committee was formed in

1949 to establish the truth of Kersten's extravagant claims of saving the
Dutch from deportation, their country from destruction, and their treasures from being looted. The committee was led by an economic historian
named N. W. Posthumus. The other members were two diplomats and a
historian. Their main informant appears to have been Baron Van Nagell.
Posthumus became convinced that Kersten's claims were essentially true.
Kersten may not have been the only reason Himmler didn't deport the
Dutch to Poland, but at least his influence had been a major factor. Because Kersten's documents were so detailed, the gentlemen of the committee had to conclude that "one cannot believe they were fictional, unless
one would wish to regard Kersten as an exceptional fantasist, which the
committee declines to do."

There have been suggestions that Posthumus was less than impartial
in his investigation because of his close personal relationship with Kersten. He might even have borrowed money from him, as well as being the
happy recipient of his soothing massages. Still, the Dutch government
accepted the committee's findings and Prince Bernhard once again was
delighted to give Kersten one of the highest Dutch honors, stating that it

was "difficult to find words for everything you have done for the Dutch people." Soon after this, Kersten bought a house in Scheveningen, near the spot where he had lived so happily before the war, a short walk away from Villa Windekind, where Jews were tortured and Weinreb tried to hoodwink the SD. His wife was still in Stockholm, and somewhat eccentrically, their sons were sent to a boarding school in Germany; Kersten believed in a solid German education, even amid the ruins of a defeated nation.

The other piece of unsolicited good fortune for Kersten was the death in 1948 of his nemesis, Count Bernadotte. That May, Bernadotte had been appointed as peace mediator between the Jews and the Palestinians in the newly founded state of Israel. His peace proposals did not go down well with some Israelis, who regarded him as an Arab stooge. On September 17, as his motorcade moved through the center of Jerusalem, Bernadotte was gunned down by members of the radical Lehi group, better known as the Stern gang, led by the future Israeli prime minister Yitzhak Shamir.

In the narrative struggle over recent history, this put Kersten in an advantageous position. He already had the Dutch, as well as the World Jewish Congress, on his side. But the Swedes still refused to grant him citizenship, and suspicions of his Nazi sympathies had not gone away, especially among left-leaning Swedes. Kersten disclosed his unhappiness to a most peculiar confidante, a Dutch faith healer and "hand layer" named Greet Hofmans, a woman who was convinced that Jesus, among other voices from higher spheres, spoke through her.

Hofmans had a few things in common with Kersten. Both found their clientele among rich and influential people. Both claimed that powerful figures had special physical and psychological problems due to the stress of their many responsibilities, and that they, as the masseur and the faith healer, had the rare means to help them. Like Madame Blavatsky, the nineteenth-century founder of theosophy, Hofmans was in touch with spirits of the dead. She had been called to the Dutch royal palace in 1948, when one of the princesses had serious eye problems. Queen Juliana, who had succeeded to the throne when her mother, Wilhelmina, abdicated, was rather susceptible to spiritual mumbo jumbo. In this case, rather too much so. Hofmans's grip on the queen became so alarming that it almost destroyed her marriage to Prince Bernhard and possibly the monarchy itself. Hofmans was deeply sympathetic to Kersten. Whether her advice helped him at all is doubtful. In a letter to him, she wrote that some people might never forget "the bestiality" of the recent past. Naturally, such people would stand in the way of his "rehabilitation." But he should pay no attention to this and "keep [his] eyes firmly on Jesus Christ, the savior of mankind."

Kersten's case was boosted by another piece of luck in 1953, when a sensational letter popped up, apparently written by Count Bernadotte to Himmler on March 10, 1945. The contents were devastating to the count's reputation, and highly flattering to Kersten. Speaking of prisoners to be released, Bernadotte insisted that "Jews are as unwelcome in Sweden as they are in Germany." Kersten, he wrote, had told him about Himmler's agreement to let five thousand Jews go to Sweden. This was most unfortunate since the count had "no desire to transport Jews to Sweden." Kersten, he continued, had "no authority to negotiate the release of Jews. He did this on his own account." Moreover, Bernadotte wrote, in one of the most damaging sentences, German rockets were not hitting the right targets in London. He, Bernadotte, would "supply a sketch indicating British military targets."

This was almost too good (or bad) to be true. The Swedes surely had to give full credit to Kersten now. But the Swedish foreign ministry dismissed the letter as a forgery. Count Bernadotte was a gentleman. This crudely worded missive couldn't possibly have been written by him. Besides, we know that Bernadotte asked Himmler to hand over Jews to the Red Cross in March. The main witness to the authenticity of the letter was Gottlob Berger, who declared that Bernadotte hated the Jews, whom he, Berger, had done his best to save. Not only that, but Kersten had been the only person responsible for helping Berger in this rescue mission. Since Berger had been an active participant in the Jewish genocide, for which he had been convicted as a war criminal, his words were hardly convincing. And because Kersten had helped Berger during his war crimes trial with an obliging testimony to his fine character, Berger was also in his debt.

Posthumus decided to send Bernadotte's letter to the distinguished British historian Hugh Trevor-Roper, later Baron Dacre of Glanton. Trevor-Roper, a counterintelligence officer during the war, had had great success with his 1947 book *The Last Days of Hitler*. He was also a lifelong student of forgers, fantasists, and mythomaniacs. He wrote a fine book, entitled *Hermit of Peking*, about the remarkable life of Sir Edmund Backhouse, a master forger of classical Chinese, whom he described as "a confidence man with few equals." Perhaps because his own father was a doctor, Trevor-Roper was also fascinated by the political influence of medical men. The perfect scholar, then, to get to the bottom of the Kersten affair.

Trevor-Roper didn't have enough evidence to authenticate Bernadotte's letter to Himmler. Which was a good thing too, since the Swedes turned out to have been right. The letter *was* too good to be true. Suspicions about its authenticity persisted. In the 1970s, Gerald Fleming, a British historian of Nazi Germany, subjected the letter to further scrutiny with the help of forensic experts at Scotland Yard. They concluded that not only did the writing style point to Kersten himself, but the letter type showed it would have come from his typewriter.

Nonetheless, Trevor-Roper was sufficiently convinced by the Dutch committee's findings, and outraged by Bernadotte's efforts to write Kersten out of history, to get involved in the case. He wrote articles for the Swedish press and *The Atlantic Monthly* in January 1953 denouncing Bernadotte's grandstanding and celebrating Kersten as "one of the great benefactors of Mankind." This caused a great stir in Sweden. The case was discussed by critics and supporters of Kersten in the Swedish parliament.

The result, as Trevor-Roper relates in his introduction to the American edition of Kersten's memoirs, was that "truth had triumphed over slander in Sweden" and Kersten finally got his Swedish passport in 1953.

Since they are particularly pertinent to the three life stories related in this book, Trevor-Roper's words in his introduction are worth quoting. "Human memory and human judgment are always fallible," he wrote, which is incontestable. He then went on to say that "as far as honesty of purpose and authenticity of documentation are concerned, I am pleased to support with such authority as I possess the accuracy of these memoirs of Felix Kersten."

As we now know, Trevor-Roper's judgment was a little too hasty. In fact, he later would distance himself from his early conclusions about Kersten. The great connoisseur of fraudsters would make a similar mistake with far greater publicity in 1983, when he vouched for the authenticity of Hitler's diaries, only to find out they were forged by a German petty crook.

One can only speculate why a great historian would allow himself to be duped in this way: vanity of the expert, too much eagerness for a good story, Kersten's undeniable charm, an animus against Bernadotte (who had been critical of *The Last Days of Hitler*)—all these things might have played a part. But a letter from Trevor-Roper to Kersten, after a visit to The Hague in October 1953, reveals something else. "Dear Dr. Kersten," it begins. "It was a great pleasure to see you again in Holland, and Lord and Lady Reay were both as delighted as I was with your hospitable entertainment of us. We all dined also with Professor Posthumus in the Hague before I returned to England, and enjoyed seeing him and hearing more from him."

Dinner with Lord and Lady Reay. Even his greatest admirers would admit that Trevor-Roper was a bit of a snob. Along with his gifts as a masseur, Kersten had always been brilliant at pleasing his social betters. That was his business, after all, to service the powerful and the wealthy. Trevor-Roper was a fine judge of the brutes in Hitler's entourage, but he was far from the only one to give too much slack to more urbane figures with greater social graces and intellectual sophistication. Albert Speer, Hitler's favorite architect and the minister of industry and armaments, was a ruthless man responsible for the deaths of countless slave workers. Although he later denied it, Speer was present when Himmler gave his notorious speech in Posen in 1943 describing the extermination of the Jews as "a difficult task" carried out "for the love of our people." But unlike more obviously criminal types, Speer was not hanged for his crimes. His polished demeanor stood out among the sullen ruffians on trial in Nuremberg. To some of his judges, he seemed almost like a gentleman.

Himmler, in Trevor-Roper's description, was "a cold-blooded inhuman ogre," but Speer's views deserved to be taken seriously: "His conclusions are never naïve, never parochial; they seem always honest; they are often profound. If he seems sometimes to have fallen too deeply under the spell of the tyrant whom he served, at least he was the only servant whose judgment was not corrupted by attendance on that dreadful master."

Kersten was not a slave driver who forced people to die in terrible conditions. But he was a courtier to that class of men who might not all have been Nazis but who had adapted themselves to Hitler's Reich, and often did very well: the industrialists and businessmen, the professors and doctors, the diplomats and bureaucrats, the "decent" men who served in the SS proudly but were supposedly shocked in private by its brutal methods. To find a loyal servant of that class, who was not only decent, but a hero, had great appeal, especially at a time when the compromised elites, in Germany and elsewhere, had to find their feet in postwar democracies, which they often served just as efficiently as they had the Third Reich.

Even as Kersten continued to thrive in his services as a masseur of the upper class, in Holland, Sweden, Germany, and elsewhere, he never severed his connections to his former comrades in Hitler's time. This was partly a matter of self-interest. Friedrich Flick, his former patient and one of the major industrialists in the Third Reich, was found guilty at

Nuremberg for using slave labor. Still, Kersten asked Flick to finance the publication of his memoirs. And Flick, by the way, after serving a short sentence, became one of the richest businessmen in West Germany. Kersten also went out of his way to supply not only Gottlob Berger but also Rudolf Brandt with helpful testimonies when they were on trial. In return, both men supported Kersten's most dubious claims.

There were, however, other, more disturbing postwar connections that cannot be so easily explained away. A Dutch amateur historian came across a cache of Kersten's correspondence from 1951 to 1954 at an auction. Most of these letters are either pleas for help from former Nazis and collaborators, or Kersten's promises that he would do what he could for them. He did his best for Friedrich Christiansen, the former commander of the German army in the occupied Netherlands, a man notorious for his savage reprisals against civilians. Kersten offered help to the ex-police chief in The Hague, who had taken an active part in the persecution of Jews. He asked a war crimes court to treat a concentration camp doctor with clemency.

Apart from one remark about the need for rehabilitation of the Waffen SS, there is no evidence in these letters that Kersten was a secret Nazi, as some have alleged. But the language of some of his correspondents suggests an assumption on their part that he was at least sympathetic. One of these was Leo Hausleiter, a journalist and publisher who joined the Nazi party in 1932 and was appointed to a high rank in the SS by Himmler. Hausleiter was arrested by the British in 1945, but he was imprisoned for only three years. He wrote a friendly letter to Kersten containing the following rather astonishing statement about Himmler: "People can say what they want about your former patient, but in his descriptions of the worst characteristics of the Jews, he was way ahead of his time." Hausleiter adds further comments on the text of Kersten's memoir, voicing his disappointment that not all Himmler's opinions could be published safely. This lends some credence to those who believe that Hausleiter helped Kersten write his books. Even if there is no proof of this, Kersten's goodwill toward Hausleiter and other former Nazis seems beyond doubt.

Goodwill does not, however, mean that Kersten was a Nazi himself. It still seems most likely that he never had strong political opinions, apart from his anticommunism. He always remained a courtier, a servant, a fixer for the high and mighty. Like gangsters and butlers, courtiers are almost always conservative. Living, as Kersten did, through bad times, many of the high and mighty were at best deeply compromised. To put his behavior in the most positive light, Kersten was a loyal servant who stuck with bad friends, especially if they could still be useful to him, but perhaps not only for that reason. He liked to say that he took all kinds of patients, high and low, without discrimination. This was never quite true. He much preferred the high, but there was room for many people in that category.

There is a story of a patient in Paris. Like so much else in Kersten's life, the story may be apocryphal, but it is no less delightful for that. The patient was the daughter of a wealthy Jewish banker, living in the Sixteenth Arrondissement. Like many people who sought Kersten's help, she suffered from unbearable stomach pains. After some light exploration, Kersten found the source of her suffering, and his healing hands soon did their magic. The young woman felt comfortable for the first time in years. To show her deep gratitude, she had a shrine put up in the family apartment with Kersten's "miraculous hands" cast in gold.

Perhaps the family of this young patient was among those who asked General Charles de Gaulle, then president of France, to honor Kersten with a Legion of Honor for his role in rescuing French prisoners from Himmler's camps. In April 1960, Kersten was driving through rural Germany, approaching the Ruhr area. He was on his way to Paris, some say, to receive his award. Others have suggested that he was just visiting Germany. Kersten and his wife stopped the car for refreshments when he suddenly crumpled after a heart attack. A death certificate in Dutch says he actually died in Düsseldorf. Some websites claim that he was not in

Germany at all, but in Stockholm, when this happened. But the one fact about Kersten that no one disputes is that he died on April 16, at the age of sixty-one.

3: *Amsterdam*

To call the career of Friedrich Weinreb, after his release from prison in 1948, "checkered" would be an understatement. He spent some years as an economic consultant, but soon got into trouble again. Accusations of cooking his expenses and of defrauding a Jewish lawyer fell short of a conviction for lack of enough evidence. But Weinreb and his flock of loyal supporters thought he might be better off leaving the Netherlands for a while. (Weinreb explained in a memoir, published posthumously in German, that he was the victim of antisemitism by the "stupid Dutch.") Between 1952 and 1955, he was professor of economics at a university in Indonesia. Weinreb compared his move from the country he now detested more than ever to the Jews' escape from the land of the pharaohs.

Weinreb appears to have gotten on well with his students in Jakarta, and he later claimed to have instructed Indonesians in spiritual matters. A diary entry on June 6, 1953, reads: "those people believe so strongly that I felt my power of healing just by entering the room." This was in line with Weinreb's freelance activities, already in Holland, as a kind of guru to socially well-connected people, many of them rich ladies, who turned to him for religious guidance based on his esoteric reading of the Hebrew Bible. Weinreb had found the key to the true meaning of the sacred words through a secret code of numbers, associated with the Kabbalah.

He also felt that the Indonesians treated him as one of their own, as a fellow victim of Dutch arrogance and stupidity. "The most radical nationalists," he claimed, "spoke to me as though I were their father; and I was only in my early forties."

The reason that Weinreb's career in Jakarta was cut short after just three years was mysterious until the 1990s, when his biographer, Regina Grüter, read Dutch Foreign Office files. Weinreb had embarked on another one of his fantastical schemes, which he turned into a form of blackmail. Like his wartime fantasies, this one had sufficient roots in reality to give it plausibility. The former Dutch colony had become independent only in 1949, and relations with the old colonial masters were still fraught. Feelings were raw after the long bloody struggle for independence. Running a Dutch business in Jakarta required a lot of tact. Weinreb exploited this by making up a story that he was being pressed by the Indonesian government to denounce Dutch companies. In exchange, he said, the Indonesians had offered him citizenship. The pressure was so severe, he claimed, that he didn't know whether he could resist much longer. To avoid trouble and protect Dutch businesses, the Foreign Office agreed to get him out of Indonesia and set him up back home with a generous financial package. This lasted, at great expense to the government, until 1958, when Weinreb left for another appointment, this time as a professor in Turkey.

But his life in Ankara, too, ended under a cloud just a few years later, when Weinreb was accused by a furious Turkish father of having molested his daughter. To prepare Turkish students for a trip to Holland, Weinreb determined that some of the young women should be subjected to a close medical examination, which, he, Weinreb, would personally take charge of. The women had to strip and were given painful injections in their thighs. To avoid further scandal, Weinreb was obliged to leave Turkey quickly, and the Foreign Office finally severed all relations with him.

At that point the story of Weinreb's eccentric life would have faded from the public view if it hadn't been for an explosive reassessment of the Dutch wartime past. Weinreb became the focus of a cause célèbre, a position he would have relished had it ended better for him. For this, he bore some of the responsibility himself. Still active as a spiritual adviser to mostly Gentile ladies and gentlemen of wealth and standing, Weinreb published his most famous book in 1963. *Roots of the Bible* (*De bijbel als schepping*) laid out Weinreb's theories about the secret codes of the Scripture. I had a glancing acquaintance with his work in the early 1970s, when I shared my student quarters with a close friend who would spend his Sundays imbibing Weinreb's wisdom with his grandmother, one of the guru's highborn disciples. I recall taking my friend's talk of primordial meanings seriously enough to bring it up in my class on classical Chinese literature. My suggestion that these texts too might be scrutinized for hidden codes resulted in much rolling of professorial eyes, which my friend and I attributed to their hopeless superficiality.

Roots of the Bible was dismissed by recognized Jewish scholars, such as Gershom Scholem, who regarded Weinreb as a charlatan. But it was taken very seriously by less rigorous spiritual enthusiasts, including Greet Hofmans, Queen Juliana's faith healer, to whom Felix Kersten had turned for solace in the late 1940s. Weinreb recalled, in a memoir published after his death, how Hofmans was bowled over by his book. She compared Weinreb's text with God's words in the Burning Bush. Even more astonishing was her belief, recounted by Weinreb, that Jesus spoke through Weinreb. He might find this repugnant, she said, considering how the Christians had treated the Jews. But that wasn't the fault of Christ: "After all, he was a Jew, just like you."

Whether she actually said this, Hofmans did view Weinreb's problems with great sympathy, as was true in the case of Kersten. All three were professionally engaged in catering to the spiritual needs of rich and powerful people. But instead of rivalry, there appears to have been a kind of esprit de corps. At the beginning of 1968, Hofmans heard voices telling her that Weinreb would be pursued by hostile forces and should pack his bags to leave the country. Perhaps Jesus was speaking through him once more. This is how Weinreb described his "persecutors": "Ah, those poor souls. They know not what they do."

Onderduiken, "diving under" in wartime parlance, was how his escape was described by sympathetic observers. Weinreb was indeed in trouble, but not for theological reasons, or even for anything to do with the war. New accusations emerged about his intimate medical examinations. His "patients" this time were drawn from his female disciples, one of whom lodged a complaint in 1966. He had already been fined for a similar offense ten years earlier. Women with stomachaches and problems with getting pregnant were frequently subjected to his painful intrusions. In April 1968, he was handed a prison sentence, but by then he had already fled to Switzerland, where he would spend the rest of his life.

Weinreb's cause célèbre began three years before his flight, with the publication of a book that caused a national sensation. Written by Jacques Presser, a Marxist historian, it was entitled *Extinction: The Destruction of Dutch Jewry, 1940–1945* (*Ondergang: Vervolging en verdelging van het Nederlandse Jodendom, 1940–1945*). Presser, of Jewish origin himself, laid out the whole terrible sequence of German policies—anti-Jewish laws, the Jewish Council, deportations, Westerbork, and the death camps. The book is a detailed chronicle in two volumes of systematic persecution and mass murder, as well as an emotional display of belated righteous indignation. Presser aimed to speak, as he put it, "for those whose voices have been silenced forever." His passionate rhetorical style owed much to his personal circumstances during the war, which he had survived in hiding, while his wife, Debora Appel, was gassed at a death camp in Poland. Survivor's guilt, according to Presser himself, and his sense of impotence in the face of catastrophe fueled his rage against the passivity of the Dutch bureaucracy, the abject obedience of the Jewish Council, his own incapacity to resist, and the years of relative public silence about the horrendous crimes that took place amid an orderly, complacent, and seemingly indifferent population.

Not everyone appreciated Presser's impassioned style. W. F. Hermans, the greatest Dutch novelist of his generation, admired and feared for his pitiless essays, which were often correct but rarely tactful, pronounced that *Ondergang* was "unreadable because of the most shameless rhetoric ever applied to such a terrible subject." But this kind of bluntness was rare. Others who might have agreed with Hermans preferred to keep it to themselves.

Presser's book became an instant bestseller. The critical reception was so effusive that one suspects the praise was less for the book itself than for the moral indictment it represented. People were shocked, as though they were learning this history for the first time, which may have been true as far as the scale of the crimes and their revolting details were concerned. But enough was known for people to have felt uneasy about something that had remained largely unspoken. Presser had broken the silence. The convenient postwar myths of collective bravery under Nazi occupation, of a plucky people standing up as one to the wicked Germans, of absolute heroes and villains, were ready for revision.

As was true in other countries, not least in Germany, student protests against the Vietnam War, "U.S. imperialism," conservative professors, and the political elites dovetailed with a new and much more critical judgment of the recent past. *The Sorrow and the Pity*, Marcel Ophuls's brilliant documentary film about French collaboration with the Nazis, came out a year after the Paris revolts in May 1968. The 1960s in the Netherlands were also when the darkest sides of Dutch colonial history began to be scrutinized. A strong motive for the youth rebellion, in Paris, Berlin, Amsterdam, and Tokyo, was the wish to do better than the previous generations, to make up for their sins of obedience, to "resist."

Even as Presser's book forced the Dutch to face the horrific fact that 70 percent of Jews in their country never came back from the camps, young people in Amsterdam were resisting the establishment by provocations (they called themselves Provos), needling the police into responding aggressively to their teasingly subversive "happenings"—blocking traffic, throwing smoke bombs at the police, threatening to lace the public water supply with LSD, and so forth—in hope of exposing the state's "repressive tolerance." "Civil disobedience" was the order of the day. And the Weinreb described by Presser in his book as a Jewish hero fitted the times perfectly.

Presser, usually so thorough in his research, had relied too much on Weinreb's own statements. One of the most often quoted chapters in *Ondergang* concerns Weinreb's treatment by Dutch courts after the war. Weinreb, Presser argues, never betrayed anyone. In fact, he actively helped many people to survive. He was not perfect, to be sure, and possibly a little too pleased with himself, but he deserved a medal, a statue even. Instead, he was punished. Why? In Presser's words: "The Jew Weinreb became the scapegoat. He had to pay for the shortcomings of many non-Jews. He had to have failed because they had failed. Since they were remiss in their duties, he had to be as well. If there were no Jewish traitors, they had to be invented."

Here again, Weinreb was cast in the role of a modern-day Dreyfus. His case was taken up by journalists of the fashionably left-wing press, who were in tune with the Provos, and the sentiments of a youth rebellion that was shocking the bourgeoisie and shaking up the political elites. Renate Rubinstein, a famous columnist sometimes called "the Dutch

Susan Sontag" (much to the annoyance of the real Susan Sontag), be-came so fascinated by Weinreb that she decided to edit his memoirs in 1969, while starting a new Weinreb Committee to restore his reputation. Even the title of the autobiography, *Collaboration and Resistance 1940–1945: An Attempt at Demythologizing* (*Collaboratie en verzet 1940–1945: Een poging tot ontmythologisering*), was a timely tip of the hat. Decon-structing historical myths was in the air.

Like Presser, however, Rubinstein and other members of the Weinreb Committee were too eager to take Weinreb's own myths at face value. Some of his stories were so implausible that one wonders why knowl-edgeable people fell for them. It may be because we are often unable to recognize the marks of our own times in forgeries. Ivo Schöffer, a well-known historian of World War II, called this the "Van Meegeren effect." Han van Meegeren was the man who duped the greatest experts in the 1930s with his fake Vermeer paintings. They couldn't spot certain stylis-tic touches that were typical of the 1930s, which seem obvious to us now. This is also true of Weinreb's memoirs, which are suffused with the jar-gon of civil disobedience, fooling the establishment through the imagi-nation ("*L'imagination au pouvoir*"), breaking with the law-abiding habits of the bourgeoisie, and subverting the institutions of power by pretend-ing to play their game. These are far more typical of the 1960s than of the 1940s. Playful happenings were hardly an option under Nazi occu-pation.

What impressed and disturbed people more than anything were Weinreb's descriptions of life continuing in a relatively normal manner, even as a horrendous crime was taking place, often in full view. This al-leged lack of concern, the thoughtless obedience, and the lazy insouci-ance were precisely the things that drove young people into the streets two decades on.

Weinreb boosted his Provo-like credentials in newspaper interviews. "I rather like those people with long hair and strange clothes," he said, "since they refuse to be hypocrites. To build a new society, you have to break down the bureaucratic society first. . . . You have to make society unlivable through sabotage and passive resistance."

That is why Harry Mulisch, the famous novelist, who wrote an admiring book about the Provos, called Weinreb "the Che Guevara of bureaucracy."* Weinreb, like Kersten, like Kawashima Yoshiko, and like all successful self-mythologizers, knew what people wished to hear, in words that were designed to appeal to their hopes and prejudices. Didn't Weinreb himself call his wartime schemes a form of blowing bubbles, of selling dreams? In his memoir, he had simply updated some of the dreams.

There were a few doubters, of course, but Rubinstein and others (including Weinreb himself) dismissed them as agents of the same establishment that let down the Jews during the war and made Weinreb into a scapegoat to cover the tracks of their betrayal. In fact, however, the doubters tended to be Jewish themselves, people who had known Weinreb and witnessed some of the consequences of his acts. One such person was J. Rakower, who wrote a letter to the main Jewish newspaper in Holland. He had met Weinreb during the war, he said, and he "didn't agree with Presser that Weinreb was innocent." Furthermore, he said, "other eastern European Jews in Scheveningen and The Hague share my view of him." There was also Henriëtte Boas, a teacher of Latin and Greek who sent countless letters to various newspaper and magazine editors pointing out factual errors in Weinreb's account. Defenders of Weinreb ridiculed her as "the schoolmistress."

Holland was not the only European country where the so-called Jewish question in the aftermath of genocide had become a kind of neurosis affecting relations between Jews and Gentiles. I can still remember a time when Gentiles would lower their voices when the word "Jew" came to their lips. But if silence and denial marked the first few decades after the war, a flood of talk beginning in the 1960s would soon place the

---

*Mulisch is best known in the U.S. for his novel *The Assault*, published in 1986 by Pantheon.

Holocaust at the center of wartime memory, a place it had never had in the actual experience of most non-Jews during the war. It took the sharp and brutal pen of Hermans to pull at a particular scab in the psyche of many of Weinreb's most ardent defenders: their own problems with a Jewish identity that was often ambivalent.

Harry Mulisch had a Jewish mother, but his father had been an Austrian Nazi. Renate Rubinstein had a Gentile mother, and a Jewish father who was murdered in Auschwitz. There were others with similar family backgrounds. Hermans suggested that some of the most ardent "Weinrebbians" were suffering from misguided feelings of guilt, the guilt of half-Jews who were treated less horribly than people with two Jewish parents. According to religious law, a person with only a Jewish father does not even qualify as a Jew. Weinreb, the Orthodox Jew with insights into the Hebrew Scripture, became a substitute father figure, a wonder rabbi who could heal the wounded identities of his followers. Using psychological speculation to question the motives of people one disagrees with is not fair, of course. But this was a credible way to understand the zeal with which Rubinstein and others defended their hero and attacked the doubters.

One of Weinreb's critics was not even a doubter. She felt positively maligned. During a panel discussion on the Weinreb affair in 1970, Rubinstein raised the matter of Weinreb's first arrest by the SD, which he attributed to Bep Turksma, the young Jewish woman who supposedly betrayed him under torture. This had to be true, Rubinstein argued, for she had seen testimonies from former SD officers and Turksma herself that proved it was so. Alas for Rubinstein, Turksma was in the audience and stunned everyone by saying that she was indeed arrested but had never mentioned Weinreb to the SD, since she hadn't even heard his name until after the war. Rubinstein stuck to her bluff and refused to believe her. This so enraged Hermans, who was on the same panel, that he became obsessed by the Turksma case, and especially by the way Weinreb's left-wing defenders disparaged her. The novelist who made his name in 1958 with *The Darkroom of Damocles* (*De donkere kamer van Damokles*), a masterpiece that boldly put everything about resistance and collaboration in doubt, became a zealot about the truth of the Weinreb affair. In article after article, interview after interview, he excoriated Rubinstein and others for being liars in a "left-wing parrot cage" who would ruin anyone who dared to question their ideological delusions, about Weinreb, about Turksma, and about the war.

The furious debates and personal attacks went on for more than a decade. Although ostensibly about the truth of Weinreb's resistance or collaboration, or both, the polemics were not only about him, or even about the Jewish fate. The argument, echoed by similar arguments in other parts of Europe, was about contemporary politics in the light of the recent past. How should postwar democracies come to terms with a brutal history of fascism, colonialism, Nazi occupation, and military conquest? What went wrong? How to atone for the past? Who or what should be blamed? What kind of society should we build to avoid similar catastrophes in the future?

Mulisch, the Provos, and others on the left had radical ideals. They looked for inspiration to the Third World of Castro and Che Guevara, and to Gramsci and Marcuse. Hermans, on the other hand, was a conservative pessimist who loathed the cant of people he saw as pampered armchair revolutionaries. Weinreb, an ultraconservative Orthodox Jew, was an odd role model for young radicals, to be sure. But he was only the catalyst. And by drawing extra attention to himself, in many interviews and a highly questionable memoir, he laid the basis for his downfall.

In 1970, when the Weinreb debate was in full fury, the government decided to commission an official report on the affair. Politicians on the left were inclined to give Weinreb the benefit of the doubt, conservatives were more skeptical. This investigation was to be far more extensive than the report on Felix Kersten two decades earlier. Two researchers, one a former resistance member named A. J. van der Leeuw, the other a distinguished lawyer named D. Giltay Veth, spent six years sifting through all the available evidence and talking to more than six hundred witnesses. They chose not to include the cases of Weinreb's sexual abuse, since these lay outside their brief. The published fruit of their investigation was 1,683 pages long, divided into eighty chapters.

The Weinreb Report reads here and there like a case for the prosecution. But the researchers were not public prosecutors. Weinreb was not on trial. This is a work of historical research. When sufficient evidence could not be found for a case of prison betrayal, for example, the writers say so and do not press their point. The amount of detail can be numbing and boring to read: every allegation is considered, every testimony vetted. The conclusion is highly damaging to Weinreb. He did betray people. He did cooperate with the SD. His lists did cause serious harm, even though the extent of the damage is difficult to quantify; if the war had ended earlier, more people might have survived. The report agrees with the judgment of the postwar Special Court that Weinreb had been guilty of recklessly playing with the fate of others. Contrary to the court, however, the report does not conclude that Weinreb's first list sprang from good intentions, but from Weinreb's desire for power, money, and sexual gratification. Indeed, the writers believe that if the court had been fully aware of all Weinreb's actions, his punishment would have been more severe.

When some of these conclusions were leaked to a newspaper in 1973, Weinreb called the investigation an "organized pogrom" and compared the report with the *Protocols of the Elders of Zion*, the notorious Russian antisemitic forgery. Some of his supporters accused the writers of the report of being biased, without evidence. A more serious criticism was that they relied too much on testimonies of former SD agents. It is true that the SD men couldn't be trusted. But there was no reason that they should have wanted to malign Weinreb. In at least one case, that of the Dutch agent Krom, Weinreb made a deal with him to confirm each other's stories to their mutual benefit, just as Kersten had done with some of his Nazi cronies. In any case, the SD men were hardly the only informants.

Most of Weinreb's keenest defenders reacted to the report with a pained reticence. Renate Rubinstein said she needed more time to digest it properly. A critical book did appear a few years later, written by Rubinstein's ex-husband, but even he now called Weinreb's memoir "autobiographical fiction." He also said that the Weinreb case would always be veiled in "insoluble doubt." A left-wing politician, who had wanted to believe in Weinreb's innocence, still couldn't quite bring himself to accept the official report's conclusion and quoted the phrase in parliament: "Insoluble doubt will be with us forever." W. F. Hermans wrote a few more angry pieces demanding that Rubinstein and others apologize for their shameless worship of a false messiah. But that, really, was that. Even Hermans finished by saying: "Mention the name Weinreb, and everyone slowly falls asleep. I'm glad that I too have nothing more to say."

Weinreb died in Switzerland in 1988. He was still revered by a loyal group of disciples who believed that his wisdom contained the keys to unlocking the mysteries of life. They looked to him for spiritual solace. And on occasion, he would still offer his medical skills to take care of their physical problems as well.

EPILOGUE

I did not write this book to condemn Kawashima Yoshiko, Felix Kersten, and Friedrich Weinreb as bad people. It is too late for that, and anyway I don't believe many people are totally good or bad, and if such people do exist, they wouldn't interest me. There was good and bad in all three main characters of my book. Good or bad behavior so often depends on circumstances.

The reason for my fascination has less to do with character than with those circumstances that still strike so many familiar chords. The collaborators' stories are surprisingly modern; their complicated backgrounds; their problems with national, sexual, and cultural identities; their resistance to and compliance with political forces that impose identities on people; and their deliberate blurring of truth and fiction. They lived in an age of propaganda when speaking the truth was dangerous.

In many parts of the world, we live in an age of dogmatism and challenges to truth-telling once more, an age in which even democratic governments create their own realities. It is an age in which braggarts and *Hochstaplers* thrive. Some of them even get elected to the highest offices of state.

There are many reasons for this, none of which can be entirely blamed on this individual or that. The notion of truth has been questioned for quite some time in academic theories. Human expression is often seen merely as a representation of power, gender, or ethnicity. Truth, therefore, becomes a very relative concept. Everything depends on who is saying what to whom. It is but a short step to assume that everything is a kind of fabrication, a construction, and any effort to distinguish facts from fiction is naive at best.

This is echoed in the arts, where some writers and filmmakers have made their names by operating deliberately in a foggy zone where facts and fiction merge. There is nothing new about this. People have always turned memories into myths, often used to justify religious beliefs, or a new dynasty in power. The great German historian Leopold von Ranke's dictum that historiography should tell us "what actually happened" (*wie es eigentlich gewesen ist*) now has a distinctly nineteenth-century ring, when people believed in science more than they do now.

Of course, history is not an exact science. We can recognize facts that really happened. But the rest is a matter of interpretation. Nor is the human mind a computer; memories are changeable, easily manipulated, and always fallible. We make up so much of our lives as we go along. We change our minds about the past. Questioning our assumptions is the only way to get a fleeting glimpse of what is true.

Dogmatic insistence that there can only be one truth is not just oppressive, but fallacious. When ideology of any kind cannot be challenged, we live, as the Czech playwright, dissident, and statesman Václav Havel put it, in falsehood. The three collaborators, like so many other people, did not live their lives in truth. They created their own realities. They did this partly from fear, to survive in bad times, and partly out of hubris, to boost their own fortunes, or just for the hell of it.

To be free, as Havel also taught us, we must learn to live in truth. His definition of dictatorship was the compulsion to repeat official lies, even in the full knowledge that they are lies. When the state—or any other source of coercive power—says that something is white, even though everyone with eyesight can see that it is black, you still must claim that it is white. The first step toward living in truth and being free is to refuse to play this game.

Both Friedrich Weinreb and Kawashima Yoshiko, each in their own way, could see through the lies they were told, and sometimes even had the courage to tell the truth. Felix Kersten claimed in hindsight that he did too, but he was more of a conformist than the other two. His form of defense in bad times was to pretend not to see what was plainly in front of his eyes. The other two made up their own truths, which is not the same thing as living in truth.

Havel's dissident claim of living in truth does not mean a belief in one absolute truth; that is the dogmatic position. Nor does it mean that there are many truths, all relative, all depending on feelings, mood, skin color, or social or political power. Some things are true or false. The distinction is not always obvious and sometimes difficult to see. There are many ways to approach the truth: scientific, artistic, philosophical, even instinctive. Science does not have all the answers about human affairs. Myths can express truth too. Not all inventions are lies. Fictions can tell the truth about many things.

The problem with my collaborators is that their deceptions, sometimes perhaps necessary deceptions to survive in a system of lies, became self-deceptions. That is the common result of living in lies. I wrote at the beginning of this book that people who resisted dictatorships and occupying powers made things up too—names, documents, identities. But in most cases, they didn't deceive themselves. They lived secretively, in the shadows, but they still lived in truth. People who live in lies, out of fear or opportunism, end up being consumed by them.

Kawashima Yoshiko, Friedrich Weinreb, and Felix Kersten were not consigned to Dante's eighth circle of hell because of their complicated backgrounds and multicultural identities. They did not even have to join other fraudsters in the eighth circle because they deceived other people. They must suffer because they conned themselves. By turning your own life into a fiction, you don't really have an identity at all. That is a melancholy state that threatens many of us, whether we live in a dictatorship or not.

ACKNOWLEDGMENTS

Even though hardly anyone is alive who could have known the characters in this book personally, I still had the great benefit of discussing their stories with several people, whose advice and expertise were invaluable. Some were kind enough to read the whole or parts of the book before it found its final form. They are in no particular order: Abram de Swaan, David Barnouw, René Zwaap, Phyllis Birnbaum, Bas Blokker, Andrew Horvat, Jos Verlaan, Joggli Meihuizen, Yanagisawa Kazuhiko, Arnon Grunberg, Harko Keizer, Phil Blumberg, David Rieff, Judith Thurman, Isabel Buruma, Oren Overman, Bas Heijne, and Ben Taylor.

In Scott Moyers, Mia Council, and Helen Rouner, I have found the best and most painstaking editors in the business. Their talents and dedication are extraordinary.

Jin Auh and Andrew Wylie of the Wylie Agency have given me the kind of sage advice and guidance without which I would frequently have been at sea.

Without the loving support of Eri Hotta I would have been even more at sea.

CREDITS

NOTES

Chapter One
12 culture of "freedom, education, universality and love": Felix Kersten, *Klerk en beul: Himmler van nabij* (Amsterdam: Meulenhoff, 1948), 25.
14 Battle of Verdun: Freek van Rijsinge, *Het Kerstenspiel: Het omstreden netwerk van de masseur van Himmler* (Amsterdam: Boom, 2006).
14 yet another account: Achim Besgen, *Der stille Befehl: Mezinalrat Kersten, Himmler und das Dritte Reich* (Munich: Nymphenburger Verlagshandlung, 1960).
16 "If you wish to hear": Friedrich Weinreb, *Ontmoetingen (1)* (Groningen: Holmsterland, 1982), 29.
19 "rebellions, riots, revolutions": Kawashima Yoshiko, *Doran no kage ni* (repr., Tokyo: Nihon Toshokan Center, 2012), 24.

Chapter Two
26 "don't have a home anywhere": Joseph Roth, "Juden auf Wanderschaft," in *Ich Zeichne das Gesicht der Zeit* (Zürich: Diogenes, 2010), 145.
26 "Identity documents are untouchable": Friedrich Weinreb, *Ontmoetingen (1)* (Groningen: Holmsterland, 1982), 71.
27 "Germany is still": Roth, "Juden auf Wanderschaft," 141.
28 "represented a disappointed Western idealism": Weinreb, *Ontmoetingen (1)*, 47.
29 "the downfall of the world": Weinreb, *Ontmoetingen (1)*, 46.
35 the Chinese refused to surrender: Kamisaka Fuyuko, *Danso no reijin: Kawashima Yoshikoden* (Tokyo: Bungei Shunju, 1984), 47.
35 "love and sincerity": Kawashima Yoshiko, *Doran no kage ni* (repr., Tokyo: Nihon Toshokan Center, 2012), 24.
37 "I am gifting you": Kamisaka, *Danso no reijin*, 65.
37 he died by: Bruce Coggeshall, "The Mata Hari of the Far East: Uncovering the Incredible Story of Yoshiko Kawashima," in *Open Source Intelligence Reports*, July 16, 2019.
37 this sinister event: Phyllis Birnbaum, *Manchu Princess, Japanese Spy: The Story of Kawashima Yoshiko, the Cross-Dressing Spy Who Commanded Her Own Army* (New York: Columbia University Press, 2015).

Chapter Three
40 "In this period of tremendous": Wilhelm Wulff, *Zodiac and Swastika: How Astrology Guided Hitler's Germany* (New York: Coward, McCann, Geoghegan, 1973), 29.
44 "From my mother's tummy": Kamisaka Fuyuko, *Danso no reijin: Kawashima Yoshikoden* (Tokyo: Bungei Shunju, 1984), 70.
45 "You are neither Chinese": Kamisaka, *Danso no reijin*, 60.
48 "necessary sacrifice for the revival": Kamisaka, *Danso no reijin*, 79.
48 "was used as a kind of pronoun": Kawashima Yoshiko, *Doran no kage ni* (repr., Tokyo: Nihon Toshokan Center, 2012), 42.

50 wrote his book: Muramatsu Shofu, *Danso no reijin* (Tokyo: Chuo Koronsha, 1933).

51 a suitor sucked the drug: Phyllis Birnbaum, *Manchu Princess, Japanese Spy: The Story of Kawashima Yoshiko, the Cross-Dressing Spy Who Commanded Her Own Army* (New York: Columbia University Press, 2015), 70.

52 "I've had all this trouble": Birnbaum, *Manchu Princess, Japanese Spy*, 72.

52 "Yoshiko has an interest": Birnbaum, *Manchu Princess, Japanese Spy*, 72.

52 "The dreamlike heroic feeling": Kawashima, *Doran no kage ni*, 70.

52 "'If I had three thousand soldiers'": Birnbaum, *Manchu Princess, Japanese Spy*, 51.

57 "lived with God": Friedrich Weinreb, *Ontmoetingen (1)* (Groningen: Holmsterland, 1982), 110.

59 "conscious of a different reality": Weinreb, *Ontmoetingen (1)*, 130.

Chapter Four

63 Kersten does not mention the duke: Felix Kersten, *Die manuelle Therapie* (Rudolstadt: Hofbuchdruckerei, 1929).

65 "A new power became visible": Felix Kersten, *Klerk en beul: Himmler van nabij* (Amsterdam: Meulenhoff, 1948), 30.

65 "intellectuals and people": Joseph Kessel, *Les mains du miracle* (Paris: Gallimard, 1960), 46.

68 "of great intellectual and moral stature": Kessel, *Les mains du miracle*, 53.

70 "In the course of my practice": Kersten, *Klerk en beul*, 32.

75 "I felt taken up": Friedrich Weinreb, *Ontmoetingen (2)* (Groningen: Holmsterland, 1982), 53.

76 "that vermin, those mockers": Weinreb, *Ontmoetingen (2)*, 13.

80 "My husband and I": Kawashima Yoshiko, *Doran no kage ni* (repr., Tokyo: Nihon Toshokan Center, 2012), 42, 82.

86 "I'm not just a spy": Quoted in Kamisaka Fuyuko, *Danso no reijin: Kawashima Yoshikoden* (Tokyo: Bungei Shunju, 1984), 124.

Chapter Five

92 "Above all, we : Bianca Stigter, *Atlas van een bezette stad: Amsterdam 1940–1945* (Amsterdam: AtlastContact, 2019), 29.

92 doing the Nazis' work: The best-known proponent of this view is Hannah Arendt, who believed that the scale of Nazi mass murder would have been much smaller without Jewish complicity. It is a doubtful premise. See her *Eichmann in Jerusalem* (New York: Viking, 1963).

93 "stupid kiss-asses": Friedrich Weinreb, *Collaboratie en verzet* (Amsterdam: Meulenhof, 1971), 70.

93 "choose to remain legal": Weinreb, *Collaboratie en verzet*, 20.

93 "To tell the truth could": Weinreb, *Collaboratie en verzet*, 17.

94 report on Weinreb's wartime operations: D. Giltay Veth and A. J. van der Leeuw, *Weinreb-rapport* (Amsterdam: RIOD, 1976).

94 the Weinreb case and its aftermath: Regina Grüter, *Een fantast schrijft geschiedenis: De affaires rond Friedrich Weinreb* (Amsterdam: Balans, 1997).

98 "I had broken through that ghastly passivity": Weinreb, *Collaboratie en verzet*, 31.

98 "All promises were soap bubbles": Grüter, *Een fantast schrijft geschiedenis*, 43.

98 "You are a *malech*": Weinreb, *Collaboratie en verzet*, 43.

99 "Yet another meeting": Weinreb, *Collaboratie en verzet*, 22–23.

100 "It takes so little to give": Weinreb, *Collaboratie en verzet*, 46.

102 "imbued with that typically German weakness": Felix Kersten, *Klerk en beul: Himmler van nabij* (Amsterdam: Meulenhof, 1948), 36.

102 "He stood before us": Curzio Malaparte, *Kaputt* (London: Picador Classics, 1982), 322.

102 vowed to eradicate "root and branch": Felix Kersten, *The Kersten Memoirs* (New York: Macmillan, 1956), 57.

102 "but nothing yet [had] been done": Kersten, *Memoirs*, 59.

103 "High-grade Masons": Kersten, *Memoirs*, 27.

103 "You take your arguments": Kersten, *Memoirs*, 36.

104 "How can you take pleasure": Kersten, *Klerk en beul*, 32.

106 "a peculiarly communist disease": Li Zhisui, *The Private Life of Chairman Mao: The Memoirs of Mao's Personal Physician, Li Zhisui* (New York: Random House, 1994), 109.

108 General Berger was one of the "moderates": Kersten, *Klerk en beul*, 46.

108 Brandt was an "idealist": Kersten, *Klerk en beul*, 128.

NOTES

108 "The Germans made here": Martha Gellhorn, *The Face of War: Writings from the Frontline, 1937–85* (London: Granta, 1993), 168.
109 "fierce longing to escape the tentacles": Kersten, *Klerk en beul*, 34.
110 make the pain go away: Such services did not always come cheaply. Kersten allegedly charged the family of an old Jewish lady fifty thousand marks to save her from deportation.
114 "I'll do anything you like'": Kersten, *Memoirs*, 174.

Chapter Six
117 book of self-inventions: Willa Lou Woods, *Princess Jin, the Joan of Arc of the Orient* (Cleveland: World, 1937).
120 the words of two British admirers: D. M. B. Collier and L. E. Malone, *Manchoukuo, Jewel of Asia* (London: George Allen & Unwin, 1936), 232.
121 "It was indeed with a fine understanding": Collier and Malone, *Manchoukuo, Jewel of Asia*, 240.
125 "the future of peace in Asia": Kawashima Yoshiko, *Doran no kage ni* (repr., Tokyo: Nihon Toshokan Center, 2012), 212.
127 "a soldier in a Chinese opera": Phyllis Birnbaum, *Manchu Princess, Japanese Spy: The Story of Kawashima Yoshiko, the Cross-Dressing Spy Who Commanded Her Own Army* (New York: Columbia University Press, 2015), 143.
128 "My volunteer corps": Kawashima, *Doran no kage ni*, 224.
128 "I was running all over Jehol": Kamisaka Fuyuko, *Danso no reijin: Kawashima Yoshikoden* (Tokyo: Bungei Shunju, 1984), 132.
130 "despite these difficulties, the removal of Jews": A. C. F. Koch et al., eds., *Nederlandse Historische Bronnen* (The Hague: Martinus Nijhoff, 1979).
131 "But I think God": Friedrich Weinreb, *Collaboratie en verzet* (Amsterdam: Meulenhof, 1971), 165.
134 "a glorious time": Weinreb, *Collaboratie en verzet*, 215.
135 "a funny sight": Weinreb, *Collaboratie en verzet*, 236.
135 A childhood friend, Herbert Kruskal: Regina Grüter, *Een fantast schrijft geschiedenis: De affaires rond Friedrich Weinreb* (Amsterdam: Balans, 1997), 172.
138 "Only a golem would do": Weinreb, *Collaboratie en verzet*, 299.
139 "A brilliant scheme, I must say": Weinreb, *Collaboratie en verzet*, 305.
139 "sat there, like a puppet": Weinreb, *Collaboratie en verzet*, 309.
140 "I was frightened": Weinreb, *Collaboratie en verzet*, 316.
140 "trembled with emotion": Weinreb, *Collaboratie en verzet*, 340.

Chapter Seven
143 On October 26, 1941: Felix Kersten, *The Kersten Memoirs* (New York: Macmillan, 1956), 113.
144 "As previously authorized by the Führer": Peter Longerich, *Heinrich Himmler: A Life* (New York: Oxford University Press, 2012), 555.
145 "it is the curse of greatness": Joseph Kessel, *Les mains du miracle* (Paris: Gallimard, 1960), 197.
146 "very indignant about this": Felix Kersten, *Klerk en beul: Himmler van nabij* (Amsterdam: Meulenhoff, 1948), 133.
146 his brilliant book: Christopher Browning, *Ordinary Men* (New York: HarperCollins, 1992).
147 "All [male] Jews": Richard Breitman, "Himmler and the 'Terrible Secret' among the Executioners," *Journal of Contemporary History* 26, no. 3/4 (1991): 440.
147 "Dined on the train": Longerich, *Heinrich Himmler*, 533.
148 "I did not consider myself justified": Longerich, *Heinrich Himmler*, 539.
149 "A soldier on leave": Robert Scott Kellner, ed., *My Opposition: The Diary of Friedrich Kellner—A German Against the Third Reich* (Cambridge: Cambridge University Press, 2018), xiv.
150 "greedy little eyes": Wilhelm Wulff, *Zodiac and Swastika: How Astrology Guided Hitler's Germany* (New York: Coward, McCann, Geoghegan, 1973), 80.
150 "a refuge for the oppressed": Kersten, *Klerk en beul*, 82.
150 "messenger from the angels": Kessel, *Les mains du miracle*, 204.
150 concentration camps in 1942: Parlementaire Enquetecommissie, September 15, 1948.
151 "We Germans are not as bad as that": Kersten, *Klerk en beul*, 83.
151 Himmler supposedly said: Kessel, *Les mains du miracle*, 210.
153 His claim to have "saved the Finnish people": Letter dated October 10, 1948, NIOD Archives, Amsterdam.

154 "As the great Germanic leader": Felix Kersten to Heinrich Himmler, March 21, 1943, NIOD Archives, Amsterdam.

155 "All they needed to do": Kessel, *Les mains du miracle*, 232.

156 "I will talk to the Führer": Kessel, *Les mains du miracle*, 235.

156 "unobtrusively distancing myself": Kersten, *Klerk en beul*, 116.

157 "incited anti-Japanese feeling": Kawashima Yoshiko, *Doran no kage ni* (repr., Tokyo: Nihon Toshokan Center, 2012), 228.

158 "a war of resistance to the end": Rana Mitter, *Forgotten Ally: China's World War II, 1937–1945* (Boston: Houghton Mifflin Harcourt, 2013), 102.

160 "build a paradise in Manchukuo": Kamisaka Fuyuko, *Danso no reijin: Kawashima Yoshikoden* (Tokyo: Bungei Shunju, 1984), 156.

161 "Every time there is war": Kamisaka, *Danso no reijin*, 153.

163 "The day will come when Japan": Kamisaka, *Danso no reijin*, 145.

165 "offering solace to the officers": Kawashima, *Doran no kage ni*, 228.

166 "we have the same name too": Yamaguchi Yoshiko, *Ri Koran: Watashi no Hansei* (Tokyo: Shinchosha, 1987), 89.

167 "She had been rejected": Yamaguchi, *Ri Koran*, 91.

169 "The vengeance of Chinese women": Yamaguchi, *Ri Koran*, 227.

Chapter Eight

171 "a provocateur, a police spy, a snitch": Friedrich Weinreb, *Collaboratie en verzet* (Amsterdam: Meulenhof, 1971), 680.

171 "betrayed many families": Fritz Koch, statement to the Dutch Political Investigation Department (PRA), March 18, 1946.

172 "they wouldn't be allowed": Weinreb, *Collaboratie en verzet*, 350.

172 "Koch hissed": Weinreb, *Collaboratie en verzet*, 353.

173 he mentioned the names of Jews: Krijna Peeren, statement to the 1980 parliamentary committee investigating the Weinreb case.

174 Weinreb's assistance in this and other matters: The official report on the Weinreb case by the National Institute for War Documentation (RIOD) in 1976, as well as a parliamentary investigation in 1980, concluded that Weinreb had indeed been guilty. The former has been published as D. Giltay Veth and A. J. van der Leeuw. *Weinreb-rapport* (Amsterdam: RIOD, 1976).

174 "And now they're pleased they were right": Weinreb, *Collaboratie en verzet*, 364.

177 the smiling "gentleman-criminal": Etty Hillesum, *An Interrupted Life: Letters from Westerbork* (New York: Henry Holt, 1996).

178 sang a song that went: Regina Grüter, *Een fantast schrijft geschiedenis: De affaires rond Friedrich Weinreb* (Amsterdam: Balans, 1997), 183.

179 "The Germans felt comfortable": Weinreb, *Collaboratie en verzet*, 467.

179 "So you are Weinreb": Weinreb, *Collaboratie en verzet*, 484.

180 "Eating may not be the most important": Grüter, *Een fantast schrijft geschiedenis*, 53.

181 "Stalingrad lay between": Weinreb, *Collaboratie en verzet*, 489.

181 "that you are all Jews!": Weinreb, *Collaboratie en verzet*, 495.

182 "What brilliance!": Weinreb, *Collaboratie en verzet*, 512.

183 the careful analysis: This report, *Weinreb-rapport*, commissioned by the Dutch government, was compiled by two distinguished scholars, D. Giltay Veth and A. J. van der Leeuw.

184 "no doubt Weinreb had been used": Giltay Veth and Van der Leeuw, *Weinreb-rapport*, 487.

186 "There are Dutch Jews": Weinreb, *Collaboratie en verzet*, 640.

187 "called me a magician": Weinreb, *Collaboratie en verzet*, 621.

187 "I am convinced": Weinreb, *Collaboratie en verzet*, 658.

187 "I feel dizzy": Weinreb, *Collaboratie en verzet*, 619.

188 the horrors inflicted: Anon., *Polens Martyrium* (Stockholm: Trotsallt!, 1942).

190 well rewarded by the employer: Freek van Rijsinge, *Het Kersten Spiel* (Amsterdam: Boom, 2006), 36.

190 conservative anti-Nazi dissidents: Jacob Wallenberg's nephew, Raoul Wallenberg, was the famous Swedish diplomat who heroically saved thousands of Jews from deportation in Hungary, only to be arrested by the Soviet Union after the war. He never emerged from Soviet captivity.

190 "Sweden's humanitarian and neutral traditions": Felix Kersten, *The Kersten Memoirs* (New York: Macmillan, 1956), 187.

192 "for the survival of our blood": Peter Longerich, *Heinrich Himmler: A Life* (New York: Oxford University Press, 2012), 695.

192 **play the role of an important diplomat:** This episode is described in detail by Richard Breitman, "A Deal with the Nazi Dictatorship: Himmler's Alleged Peace Emissaries in Autumn 1943," *Journal of Contemporary History*, 30 (July 1995): 410–30.

193 **"This morning I tried to make Himmler":** Kersten, *The Kersten Memoirs*, 192.

194 **"emphasized especially the great danger":** John H. Waller, *The Devil's Doctor: Felix Kersten and the Secret Plot to Turn Himmler Against Hitler* (New York: John Wiley, 2002), 151.

195 **"likely that the sentiments expressed [purportedly by Hewitt]":** Waller, *The Devil's Doctor*, 152.

197 **"prevent or mitigate some":** Wilhelm Wulff, *Zodiac and Swastika: How Astrology Guided Hitler's Germany* (New York: Coward, McCann, Geoghegan, 1973), 92.

200 **"bore a grudge toward Japan":** Kamisaka Fuyuko, *Danso no reijin: Kawashima Yoshikoden* (Tokyo: Bungei Shunju, 1984), 160.

200 **"My dear little Yoshiko":** Yamaguchi Yoshiko, *Ri Koran: Watashi no Hansei* (Tokyo: Shinchosha, 1987), 217.

201 **the "world's richest fascist":** *Time*, August 26, 1974.

202 **whose book is so fawning:** Yamaoka Sohachi, *Hatenko: Ningen Sasakawa Ryoichi* (Tokyo: Yuhosha, 1978).

202 **"two-bit generals":** Phyllis Birnbaum, *Manchu Princess, Japanese Spy: The Story of Kawashima Yoshiko, the Cross-Dressing Spy Who Commanded Her Own Army* (New York: Columbia University Press, 2015), 186.

203 **"I want to be held":** Birnbaum, *Manchu Princess, Japanese Spy*, 188.

204 **folded away his kimono trousers:** Kamisaka, *Danso no reijin*, 167.

204 **"I, your little Yoshi":** Kamisaka, *Danso no reijin*, 168.

204 **"heart had been greatly moved":** Birnbaum, *Manchu Princess, Japanese Spy*, 189.

Chapter Nine

210 **"We are received with such warmth":** Friedrich Weinreb, *Collaboratie en verzet* (Amsterdam: Meulenhof, 1971), 729.

211 **hit the Dutch where it hurt:** Friedrich Weinreb, *De gevangenis: Herinneringen 1945–1948* (Amsterdam: Meulenhof, 1989).

213 **"We have the power to decide":** Weinreb, *De gevangenis*, 35.

217 **But Krom withdrew:** This is described in Regina Grüter, *Een fantast schrijft geschiedenis: De affaires rond Friedrich Weinreb* (Amsterdam: Balans, 1997) and, in even more detail, in D. Giltay Veth and A. J. van der Leeuw, *Weinreb-rapport* (Amsterdam: RIOD, 1976), 1434–72.

218 **"a little too impulsive":** Grüter, *Een fantast schrijft geschiedenis*, 65.

218 **"A conviction of Weinreb":** Grüter, *Een fantast schrijft geschiedenis*, 206.

219 **an article aimed at American readers:** Grüter, *Een fantast schrijft geschiedenis*, 210.

219 **"almost every Jew in Holland":** Records of the Special Court of Cassation, September 27, 1948.

220 **"If collective guilt":** H. Drion, "Presser over de zaak Weinreb." *Hollands Maandblad*, January 1966, 224–25.

220 **"resulted in the sacrifice":** Grüter, *Een fantast schrijft geschiedenis*, 71.

221 **"as a combination of an operator":** Giltay Veth and Van der Leeuw, *Weinreb-rapport*, 1516–17.

222 **the torture instruments:** Yamaguchi Yoshiko, *Ri Koran o ikkite* (Tokyo: Nihon Keizai Shimbunsha, 2004), 189.

223 **2.7 million Chinese civilians:** See the work of one Japanese historian in particular: Himeta Mitsuyoshi's book *Mo Hitotsu no Sanko Sakusen* (Tokyo: Aoki Shoten, 1989).

224 **"made into a public spectacle":** Yamaguchi, *Ri Koran o ikkite*, 179.

225 **"China's number one singer":** Yamaguchi Yoshiko, *Ri Koran: Watashi no Hansei* (Tokyo: Shinchosha, 1987), 315.

227 **"to put a smile":** Ohta Naoki, *Manchu Urashi: Amakasu Masahiko to Kishi Nobusuke ga Seotta Mono* (Tokyo: Kodansha, 2005), 461.

227 **"They only make trouble":** Phyllis Birnbaum, *Manchu Princess, Japanese Spy: The Story of Kawashima Yoshiko, the Cross-Dressing Spy Who Commanded Her Own Army* (New York: Columbia University Press, 2015), 224.

228 **"According to the Chinese guard":** Kamisaka Fuyuko, *Danso no reijin: Kawashima Yoshikoden* (Tokyo: Bungei Shunju, 1984), 222.

228 **"a man feared by millions":** Wilhelm Wulff, *Zodiac and Swastika: How Astrology Guided Hitler's Germany* (New York: Coward, McCann, Geoghegan, 1973), 257.

229 **"his selfish plans":** Wulff, *Zodiac and Swastika*, 139.

231 "tarnished in the history books": Felix Kersten, *Klerk en beul: Himmler van nabij* (Amsterdam: Meulenhoff, 1948), 162.

231 "a Nazi and a thoroughly bad man": Victor Mallet to Foreign Office, FO 370, 48026, February 25, 1945, quoted by Steven Koblik in "No Truck with Himmler: The Politics of Rescue and the Swedish Red Cross Mission, March–May 1945," *Scandia* 51, no. 1 (June 2008): 175.

231 "from that moment on": FO 370, 48026, February 25, 1945, quoted by Koblik, in Kersten, *Klerk en beul*, 162.

232 "liked to make a joke": Peter Longerich, *Heinrich Himmler: A Life* (New York: Oxford University Press, 2012), 724.

233 "obliged to carry out": Felix Kersten, *The Kersten Memoirs* (New York: Macmillan, 1956), 283.

233 "devotion to the good cause": Kersten, *Klerk en beul*, 187.

233 "lay slumped on his metal bed": Joseph Kessel, *Les mains du miracle* (Paris: Gallimard, 1960), 356.

234 "in the name of humanity": Kersten, *Memoirs*, 277.

234 "this benevolent act": Kersten, *Klerk en beul*, 172.

234 Count Bernadotte claimed: Folke Bernadotte, *The Curtain Falls: The Last Days of the Third Reich* (New York: Knopf, 1945).

236 He was sure that: Himmler's letter of March 25, 1945, to Kersten is in the NIOD archives in Amsterdam.

236 "a political event of global importance": Kersten, *Memoirs*, 283–84.

236 "My goodness!": Kessel, *Les mains du miracle*, 368.

237 Himmler also told the commandants: Longerich, *Heinrich Himmler*, 731.

237 "For me, as a Jew": Masur immediately recounted this extraordinary episode in his "Report to the World Jewish Congress," April 20, 1945.

238 his reconstructed diary: Kersten, *Memoirs*, 286.

240 "Please help my poor family": Kersten, *Klerk en beul*, 188.

240 "I was grateful to the Eternal One": Kersten, *Klerk en beul*, 189.

Chapter Ten

252 "The gloves were off": Folke Bernadotte, *The Curtain Falls: The Last Days of the Third Reich* (New York: Knopf, 1945), 67.

252 "always be grateful": Bernadotte, *The Curtain Falls*, 29.

252 "*The Labyrinth* throws into relief": Clinton Gallagher, "Critiques on Some Recent Books on Intelligence," *Studies in Intelligence*, Fall 1957, 119.

252 "dared to make a criticism": Raymond Palmer, "Felix Kersten and Count Bernadotte: A Question of Rescue," *Journal of Contemporary History* 29 (January 1994): 39–51.

254 "utterly unreliable witness": L. de Jong, *Tussentijds: Historische Studies* (Amsterdam: Querido, 1977), 212.

254 "grandiose propaganda for himself": A. J. Th. van der Vlugt to Dutch Foreign Ministry October 18, 1948, in NIOD Archives, Amsterdam.

255 "an exceptional fantasist": De Jong, *Tussentijds: Historische Studies*, 133.

257 never forget "the bestiality": Freek van Rijsinge, *Het Kersten Spiel* (Amsterdam: Boom, 2006), 59.

257 "Jews are as unwelcome": Van Rijsinge, *Het Kersten Spiel*, 66.

258 forensic experts at Scotland Yard: Gerald Fleming, "Die Herkunft des Bernadotte-Briefs an Himmler," *Vierteljahrshefte für Zeitgeschichte* 26 (1978): 582–84.

259 "Human memory and human judgment": Hugh Trevor-Roper, introduction to *The Kersten Memoirs*, by Felix Kersten (New York: Macmillan, 1956), 21.

259 "It was a great pleasure": Van Rijsinge, *Het Kersten Spiel*, 70.

260 Speer was present: Himmler's speech was delivered on October 4, 1943.

260 "a cold-blooded inhuman ogre": Hugh Trevor-Roper, *The Last Days of Hitler* (London: Macmillan, 1947), 120.

260 "his conclusions are never naïve": Trevor-Roper, *The Last Days of Hitler*, 120.

261 a cache of Kersten's correspondence: The historian was Freek van Rijsinge, author of *Het Kersten Spiel*.

261 "People can say what they want": Van Rijsinge, *Het Kersten Spiel*, 87.

263 the "stupid Dutch": *Meine Revolution* (Weiler im Allgäu: Thauros, 1990), 48.

263 "I felt my power of healing": W. F. Hermans, *Het sadistische universum* (Amsterdam: De Bezige Bij, 1966), 389.

264 "The most radical nationalists": *Meine Revolution*, 69.

265 dismissed by recognized Jewish scholars: Regina Grüter, *Een fantast schrijft geschiedenis: De affaires rond Friedrich Weinreb*, (Amsterdam: Balans, 1997), 98.

265 "After all, he was a Jew": "Meine Revolution," 269.

266 "for those whose voices": Jacques Presser, *Ondergang: Vervolging en verdelging van het Nederlandse Jodendom, 1940–1945* (The Hague: Nijhoff, 1965), 1: vii.

267 "unreadable because of the most shameless rhetoric": Hermans, *Het sadistische universum*, 372.

268 state's "repressive tolerance": The phrase was coined by Herbert Marcuse, the Marxist philosopher and one of the heroes of the youth rebellion.

268 "If there were no Jewish traitors": Presser, *De ondergang*, 110.

270 "To build a new society": Grüter, *Een fantast schrijft geschiedenis*, 277.

270 "didn't agree with Presser": J. R. Rakower, letter to *Nieuw Israelitisch Weekblad*, July 16, 1965.

273 "organized pogrom": Interview with Friedrich Weinreb, *De Nieuwe Linie*, June 6, 1973.

274 "autobiographical fiction": Aad Nuis, *Het monster in de huiskamer: Een analyse van het Weinreb rapport* (Amsterdam: Meulenhoff, 1980), 87.

274 "Mention the name Weinreb": Hermans, *Het sadistische universum*, 428.

INDEX

Note: Italicized page numbers indicate material in photographs or illustrations.

"administrative guerrilla" role, 93–94
Adolf Friedrich, Duke of Mecklenburg-
    Schwerin, 62, 65, 154–55
Adolfus lizards, 63
Agudath Yisrael movement, 76, 101, 230
Ahnenerbe, 42, 108
Aisin Gyoro Shanqi. *See* Prince Su
Aisin Gyoro Xianyu. *See* Kawashima
    Yoshiko
Akabane Matsue, 45
Alexander I of Yugoslavia, 62
Amakasu Masahiko, 82, 166–68, 227
Amsterdam, 91–93, 95–96, 175–76,
    212, 268
Amsterdam Concertgebouw Orchestra,
    176
ancient texts, 75
Anglo-Saxons, 190, 193
Ankara, Turkey, 264
anthroposophy, 163
anticommunism, 7, 15, 50, 106, 146,
    201, 223, 250, 262
antisemitism
    of Berger, 108
    and conspiracy theories, 273
    of Himmler, 103
    in the Netherlands, 211–12
    and occult influences in German
        culture, 43
    parallels in Asia, 7
    of Seyss-Inquart, 90
    in Sweden, 232
    and Thule Society, 68–69

    in Vienna, 25–27
    and Weinreb's background, 56
    and Weinreb's trials and defense,
        215–16, 218–20, 263, 273
Appel, Debora, 267
Arbeitseinsatz, 177
Arendt, Hannah, 241
Army Group Upper-Rhine, 228
Army of Shadows (Kessel), 13
art collectors, 47, 126, 195. *See also* looted
    property
Arthur, William C., 30
Aryan racial ideology, 42–43, 66, 90,
    103, 110
Asahi Shimbun, 128, 169, 226
Asia Express, 120, 122
Asian modernity, 248
Asian religions, 42
assassination plots, 27, 104, 109, 196, 198
Associated Press, 227
Astor House Hotel, 81
astrology, 40, 43, 58, 106, 150, 162,
    196–97, 228
Atlantic Monthly, 258
atrocity propaganda, 188
Auden, W. H., 89
Auschwitz concentration camp
    and accusations against Weinreb, 213
    and Bach-Zelewski's role in Holocaust,
        147
    and Gemmeker's role in Holocaust,
        175
    and guilt of half-Jews, 271

Auschwitz concentration camp (cont.)
Hungarian Jews at, 239
Nanjing Massacre compared with, 159
and Nazi control of Netherlands, 90
and Slovakian uprising, 199, 231
survivors, 212
and Weinreb's efforts to halt
deportations, 132, 175, 181–82,
184, 186–87
Australia, 247
Austro-Hungarian empire, 16–17, 54–55
Avreimel (Weinreb's
great-grandfather), 29

Bach-Zelewski, Erich von dem,
147, 153
Backhouse, Edmund, 258
Bakhoven, W. P., 219, 221
Battle of Jehol, 126
Battle of Shanghai, 158, 170, 226, 247
Battle of Stalingrad, 156, 181, 187–88
BBC, 209
Beatrix, Queen, 96
The Beauty in Men's Clothes (Muramatsu
Shofu), 50, 79, 83, 118, 226–27
The Beauty in Men's Clothes: Kawashima
Yoshiko Was Still Alive! (television),
244
Beck, Ludwig, 195
Beckmann, Max, 71
Beethoven, Ludwig van, 84
Beijing, China, 36, 164–66, 202–3, 206,
222, 225, 242
Belgium, 155–57, 185
Belle de Jour (Kessel), 13
Bełżec extermination camp, 17
Bergen-Belsen concentration camp, 176,
212, 229, 234, 236–37
Berger, Gottlob, 107–8, 146, 198–99,
231, 251, 257–58, 261
Berlin, Germany, 61–70, 237–38
Bernadotte, Folke, Count of Wisborg
and case against Kersten, 256–59
death, 256
efforts to free prisoners, 191, 232
on exterminations in concentration
camps, 237
and fall of Third Reich, 251–53

and Kersten's wish for Swedish
citizenship, 251
and negotiations to free Jews at end of
war, 234–35
peace talk efforts, 232
Bernhard, Prince, consort of Juliana, 115,
253, 255, 257
Besgen, Achim, 14–15
Bettauer, Hugo, 27
bidan, 118–19, 125–26, 128–29, 165
Bier, August, 41
Bignell, Charles, 111
Binswanger, Otto, 41
Birnbaum, Miriam, 210, 212
Birnbaum, Phyllis, 37, 49, 51–52,
118, 202
Birnbaum, Uriël, 210, 212, 218–19
Black Dragon Society, 35, 46, 164
Black Ocean Society, 35
Blavatsky, Helena Petrovna, 42, 256
Blik, 174
Blue Express, 81
Boas, Henriëtte, 270
Bolland (collaborator), 179–85, 217
Bolsheviks, 14, 67, 195
bombs and bombing plots, 21–22, 86,
234, 254
Boxer Rebellion, 35–36
boycotts, 86
Brandt, Rudolf
and fall of Third Reich, 251
and Himmler's concessions on Jewish
prisoners, 234, 238
on Hunger Plan, 155
Kersten's defense of, 146, 150, 233, 261
and Kersten's wartime activities,
107–10, 112–15
and negotiations to free Jews at end of
war, 236
Brigadier General Yuri, 202–3
British Foreign Office, 231
Browning, Christopher, 146
Brownshirts, 69, 72
Buchenwald concentration camp, 68,
95, 237
Buddhist monks, 86
Buñuel, Luis, 13
Burgundian Free State, 155

Calmeyer, Hans Georg, 97, 176
Calmeyer List, 176
Carroll, Lewis, 210
Castro, Fidel, 272
Central Intelligence Agency (CIA), 192,
    195, 252
Chagall, Marc, 28
Chanel, Coco, 194
Chang, Peter H. L., 78
Channa (Weinreb's grandmother), 29
Chaplin, Charlie, 46, 71
Chiang Kai-shek, 78, 82, 86–87, 157–60,
    204, 224
China Nights (film), 199
Chinese Nationalists
    and arrest of Yoshiko, 222
    and Battle of Jehol, 126–27
    and Chinese civil war, 224
    and conspiracy theories on Yoshiko's
        death, 242
    and founding of Manchukuo Republic,
        82–84
    and Han chauvinism, 20
    and onset of war in Asia, 157–58
    resistance to Kwantung Army
        advances, 124
    and Yoshiko's public persona, 167
Chizuko, 118, 123, 165
chochem (*goochem*), 75–76, 98
Chopin, Frédéric, 147
Christian mythology, 241
Christiansen, Friedrich, 261
Churchill, Winston, 53, 71, 194,
    232, 236
Ciano, Galeazzo, conte, 69, 78, 143
The City Without Jews (Bettauer), 27
clemency requests, 221
Clerk and Butcher (Kersten), 12, 254
Cleveringa, Rudolph, 91
Clouds of War: The Queen of Asia (film),
    244
Cold War, 201
collabo figures, 5
Collaboration and Resistance 1940-1945
    (Weinreb), 269
collective guilt, 220
collective identities, 9, 26
Columbia University, 45

Communist Party, 83, 96, 212, 224.
    See also anticommunism
concentration camps. *See specific camp
    names*
concubines, 37
conspiracy theories, 3, 9, 103, 273
Cooper, Gary, 112
Cossacks, 17
Cousens, Charles, 205–6
Cultural Revolution, 80
The Curtain Falls (Bernadotte), 251–52
Czechoslovakia, 181
Czernowitz, 17–18

Dachau concentration camp, 108, 141,
    195, 235, 237
*Danso no reijin: Kawashima Yoshiko wa
    ikiteita!* (television), 244
The Darkroom of Damocles (Hermans),
    138, 272
Datsu A ("Leave Asia") motto, 247
David, King of Israel, 29
death camps. *See specific camp names*
death squads (*Einsatzgruppen*), 109, 147
de Beaufort, Marius, 253
De bijbel als schepping (Weinreb), 265
de Gaulle, Charles, 4, 262
Degrelle, Leon, 155
de Gruyter, P. S., 217
de Jong, Loe, 113, 115, 254
Denmark, 157, 235
deportations
    of Dutch Jews, 90–91, 130, 175–78
    and Kersten's background, 14
    Kersten's claim of saving the Dutch,
        12, 112–15, 145, 152, 154, 210, 217,
        219, 234, 254–55
    and Łódź ghetto, 199
    and logistics of Final Solution, 145
    and postwar bureaucracy, 212
    and Slovakian uprising, 199, 231
    strikes protesting, 96–97
    Weinreb's efforts to halt, 1, 94, 99,
        133, 135, 182–87
    and Weinreb's family, 74, 141, 178
    and Weinreb's trial, 266
Der Stürmer, 216
Diehn, August, 68, 70

Die Stadt ohne Juden (Bettauer), 27
Dirlewanger, Oskar, 108
Disraeli, Benjamin, 45
"diving" (going underground), 133–34,
   208, 266–67
Dohnanyi, Hans von, 195
Doihara Kenji (Lawrence of Manchuria),
   34, 77, 82
Dongzhen. *See* Kawashima Yoshiko
Dora-Mittelbau concentration
   camp, 237
Douglas-Hamilton, Douglas, Duke of
   Hamilton, 107
Dresdner Bank, 231
Drion, H., 220
Dulles, Allen, 194
Durlacher, Evan, 210–12
Durlacher, Jetty, 210, 218
Durlacher, Leo, 210–12
Dutch East Indies, 210
Dutch Foreign Office, 264
Dutch Jews, 55–56, 90, 92, 175,
   179, 186
Dutch National Institute for War
   Documentation, 94
Dutch Nazi party (NSB), 72,
   104, 110–11
Dutch Red Cross, 255
Dutch resistance, 110, 130, 151, 185
Dutch Supreme Court, 91
Du Yuesheng, 87

Eastern exoticism, 117
East Prussia, 148
Eco, Umberto, 89
Edward VIII, King of England, 71
Eichmann, Adolf, 91, 144, 230, 231
Eisenhower, Dwight, 236
Ekman, Dr., 15–16, 39
Elders of Zion, 103
Elijah, Prophet, 29
The End (Bernadotte), 251–52
Estonia, 13–15, 195
eugenics, 66, 103
Eulenspiegel, Till, 89
Extinction: The Destruction of Dutch Jewry,
   1940-1945 (Presser), 266–67
extraterritorial rights, 192

fake documents. *See* identity documents
Fang Yongchang, 126–27
Fiddler on the Roof (Chagall), 28
Final Solution, 106, 144–45
Finland
   and anti-Russian sentiment, 195
   and fall of Third Reich, 228
   Finnish Army, 191
   Finnish perceptions of Kersten, 254
   German wartime relations with,
      152–54, 156, 191
   Kersten's citizenship and cultural
      identity, 8, 13–16, 104–6, 151–53,
      191, 250, 252
   massage in Finnish culture, 15–16, 39,
      43–44, 102, 240
Fischer, Franz (*Judenfischer*) 186
Fischl (Weinreb's grandfather), 55, 74
Fleming, Gerald, 258
Flick, Friedrich, 67, 104, 260–61
Flossenburg concentration camp, 237
Forbidden City, Beijing, 35, 81, 164
Ford, Gerald, 206
Forgács, Péter, 89–90
forgers, 138–39, 258, 269, 273. *See also*
   identity documents
fortune tellers, 222. *See also* astrology
France
   Allied liberation of, 228, 234
   Free French, 213
   French resistance, 13, 145
   German occupation of, 136
   and myth of resistance to Nazi
      occupation, 4, 209
   and Nazi plans to loot food, 155–56
   and persecution of Dutch Jews, 94
   and postwar accounts of Kersten's
      activities, 262
   and retribution against collaborators,
      212, 224
   and Turksma's escape from Nazis, 132
   and Weinreb's background, 18, 55
Frank, Anne, 96, 176, 199, 209
Frankfurt Art School, 71
Franz Joseph I of Austria, 25–26, 55
Freemasons, 152
Frentz, Walter, 147
Freud, Sigmund, 26

Friedenau district of Berlin, 61
Friedrich Franz, Hereditary Grand Duke of Mecklenburg-Schwerin, 155
Friends of Heinrich Himmler, 66–67, 70
Fujin Koron, 128
Fukushima Yasumasa, 34, 36
Fukuzawa Yukichi, 247
Fumio Nanri, 46
Funk, Walter, 67
Fünten, Ferdinand Hugo aus der, 135–36

Galicia, 54
Ganjurjab, 78–80
gas chambers, 90, 95, 199, 209. *See also specific camp names*
gelernter, 75–76, 98
Gellhorn, Martha, 108
Gemmeker, Albert Konrad
  and arrests of hiding Jews, 209
  command of Westerbork, 176–80
  and Special Court trials, 221–22
  and Weinreb's efforts to halt deportations, 179, 182, 186–87
  Weinreb's memoir on, 207
gender norms and identity
  in Meiji Japan, 21
  retribution targeting female collaborators, 6, 212
  Ri Koran's relationship with Yoshiko, 166, 168
  third sex identity, 52, 250
Genghis Khan, 80, 242
Genyosha (Black Ocean Society), 34
Georg Alexander, Duke of Mecklenburg, 155
George VI, King of Great Britain, 107
German culture and language, 17–18, 27–28, 40–41, 55, 72
German Jews, 72, 179, 186
German Olympic Committee, 62
Gestapo
  and aftermath of war in Netherlands, 213–14
  and arrest/deportation of Dutch Jews, 155, 176, 208–9
  and arrest/interrogation of Weinreb, 138, 140
  Berlin headquarters, 70
  and Bernadotte's account of the war, 252
  and invasion of Poland, 157
  Kaltenbrunner as head of, 189
  and Kersten's connections with Nazi leadership, 106
  and Kersten's influence with Himmler, 111, 191
  and perceptions of Weinreb, 2
  and proclamation of Third Reich, 65
  and role of *Vertrauensmann,* 171
  and Special Court trials, 216, 219
  threat to Kersten, 198
  and Weinreb's crimes, 2
Gleiwitz Incident, 157
Goebbels, Joseph, 3, 68, 145–46, 154–55, 253
Goerdeler, Carl, 195
Golem, 137–40
Goltz, Rüdiger von der, 15
Gone with the Wind (film), 250
Göring, Hermann, 66, 190, 195–96
Gramsci, Antonio, 272
Grand Duchy of Livonia, 62
"Grandmother Died" (Gleiwitz Incident), 157
Green Gang, 87
Green Police, 175
Grüter, Regina, 94, 264
Guevara, Ernesto "Che," 272
Günther, Christian, 190, 236, 251
Gutwirth, Esther. *See* Weinreb, Esther
Gutwirth, Lili, 136
gymnastics clubs, 40–41

The Hague
  and aftermath of war in Netherlands, 212, 214
  and Bignell, 111
  bombing plot, 234, 254
  and complexity of Kersten's identity, 8
  and deportation of Jews, 175
  and final years of the war, 207–12
  and Kersten's prewar life, 63
  and persecution of Dutch Jews, 130, 134–35
  and postwar accounts of Kersten's activities, 259, 261

The Hague *(cont.)*
    and postwar accounts of Weinreb's
        activities, 270
    Reinkenstraat raid, 173
    and Special Court trials, 217
    threat to Kersten in, 104
    and Weinreb's background, 53
    and Weinreb's efforts to halt
        deportations, 98–100, 182–83, 187
Han Dynasty, 20, 32, 119–20
Han Gaozu, Emperor of China, 32
Hartzwalde estate
    and Kersten's departure from
        Germany, 240
    and Kersten's influence with Himmler,
        191–92
    and Kersten's life in Berlin, 104
    Kersten's purchase of, 67
    and negotiations to free Jews at end of
        war, 237–38
    and Soviet control Germany,
        250–51, 254
    and threats to Kersten, 198
    Wulff on, 150
Hassidism, 29, 55, 57, 73
Hausleiter, Leo, 261–62
Havel, Václav, 276
Hebrew language, 56
Hebrew Scripture, 263, 271
Hendrik, Prince, consort of Wilhelmina,
    63, 68, *101*, 114, 253
Henry the Fowler, 102, 229
Hermans, W. F., 138, 267, 271, 274
Hermit of Peking (Trevor-Roper), 258
Hess, Rudolf, 105–7, 152, 251
Hewitt, Abram Stevens, 192–95
Heydrich, Reinhard, 106–7, 109, 113,
    144, 152, 156–57, 189
Hillesum, Etty, 177
Himmler, Heinrich, *101*
    Amakasu compared to, 82
    antisemitism, 103
    attempted Holocaust coverup, 17
    and Edda Ciano, 78
    and final years of Third Reich,
        188–99
    as focus of *The Kersten Memoirs*, 11–12

Gestapo headquarters office, 70
    and Kersten's claim of saving the
        Dutch, 114–15
    Kersten's relationship with, 101–12
    and Langbehn, 188–89
    and negotiations to free Jews at end of
        war, 228–39
    nickname for Kersten, 1
    and occult influences in German
        culture, 40, 42–43
    and origins of Final Solution, 143–56
    pain problems, 145, 153, 156
    and persecution of Dutch Jews, 90
    and postwar accounts of Kersten's
        activities, 253–55, 257–58, 260–62
    and rise of Third Reich, 66–68
    and SD annual reports, 129
    shooting party at Ribbentrop's estate,
        143, 146–47
    suicide, 251
Hindenburg, Paul von, 66
Hinduism, 43, 58
Hirohito, Emperor, 78
Hishikari Takashi, 121–22
Hitler, Adolf
    and Bier, 41
    and British culture, 112
    connections with Dutch royalty, 156
    deportation orders, 113–14
    diary forgeries, 259
    Diehn's attempt to influence, 68
    Dutch response to rising power of,
        71–73
    and final years of Third Reich, 190
    and Hess's peace efforts, 107
    negotiations on post-Hitler Germany,
        192–99
    and negotiations to free Jews at end of
        war, 231, 233–35, 238–39
    and occult influences in German
        culture, 40, 58
    and origins of Final Solution, 144–46,
        147–48, 151–55
    and persecution of Dutch Jews, 90
    plots against, 109, 196, 228
    rise to power, 65–66
    stomach pains, 106

and Venlo Incident, 109
in Vienna, 25–26
and Weinreb's political beliefs, 76
Hitler Youth, 102
Hochstapler description, 3, 6, 9, 221, 275
Hofmans, Greet, 256–57, 265
Holland, 71–72, 112, 155–57, 270.
    See also Netherlands
Hollander, F., 215–16
homeopathy, 41
homophobia, 102
human weakness, 8
Hunger Plan, 156

identity documents
    and arrest/interrogation of Weinreb,
        131, 137–39
    and Calmeyer's role, 97
    and destruction of Kersten's archive,
        105
    and Durlacher family, 210
    and persecution of Dutch Jews, 92
    and self-deception of collaborators,
        277
    Weinreb on, 26
    and Weinreb's exemption lists, 94, 208
    and Yoshiko's trial as Chinese traitor,
        225
ideology, 276
Indonesia, 210, 263
informants, 110, 207–8, 242, 255, 274
Inner Mongolia, 31, 33, 46–47, 124, 126
Internal Armed Forces, 213
International League for Human Rights,
    218
In the Shadow of Chaos (Kawashima),
    19, 157
Ishiwara Kanji, 77
Israel, 75, 256
Issberner-Haldane, Ernst, 43
Itagaki Seishiro, 77, 121–23
Italy, 69, 205
Ito Hanni (Matsuo Masanao), 162–64
Iwata Ainosuke, 50, 51

Jahn, Friedrich Ludwig, 40
Jakarta, Indonesia, 263, 264

Jamenfeld, Nosen, 28–29
Janowska concentration camp, 17
Japan
    Japanese culture and heritage, 20,
        119–20
    and Nanjing Massacre, 158–60,
        169–70, 247
    occupation of Manchuria, 77–88
    Pearl Harbor attack, 124, 162, 199,
        205–6, 247
    propaganda efforts, 80, 83
    See also Kwantung Army; Manchukuo
        Republic
Japanese 14th Division, 125
Japanese Foreign Ministry, 50
Japanese Imperial Army, 19, 77, 162
Japanese Imperial Navy, 118
The Japanese People (journal), 163
Jaremca, Ukraine, 18
jazz, 84, 162
Jehol/Chengde, 126–28
Jehovah's Witnesses, 67, 149–50, 238
Jewish Council, 92–94, 96, 129, 137–38,
    179, 266–67
"Jewish problem"/"Jewish question," 13,
    96, 154, 192, 233, 239, 270
Jin Bihui. *See* Kawashima Yoshiko
Jing Garden House, 81
Joop den Uyl (Johannes Marten den
    Uijl), 12
Judah Loew ben Bezalel, 137
Juliana, Queen of the Netherlands,
    257, 265

Kabbalah, 263
Kakania, 26
Kalker, Joseph, 183–84
Kaltenbrunner, Ernst, 107, 189–91,
    198–99, 252
Kamisaka Fuyuko, 49, 52, 129, 242
Kaputt (Malaparte), 154
Karl Alexander, Archduke of
    Saxony-Weimar-Eisenach, 53
Katzenellebogen, Shaul Wahl, 29
Katzmann, Fritz, 17
Kawashima Naniwa, 19, 23, 33–38,
    45–52, 79, 225, 243

Kawashima Yoshiko
  arrest, trial, and execution of, 2, 6,
    222–28, *226*
  background, 8, 19–23
  burial place, 250
  celebrity of, 161
  childhood and upbringing, 44–45,
    47–52
  Chinese name, 222, 225, 228
  citizenship status, 45, 225
  and complexity of collaborator figures,
    8, 9–10, 275
  contrasted with other collaborator
    subjects, 1
  cultural/political background of
    family, 31, 35, 37–38
  domestic arrangements in Shanghai,
    118
  drug problem, 204
  education, 49
  and end of war, 199–206
  family's exile from Beijing, 31
  as *Hochstapler* figure, 9
  "Joan of Arc" identity, 52, 80, 83, 117,
    123, 125, 167
  and Manchu heritage, 19–22, 78–80,
    87, 124–25, 164–65
  marriage to Mongolian, 79–80, 244
  "Mata Hari of the Orient" identity, 85
  modern perspective on, 4–5
  nonbinary gender identity, 49, *51,*
    51–52, 168, 250
  and onset of war in Asia, 157–69
  poetry of, 243
  in popular culture, 243–46, 249–50
  in postwar popular culture, 242–47,
    249–50
  and Puyi's court in Shinkyo, 117–20,
    123–29
  return to Japan, 159–60
  and self-deception of collaborators,
    277
  sexual abuse suspicions, 49–50
  in Shanghai, 78–88
  suicide attempts, 51, 204
Kawashima Yoshiko Wants to Be a Man
    (Tanaka Hosana), 249
Kelder, D., 214

Kellner, Friedrich, 149
Kempeitai, 168, 202
Keppler, Wilhelm, 66
Keppler Circle, 66
Kershaw, Ian, 148
Kersten, Felix
  apolitical nature of, 73
  background, 8, 11–16
  citizenship status, 2, 11, 15, 64, 104,
    106, 228, 250–54, 256
  and complexity of collaborator figures,
    2–4, 7–10, 275
  connections with Nazi leadership,
    101–12
  contrasted with other subjects, 1
  death, 262–63
  diaries, 105
  and Dutch deportation tale, 112–15,
    145, 152, 154, 254–55
  family background, 12
  and German cultural influences,
    39–40
  and German *Kultur*, 18
  as *Hochstapler* figure, 9
  and Hofmans, 256–57, 265
  influence with Himmler, 104, 111,
    143–56, 188–99
  introduction to massage, 15–16
  and "living in truth," 277
  marriage, 41, 69
  medical and massage training,
    41–44, 63
  memoirs, 113
  military career, 14–15
  and negotiations to free Jews at end of
    war, 228–40
  nickname, 1
  and occult influences in German
    culture, 41–44
  offered SS rank, 105
  political opinions, 262
  postwar accounts of activities, 250–63
  prewar life, 61–70
  Scheveningen home, 64
  and self-deception of collaborators,
    277
  and shooting party at Ribbentrop's
    estate, 143

Kersten, Friedrich, 12
Kersten, Irmgard, 150
The Kersten Memoirs (Kersten), 11, 254
Kessel, Joseph
    on Allied pressure on Sweden, 190–91
    on Bier, 41
    on Diehn's fear of Himmler, 70
    on Himmler's train, 148
    on Kersten's clientele, 67–68
    on Kersten's influence with Himmler,
        104, 144, 233
    on Kersten's wartime activities,
        112–13
    on Kersten's apolitical nature, 65
    on Nazi plans to loot food, 155–56
    on negotiations on post-Hitler
        Germany, 196
    on negotiations to free Jews at end of
        war, 236
    on prisoners at Hartzwalde estate,
        150–51
    on threats to Kersten, 198
Kharchin people, 33
Kleist, Paul Ludwig Ewand von, 181–82
Klerk en beul (Kersten), 12, 254
Kneipp, Sebastian, 102
Knesset, 96
Knieriem, Ottokar von, 231
Ko, B., 41–44, 61
Kobayashi Takiji, 128
Koch, Fritz
    and arrests of hiding Jews, 208
    and Weinreb's arrest/interrogation,
        130–34, 136–37, 140–41, 171–74,
        179
    and Weinreb's efforts to halt
        deportations, 183–84, 186–87
Koolhaas, Rem, *101*
korban, 214
Korean heritage, 119–20
Kormis, Fritz, 70–71
Kormis, Rachel, 71
Kotte, Hendrik, 139–40
Kraus, Karl, 26, 28
Kristallnacht, 69, 76, 146
Krom (Dutch agent), 184, 185, 273
Krupp (German arms manufacturer), 30
Krupp, Gustav, 66

Kruskal, Herbert, 135
Kurhaus hotel, 53
Kwantung Army
    and Amakasu's suicide, 227
    and Battle of Jehol, 126, 128
    and founding of Manchukuo Republic,
        81, 85
    occupation of Manchuria, 78
    and postwar Japanese culture, 246
    and postwar retribution against
        Japanese, 223
    and Puyi's court in Shinkyo, 119, 121,
        123–24
Kyushu, 199, 200

labor camps. *See specific camp names*
The Labyrinth (Schellenberg), 252
Landau, Mendel, 184
Langbehn, Carl, 188–89, 190, 194,
    196, 198
Lange, I. G., 136
The Last Days of Hitler (Trevor-Roper),
    258–59
Latvia, 147
Lawrence, T. E., 34
League of Nations, 247
lebensraum, 31, 35–37, 147
Legion of Honor, 262
Lehi group (Stern gang), 256
Lemberg, Ukraine, 16–18
Lemke, 172, 179, 180, 183
Lenin, Vladimir, 3
Leopoldstadt, Vienna, 27, 28
Ley, Robert, 105–7, 251
Leyden University, 91
The Lives of a Bengal Lancer (film), 112
Livonia, 12–14, 18
Li Xianglan, 224. *See* Yamaguchi
    Yoshiko
Li Zhisui, 106
Łódź, Poland, 199
Longerich, Peter, 197
looted property
    and Bignell, 111
    and complexity of collaborator
        figures, 7
    and final years of Third Reich, 190
    and Flick, 67

looted property *(cont.)*
  German extortion of Jewish wealth,
    132–33
  and Hunger Plan, 156
  and postwar retribution against
    Japanese, 223
  and Weinreb's efforts to halt
    deportations, 181
Lüben, Elisabeth, 41, 61, 69, 104,
  191, 254
Lüben, Irmgard, 104
Lueger, Karl, 25–26
luftmensch identity, 74, 76
Lugou Bridge (Marco Polo Bridge), 157
Lüshun. *See* Port Arthur

macher identity, 98–99, 107, 124, 135
Machiel (newborn, prisoner), 177
Madagascar, 145
Madoff, Bernie, 100
The Maelstrom (Forgács), 89–90
Maeterlinck, Maurice, 58–59
Maggid of Nadvirna, 29
Majdanek death camp, 153, 154
Malaparte, Curzio, 102, 154
malaria, 34
Mallet, Victor, 231
Manchu heritage
  and founding of Manchukuo Republic,
    80–83
  and Manchukuo flag, 119–20
  and Russo-Japanese War, 31–32
  and Sasakawa's interest in Yoshiko,
    204
  and Yoshiko's background, 19–22
  and Yoshiko's marriage to Ganjurjab,
    78–80
  and Yoshiko's motives, 87
  and Yoshiko's negotiations with
    General Su, 124–25
  and Yoshiko's public persona, 164–65
  See also Manchukuo Republic;
    Manchuria
Manchukuo Republic
  and Amakasu's suicide, 227
  arrest of emperor Puti, 223
  and final years of the war, 205
  founding and purpose of, 80–82

and onset of war in Asia, 159–62
  and postwar Japanese culture, 246–49
  Puyi's court in Shinkyo, 119–26
  and racial harmony propaganda, 162
  and Shanghai Incident, 85–88
  and threats against Yoshiko, 201–2
  wei Manzhou (fake Manchuria), 119
  Westerbork compared with, 176
  Yoshiko's promotion of, 129
  and Yoshiko's public persona,
    164–68
  See also Manchuria
Manchuria
  anti-Chinese uprisings, 46–47
  and founding of Manchukuo Republic,
    84–85
  Japanese occupation of, 77–79
  and Kawashima's pan-Asianism, 36
  and postwar Japanese culture, 249
  and Russo-Japanese War, 31
  and Shanghai Incident, 88
  and Yoshiko's cultural background,
    31–33
  See also Manchu heritage; Manchukuo
    Republic; Port Arthur
manga featuring Yoshiko, 249–50
Mann, Thomas, 58
The Man with the Miraculous Hands
  (Kessel), 13
Mao Zedong, 106, 209, 224
Marco Polo Bridge Incident, 157–58
Marcuse, Herbert, 209, 272
Marie, Queen of Romania, 62
"Marx boys," 46
Masonry, 103
Masur, Norbert, 237, 238–39
"Mata Hari" legend, 85, 123, 242, 244
Matsumoto, Japan, 160, 164
Matsumoto Castle, 48
Matsuoka Yōsuke, 204, 205
Mauretania file, 216
Mauthausen concentration camp, 73, 95,
  151, 235
Max, Prince of Baden, 53
medical experimentation, 39–40, 108
Meijers, Eduard, 91
Meiji Japan, 21, 33
Melville, Jean-Pierre, 13

"Memorandum about My Helpful Acts in the Years 1940-1945" (Kersten), 114
Mikado, 122
Minamoto no Yoritomo, 242
Minamoto no Yoshitsune, 242
Ming Dynasty, 20
Mizoguchi Kenji, 226–27
Moeru Shanghai (film), 244
Mongolia and Mongol heritage, 31–33, 36, 46–47, 78–80, 83, 119–20, 222, 244
Monnoson, 57
Moonlight Sonata (Beethoven), 84
Moosa, Spencer, 227
morphine, 51, 81, 160. *See also* opium
Mr. Smith Goes to Washington (film), 162
Mukden Incident, 77, 82, 88, 157
Mulisch, Harry, 270–72
Muramatsu Shofu, 79, 83–86, 129, 161, 226, 244
Museum of the Puppet Empire, 122
Mussert, Anton, 72, 104
Mussolini, Benito, 201
Mussolini, Edda (wife of Count Galeazzo Ciano), 78
Musy, Benoît, 230
Musy, Jean-Marie, 230
My Opposition (Kellner), 149
myths and mythmaking
    and charges against Yoshiko, 227
    and complexity of collaborator figures, 2–5, 83, 200
    and countermyths, 5
    "demythologizing" conventional narratives, 209, 269
    and denialism, 241
    as expression of truth, 277
    and founding of Han dynasty, 32
    and postwar accounts of Weinreb's activities, 270
    and postwar Japanese popular culture, 241–50
    resistance to Nazi occupation myth, 4, 208–12, 267
    and role of historiography, 276
    and self-delusion, 100
    Tokyo Rose myth, 205–6

and Trevor-Roper, 258
and Weinreb's tales, 134
and Yoshiko's arrest, 225
and Yoshiko's childhood, 19
and Yoshiko's social connections, 85

Nagano Prefecture, 48
Nanjing Massacre, 158–60, 169–70, 247
National Army, 127–28
National Institute for War Documentation (RIOD), 132, 183–84, 214
nationalism, 45, 248
national morality tales, 5
nativism, 46
Nazi Culture Chamber, 216
Nazism, 40, 41, 63, 65–66, 76, 106. *See also specific groups and individuals*
Netherlands
    antisemitism in, 212, 215–16
    colonial legacy, 268
    complacency to Hitler's rise, 71–73
    and complexity of Kersten's identity, 8
    deportation of Dutch population tale, 12, 112–15, 145, 152, 154, 254–55
    Dutch edition of Kersten's memoir, 12
    Dutch elite's connections with Germany, 195–96
    Dutch resistance, 110, 130, 151, 185
    extent of Holocaust deaths, 99
    German persecution/deportation of Dutch Jews, 89–96, 129–30
    and Kersten's connections with Nazi leadership, 109–15
    and Kersten's prewar life, 63–64
    myth of resistance to Nazis, 4, 208–12, 267
    Nazi occupation of, 104–5
    and Turksma's postwar service, 132
    and Weinreb's family background, 54–56
Netherlands Ministry of Foreign Affairs, 153
Neuschaffer, Irmgard, 69
New Asianism, 163, 166
Nietzsche, Friedrich, 46
Nieuwenhuis, Jacob, 110–11
Nippon Foundation, 201

Nobel Prizes, 74, 201, 255
Nojiri Lake, 48
Norway, 188
Norwegian Jews, 232
Nuremberg racial laws, 76
Nuremburg War Crimes Trials, 67, 109, 252, 261

occultism and mysticism, 40–44, 58–59, 75
Office of Strategic Services (OSS), 192, 194
Okamura Yasuji, 223–24
Okura Kihachiro, 46–47
Onderduiken. See "diving" (going underground)
"Only in Lwów!" (song), 16
Operation Modellhut, 194
Ophuls, Marcel, 267
opium, 34, 78, 81, 126–27, 168, 201. *See also* morphine
Opium Wars, 247
Orange Hotel, 131, 135, 172, 180, 214
Order of the White Rose, 152
Ordinary Men (Browning), 146
Oriental cults, 58
"Orphan Annie." *See* Toguri, Iva (Tokyo Rose)
Orthodox Judaism, 74, 76, 230, 271
Ostjuden, 26–28, 55, 179

Palestina List, 176
Palestine and Palestinians, 56, 75, 176, 256
pan-Asianism, 20–21, 23, 36, 163
Pan Shuhua. *See* Yamaguchi Yoshiko
Pan Yugui, 165–66
passports, 71, 97, 106, 154, 212, 237, 250, 254, 259. *See also* identity documents
The Patriot (aircraft), 201–2
Patriotic Association, 50
Patriotic People's Party, 201
Patton, George, 195
Pavillon Riche, 54
Peaceful Nation Army, 127–28
Pearl Harbor attack, 124, 162, 199, 205, 206, 247

peasantry, 13, 18, 32, 120, 129, 210, 223
Peeren, Krijna, 172
Peking Opera, 20
Pélleas et Mélisande (Maeterlinck), 58–59
People's Republic of China, 249
Petäys resort, 154
PM, 218
pogroms, 17, 18, 137
Poland
    and deportation of Dutch Jews, 176
    and Dutch deportation tale, 12, 112–15, 145, 152, 154, 254–55
    Kellner on murder of Polish Jews, 149
    and Nazi plans to loot food, 156
    and Swedish resistance to Germany, 188
Poland's Martyrdom, 188
polio, 182
Polish Hearth Club, 17
Polish Jews, 186, 232
Polish resistance, 188
Ponzi schemes, 100
Popitz, Johannes, 194, 196
popular culture, 243–44
Port Arthur, 22–23, 30–38, 47, 50, 120
Portugal, 94–95, 136
Posthumus, N. W., 255, 258–59
Presley, Elvis, 241
Presser, Jacques, 266–67
Princess Jin, the Joan of Arc of the Orient (Woods), 117
Prince Su (Aisin Gyoro Shanqi)
    Boxer Rebellion service, 35
    death of, 37, 50
    dream of Qing restoration, 22–23, 32, 37
    exiled, 30–33
    Manchu heritage, 19–20
    and pan-Asianism, 36
    and Rungsangnoerhbu, 33
    support for anti-Chinese uprisings, 46–48
    and Yoshiko's background, 19–20, 22–23, 30–33, 35–37, 50
prisoner exchanges, 176, 181, 229–31
prisoners of war, 71

propaganda
and charges against Yoshiko, 227
and complexity of collaborator figures, 275
and postwar Japanese culture, 245–46
and postwar life in Netherlands, 212
and reactions to abuses in camps, 151
and Russo-Japanese War, 21
as tool of dictatorships, 3
and Weinreb's trial, 218–19
and Yamaga, 51
and Yoshiko's public persona, 166–68
Yoshiko's role, 161–62
and Yoshiko's trial, 2, 226
Propaganda Ministry, 68
prostitution, 34
Protocols of the Elders of Zion, 273
Provos, 268, 270, 272
Prussian militarism, 12
psychoanalysis, 26
public health and hygiene, 102, 122
Puyi (Qing emperor), 81–83, 119–22, 126, 223, 226, 246

Qin Dynasty, 32, 244
Qing Dynasty
and Boxer Rebellion, 35
and charges against Yoshiko, 226
and current Japan/Asia relations, 249
and Japanese creation of Manchukuo, 81–82, 121, 124
and Opium War, 30
and Prince Su's financial ties, 37
and Prince Su's hopes for restoration, 32, 45, 47–48
and Yoshiko's background, 19–23
Yoshiko's potential role in restoration, 45, 52, 83, 127–28, 204, 244
Qiqihar, Japan, 124–25, 225
Qiu Jin, 21–22

Rabinow (Scheveningen gelernter), 76
Racial Harmony Society, 227
racial identity
racial equality clause in League of Nations, 247

racial harmony propaganda in Manchukuo, 81, 120, 124, 162, 223, 227, 246
racial purity theories, 68–69, 90, 105, 108, 110, 247
Radetzky March (Roth), 26
Rakower, J., 270
Rangell, Johan Wilhelm, 154
Ranke, Leopold von, 276
rape and sexual violence, 97–98, 136, 159, 216–17, 223, 266, 273
rassolnik, 69
Rauter, Hanns, 111, 113
Ravensbrück concentration camp, 67, 149, 234–35, 239, 253
Red Cross movement and groups, 191, 229, 232, 235, 255, 257
Reichskommissar, 90
Reinkenstraat raid, 173
Republic of China, 22, 31
Republic of Estonia, 14
Reserve Army (German), 197, 228
Revolutionary Alliance, 20–22
Ribbentrop, Joachim von
and fall of Third Reich, 251–52
and German Finnish relations, 156
and Kersten's connections with Nazi leadership, 105–7
relationship with Himmler, 143
shooting party at estate of, 143, 146, 149, 156
Richard III (Shakespeare), 106
Ri Koran. See Yamaguchi Yoshiko
Ri Koran: The Musical, 245
Ringeling (accountant), 137
Rolling Stones, 53
ronin, 33, 35–36, 50, 167
Roosenburg, Dirk, 101
Roots of the Bible (Weinreb), 265
Rosterg, August, 67–68, 70, 110
Roth, Joseph, 26, 27
Rothstock (dental technician), 27
Rubinstein, Renate, 268–71, 274
Rungsangnoerhbu, Prince of Khallachin, 33
Russia, 18, 54, 195
Russian Revolution, 32
Russo-Finnish War, 152–53

Russo-Japanese War, 21, 30–31, 77
Ryojun. *See* Port Arthur
Ryti, Risto, 152, 153
Ryukichi, Tanaka, 202

Sachsenhausen concentration camp, 237
samurai, 21, 33, 34, 80, 226
Sanko Sakusen (Three Alls) strategy, 223
Sanno Hotel, 205
Sanskrit, 42, 43
Sant, François van 't, *101*
Sartre, Jean-Paul, 209
Sasakawa Ryoichi, 201–4
sauna baths, 39, 102
scapegoating, 1–2, 268, 270
Schellenberg, Walter
  and fall of Third Reich, 252
  and Kersten's wartime activities, 107–9
  Masur on, 238
  negotiations and machinations near
    war's end, 189, 193–97, 230, 233,
    235–36, 238–39
  and threats to Kersten, 198
Schellevis (Weinreb's cellmate), 174
Scheveningen, 53–59, 130, 172, 256
Schindler, Oskar, 150
Schnitzler, Arthur, 26–27
Schoenberg, Arnold, 27
Schöffer, Ivo, 269
Scholem, Gershom, 265
Schopenhauer, Arthur, 58–59
Schumann, Herbert Joachim von
  (fictional), 95–96, 130–33, 135–36,
    139–40, 172, 211
Schutzstaffel (SS)
  and arrest/interrogation of Weinreb,
    135
  and death of Weinreb's brother, 73
  Edda Ciano given honorary rank, 78
  internal purges, 72
  and Kersten's connections with Nazi
    leadership, 105
  and negotiations to free Jews at end of
    war, 236
  and occult influences in German
    culture, 42
  and origins of Final Solution, 146
  and Weinreb's lists, 207

Scotland Yard, 258
SD. *See* Sicherheitsdienst
Second Opium War, 30
Second Sino-Japanese War, 86
Segev, Tom, 96
Seishiro, Itagaki, 121
Seitz, Karl, 198
Sen'un: Ajia no jo-o (film), 244
sexual abuse allegations. *See* rape and
  sexual violence
Seyss-Inquart, Arthur, 90, 96, 115
Shakespeare, William, 106
Shamir, Yitzhak, 256
Shanghai, 78, 81, 83–88, 201, 246. *See
  also* Battle of Shanghai; Shanghai
  Incident
Shanghai Incident, 85–88, 95, 117–19,
  157–58
Shanghai Is Burning (film), 244
Shanghai Municipal Council, 86, 170
shiatsu, 43
Shinkyo, 123, 126
Shoji Hisako, 245
Sicherheitsdienst (SD)
  and accusations against Weinreb,
    214–15
  and arrest/interrogation of Weinreb,
    136–38, 171–75, 271
  and deportation of Dutch Jews,
    129–35
  and Kotte arrest plan, 140
  and liberation of Netherlands, 211
  and postwar accounts of Kersten's
    activities, 256
  and postwar accounts of Weinreb's
    activities, 271, 273–74
  and scrutiny of Weinreb's lists, 101
  and Special Court trials, 217, 219, 221
  and Weinreb's arrest and interrogation,
    180–87
  and Weinreb's efforts to halt
    deportations, 185, 207–9
Sicily, 181
Sino-Japanese War, 30, 157–61
Six (fictional), 133, 136, 138, 140, 173
slave labor, 67, 68, 261
Slovakian uprising, 199, 231
Slutet (Bernadotte), 251–52

Smit, C., 216, 219
Sobibór concentration camp, 132, 134, 173, 175
Social Democrats (Sweden), 251
The Sorrow and the Pity (Ophuls), 267
Sottens (forger), 138–39
South America, 181
South Manchurian Railway Company, 77, 120, 124, 166
Soviet Red Army, 223, 254
Soviet Union, 114, 147, 156
Spain, 136
Spanier, Dr., 178–79
Special Courts, 1, 214–16, 219, 273
Speer, Albert, 260
SS. *See* Schutzstaffel
Stahlhelm, 41
Stalinism, 7
Steiner, Rudolf, 163
Sternbuch, Recha, 230
Sternbuch, Yitzchak, 230
Sternhell, Hermine, 18
Stockholm, Sweden, 190–98
Storch, Hillel, 232–33, 237
strikes, 96, 112
Stubbing, Olga, 12, 13
student resistance, 131–32
Su Bingwen, 124–25, 169
suicides, 37, 118
Sun Yat-sen, 20–23, 35
Swart, H. L., 214
Swastika Circle, 43
swastika symbol, 42–43
Sweden
    and gestapo threat to Kersten, 198
    and Kersten's background, 11–12
    Kersten's desire for citizenship, 11–12
    and Kersten's postwar life, 250–53
    and Kersten's prewar life, 64
    negotiations on post-Hitler Germany, 195
    and negotiations to free Jews at end of war, 229–39
    Nieuwenhuis's escape to, 111
    and postwar accounts of Kersten's activities, 256–60
    relationship with Third Reich, 188–92

Rosterg's move to, 68
Swedish Red Cross, 191, 232, 235
Switzerland
    Kersten's death, 8
    Kormis's escape to, 71
    negotiations on post-Hitler Germany, 194–95
    and negotiations to free Jews at end of war, 230–31, 234
    Swiss bank accounts, 230
    Swiss Red Cross, 229
    and Weinreb's death, 211, 274
    and Weinreb's exemption lists, 94–95
    and Weinreb's memoir, 73
    and Weinreb's postwar life, 266
symbolic representation, 58–59

Tada Hayao, 123–25, 128, 165–66, 202–3
Taiping Rebellion, 20
tairiku ronin, 33, 35, 50
Taisho democracy, 46
Takarazuka Revue, 250
Tanaka Hosana, 249
Tanaka Ryukichi, 84–86, 118–19, 202, 223
Tang Yulin, 126
Tempelhof airport, 237
Temple of Heaven, 121
theosophy, 42, 256
Theresienstadt, 181–82, 199, 229–30, 232
Third Reich, 65
third sex identity, 52, 250. *See also* gender norms and identity
Third World, 272
Three Alls (*Sanko Sakusen*) strategy, 223
Through the Looking-Glass (Carroll), 210
Thule Society, 68
Tianjin, 81–83, 157
Tibetan Buddhism, 33, 61
Tibetan healing and massage, 42
Tinbergen, Jan, 74
Togoland, 62
Toguri, Iva (Tokyo Rose), 205–6, 224
Tojo Hideki, 202
Tokoro restaurant, 165–66
Tokyo, Japan, 162
Tokyo War Crimes Tribunal, 34, 84, 159

Tolstoy, Leo, 21
Torah, 75
Toyama Mitsuru, 35, 164
transgender identity. *See* gender norms and identity
Treblinka concentration camp, 74, 90
Trevor-Roper, Hugh, 115, 258–59
trickster identity, 95, 99
Turksma, Bep, 131, 271
typhoid fever, 239
typhus epidemics, 237

Ukraine, 16–18, 115, 149
ultranationalism, 45
United Nations, 201
U.S. Department of Justice, 206
U.S. National Archives, 243

V-2 rockets, 234
van Boetzelaer van Oosterhout, Carel Godfried Willem Hendrik, Baron, 253
van Creveld, Simon, 177
van den Hout, W. H. M., 219
van der Leeuw, A. J., 272
van der Vlugt, A. J. Th., 254
van Dijk, Ans, 215, 221
van Heukelom, J. C., 214
Van Lier (medical student), 97–98
Van Maaswijk (BS commandant), 213–14
van Meegeren, Han, 269
van Nagell, J. E. H., Baron, 253–54
Van Walt van Praag (false document purveyor), 137
Venlo Incident, 109
Vermeer painting forgeries, 269
Veth, D. Giltay, 273
Vichy France, 136
Vietnam War, 267
Vieyra, Anthony, 186
Vieyra, Nanny Marie, 185–86
Villa Windekind, 101, 130–32, 136, 172, 256
Visser, Lodewijk, 91
V-Mann (*Vertrauensmann*), 171–72, 183
von Rath (fictional), 133, 136
Vries, Coen de, 130, 134
Vught concentration camp, 141

Waffen SS units, 105–6, 108, 114, 152–53, 155, 198, 231, 261
Wahlbeem, Sarah, 173, 220
"walking dance," 163
Wallenberg, Jacob, 190, 192, 195
Waller, John H., 195
Wall Street crash (1929), 162
Wang Jiaheng, 168
Wannsee Conference, 147
Wanrong ("Elizabeth," wife of Puyi), 81, 83, 119–21
Warsaw, Poland, 74, 147, 153
Warsaw Uprising, 147
Wehrmacht, 95, 132, 140, 148, 181, 197
wei Manzhou (fake Manchuria), 119
Weimar Germany, 40, 42, 46, 58
Weinreb, David, 27–29, 54
Weinreb, Edmond, 73, 95, 99
Weinreb, Esther, 76, 178–80, 183, 209
Weinreb, Friedrich
    as "administrative guerrilla," 93–94
    arrest and interrogation of, 101, 130–41, 171–74, 179–80, 211
    background, 8, 16–18, 25–30
    and *chochem (goochem)* identity, 75–76, 98
    citizenship status, 264
    and complexity of collaborator figures, 8–10, 275
    contrasted with other subjects, 1
    death, 274
    "diving" (going underground), 133–34, 208, 266
    Dreyfus comparisons, 1, 218–19, 268
    and Dutch complacency to Hitler's rise, 72–73
    education, 73–76
    gelernter identity, 75–76, 98
    as *Hochstapler* figure, 9
    on identity documents, 26
    Jewish heritage, 174
    lists of exempted people, 94–101, 131–35, 172–78, 181–87, 208, 210–11, 213–14, 220, 273
    and "living in truth," 277
    luftmensch identity, 74, 76
    macher identity, 98–99, 107, 124, 135
    memoirs, 29, 94, 174

and motivations to collaborate, 3
and persecution of Dutch Jews, 89–91
religious zeal, 57
report on actions of, 272–74
Scheveningen home, 53–59, 64
schooling, 55–57, 73–74
and self-deception of collaborators, 277
sexual abuse allegations, 97–98, 136, 216–17, 266, 273
trials, 216–22
trickster identity, 95, 99
as "V-Mann," 171
Weinreb, Hermine, 27, 28
"The Weinreb Case: A Dutch Dreyfus Trial" (article), 218
Weinreb Committee, 218, 269
The Weinreb Report, 132, 272–74
Westerbork concentration camp
and arrest of Dutch Jews, 210
and deportation of Dutch Jews, 175–78
Gemmeker's command of, 176–80
and internment of Weinreb's family, 141
last transports from, 199
SD reports on, 129
and Special Court trials, 221
and Weinreb's arrest and interrogation, 180
and Weinreb's efforts to halt deportations, 180, 182–83, 185–87
and Weinreb's exemption lists, 131–32
and Weinreb's lists, 207
Wilhelm II, German Emperor, 40, 63
Wilhelmina, Queen of the Netherlands, 63, *101*, 104, 114, 221, 253
Witting, Rolf, 153
Wiznitz, Ukraine, 18

Wolff, Karl, 104, 153
women collaborators, 6, 224. *See also* Kawashima Yoshiko
Woods, Willa Lou, 117
World Jewish Congress, 218, 232, 235–37, 253, 256
World War I, 14, 56, 71
Wright, Frank Lloyd, 101
Wulff, Wilhelm, 40, 43, 107, 150, 196–97, 228–29, 235
Wüst, Walter, 42

Xianli (Yoshiko's elder brother), 37, 47–50, 79, 124, 242

Yad Vashem (Holocaust memorial), 97
Yalta Conference, 228
Yamaga Toru, 51, 168–69, 203
Yamaguchi Fumio, 166
Yamaguchi Yoshiko (Ri Koran), 166–69, 199, 203–4, 224–27, 243, 245–47, 249
Yamaoka Sohachi, 202
Yamato Hotel, 78
Yasuhito, Prince Chichibu, 122
Yiddish, 17–18, 55, 75–76
yoga, 43
Yomiuri, 228
Yoshiko. *See* Kawashima Yoshiko
youth rebellion, 268–70
Yuan Shikai, 46, 47

Zen Buddhism, 43
Zhang Xueliang, 78
Zhang Zongchang, 127
Zionism, 25, 55–56, 73, 75–76, 92, 176, 232
Zionist Jewish Agency, 232